W9-BNM-797

Your *Best Life* Now

Your *Best Life* Now

---

7 Steps to Living at Your Full Potential

10th Anniversary Edition: Updated
with New Chapter & Foreword

Joel Osteen

Faith Words

New York • Boston • Nashville

Scriptures noted AMP are taken from the Amplified® Bible. Copyright © 1954, 1958, 1962, 1964, 1965, 1987 by The Lockman Foundation. All rights reserved. Used by permission.

Scriptures noted NKJV are taken from the New King James Version. Copyright © 1979, 1980, 1982, Thomas Nelson, Inc., Publishers.

Scriptures noted NASB are taken from the New American Standard Bible®. Copyright © 1960, 1962, 1963, 1968, 1972, 1975, 1977, 1995 by The Lockman Foundation. Used by permission.

Scriptures noted TLB are taken from The Living Bible, copyright © 1971. Used by permission of Tyndale House Publishers, Inc., Wheaton, Illinois 60189.

FaithWords
Hachette Book Group
237 Park Avenue
New York, NY 10017

www.faithwords.com

Printed in the United States of America

RRD-C

Originally published in hardcover by Warner Faith.

10th Anniversary Hardcover Edition: August 2014

10 9 8 7 6 5 4 3 2 1

FaithWords is a division of Hachette Book Group, Inc.
The FaithWords name and logo are trademarks of Hachette Book Group, Inc.

The Hachette Speakers Bureau provides a wide range of authors for speaking events. To find out more, go to www.hachettespeakersbureau.com or call (866) 376-6591.

The publisher is not responsible for websites (or their content) that are not owned by the publisher.

The Library of Congress has cataloged the 2004 hardcover edition as follows:

Osteen, Joel.
    Your best life now : 7 steps to living at your full potential / Joel Osteen.—1st Warner Faith ed.
        p. cm.
    ISBN 978-0-446-53275-4
    1. Self-actualization (Psychology)—Religious aspects—Christianity.   2. Success—Religious aspects—Christianity.   I. Title.
        BV4598.2.O88 2004
        248.4—dc22   2004011442

ISBN 978-1-4555-5057-9 (10th anniversary hardcover edition),
ISBN 978-1-4555-8405-5 (international edition)

This book is dedicated to my father, John Osteen (1929–1999). My dad's integrity, humility, love, and compassion for all people left an indelible impression on my life. I will be eternally grateful for his example.

To my wife, Victoria, the woman of my dreams and my best friend, I dedicate this book, and my life, to you. You amaze me more every day. When God gave you to me, He gave me the very best. Your unconditional love and enthusiastic spirit have made me into the man that I am today. I love you.

To Jonathan and Alexandra, my two precious treasures. You bring me more joy than I could have ever hoped for! Being your dad is my greatest reward.

And to the people of Lakewood Church, your love, loyalty, support, and enthusiasm are second to none. I am committed to you—committed to helping you to live your best life now. Our greatest days are ahead!

Acknowledgments

As with any major building project, it takes a great team to make all the elements come together in a book. I want to extend my personal and sincere thanks to:

Ken Abraham—without your expertise, this project wouldn't have been possible. Thanks for encouraging me to "put my heart on paper."

Rolf Zettersten, FaithWords, and the staff and sales "force" of Hachette Book Group—for believing so passionately. Your enthusiasm and excitement is contagious.

Michelle Trevino and the staff of Lakewood Church, as well as our many teachers and volunteers—just as David had his "mighty men," I have been blessed to work alongside you, the mighty men and women of Lakewood! You are the greatest church on the face of the earth.

To my immediate family—you know me the best; you love me the most and have supported me in all my endeavors. I love you all very much. And to those who serve alongside me at Lakewood...

Paul and Jennifer Osteen—for your sacrificial, unconditional love expressed to us on a daily basis.

Kevin and Lisa Comes—for your steadfast support and persevering love. Thank you for modeling "real-world" faith.

Don and Jackelyn Iloff—for your unwavering enthusiasm and constant encouragement.

And most of all, to Dodie Osteen, my mother—for teaching us what really matters in life and for showing us what "faith" really is. Thank you for providing an example of what a life totally committed to God can achieve.

Contents

Your Best Life Now
10th Anniversary Edition

You've probably heard me say that God wants to take us places that we've never dreamed. When you keep Him in first place, are your best each day, and take steps of faith you will see His goodness in new ways.

Sometimes the next step God asks us to take is a small one, but at other times the step to the next level becomes a leap of faith. This is what happened when I trusted God and decided to write *Your Best Life Now*.

Only seven years before, I was working in TV production for our church. I was not even thinking about being a pastor, much less an author. In fact, when I was first approached about writing a book, I declined the offer simply because I didn't think of myself as a writer. But I know that God has placed more promise and potential in each of us than we know. So, about a year after I declined the first offer to write a book, the opportunity arose again. This time, I decided to trust God, take a leap of faith, and expect good things to happen.

As I look back on this—the tenth anniversary of the release of *Your Best Life Now*—I believe now more than ever that when we trust God, He will take us where we need to be. I will admit that it was a bit intimidating to me. As I was writing this book originally, I found myself wondering if anyone would even be interested. I imagined how embarrassed I'd be if the publisher set up a big book signing and no one showed up. I had to keep telling myself that God is in control and it was my job to shake off the doubts and remain faithful.

I was amazed when *Your Best Life Now* was released in 2004, selling millions of copies worldwide and becoming a *New York Times* bestseller for almost 100 weeks. Our message of God's goodness has helped millions more than we would have reached if this book had not been written. It proved to me, once again, that God's dream for our lives is much bigger than our own, and when you believe, you will rise higher, accomplish more, and live your best life now.

—Joel Osteen, August 2014

Introduction

The future is yours for the taking!" is an often quoted expression of hope passed on to graduating seniors, new employees, and wide-eyed couples on their wedding days. Yet we all know that while some people grab life with enthusiasm and take control of their futures, such a grandiose promise doesn't always pan out for everybody. Why is that? What makes the difference?

Happy, successful, fulfilled individuals have learned how to live their best lives *now*. They make the most of the present moment and thereby enhance their future. You can, too. No matter where you are or what challenges you are facing, you can enjoy your life right now!

Many people go through life with low self-esteem, focusing on the negative, feeling inferior or inadequate, always dwelling on some reason why they can't be happy. Others put off their happiness till some future date:

- *Someday, things will be better in my life.*
- *Someday, I will be caught up with my work long enough to enjoy making memories with my family.*
- *Someday, I'll earn more money, and I won't have to worry about how I will pay the bills.*
- *Someday, I'm going to get in better physical condition.*
- *Someday, I'll have a better relationship with God and enjoy more of His goodness.*

Unfortunately, "someday" never comes. Today is the only day we have. We can't do anything about the past, and we don't know what the future holds. But we can live at our full potential right now!

In this book, you will discover just how to do that! Within these pages, you will find seven simple, yet profound, steps to improve your life, regardless of your current level of success or lack of it. I know these steps work, because they have worked in the lives of my family members, friends, and associates, as well as in my own life. I'm confident that if you will take these steps along with me, you ultimately will be happier than ever before, living with joy, peace, and enthusiasm—not just for a day, or a week, but for the rest of your life!

In *Your Best Life Now*, we'll explore how to:

- *Enlarge your vision;*
- *Develop a healthy self-image;*
- *Discover the power of your thoughts and words;*
- *Let go of the past;*
- *Find strength through adversity;*
- *Live to give; and*
- *Choose to be happy.*

In each of these areas, you will find practical suggestions and simple choices that will help you to stay positive in your lifestyle and believe for a brighter future.

You may have experienced adversity or trials in your past. Perhaps you've had more than your share of setbacks and heartaches. But today is a new day! By following the principles I'm going to share with you in *Your Best Life Now*, you can be happy and fulfilled, starting *today*.

I will challenge you in this book to break out of a "barely-get-by" mentality, to become the best you can be, not merely average or ordinary. To do that, you may have to rid yourself of some negative mindsets that are holding you back, and start enlarging your vision, seeing yourself as doing more, enjoying more, being more. That, my friend, is what it means to live your best life now.

Are you ready to develop your full potential? Let's get started! It's time to begin living your best life now!

PART 1

ENLARGE YOUR VISION

CHAPTER 1

Enlarging Your Vision

I heard a story about a man on vacation in Hawaii with his wife. He was a good man who had achieved a modest measure of success, but he was coasting along, thinking that he'd already reached his limits in life. One day, a friend was driving the couple around the island, showing them the sights. They stopped to admire a gorgeous house set high on a hill. The property was replete with beautiful palm trees and lush green gardens in a picturesque, peaceful setting with a panoramic view overlooking the ocean.

As the man gazed at the magnificent home, he commented to his wife and friend, "I can't even imagine living in a place like that."

Right there, something inside him said, *Don't worry. You won't. You will never live in a great place like that.*

Startled at his own thoughts, he asked himself, *What do you mean?*

As long as you can't imagine it, as long as you can't see it, then it is not going to happen for you. The man correctly realized that his own thoughts and attitudes were condemning him to mediocrity. He determined then and there to start believing better of himself, and believing better of God.

It's the same way with us. We have to conceive it on the inside before we're ever going to receive it on the outside. If you don't think you can have something good, then you never will. The barrier is in your mind. It's not God's lack of resources or your lack of talent that prevents you from prospering. Your own wrong thinking can keep you from God's best.

Your own wrong thinking can keep you from God's best.

You, too, may have assumed that you've already peaked, that you've reached your limits in life, that you will never be more successful. *I'll never achieve significance, do something meaningful, or enjoy the good things in life that I've seen others enjoy.*

Sad to say, you are exactly right . . . *unless* you are willing to change your thinking. That's why the first step to living at your full potential is to *enlarge your vision.* To live your best life now, you must start looking at life through eyes of faith, seeing yourself rising to new levels. See your business taking off. See your marriage restored. See your family prospering. See your dreams coming to pass. You must conceive it and believe it is possible if you ever hope to experience it.

To conceive it, you must have an image on the inside of the life you want to live on the outside. This image has to become a part of you, in your thoughts, your conversation, deep down in your subconscious mind, in your actions, in every part of your being.

Envision Your Success

From the time she was a little girl, Tara Holland dreamed of becoming Miss America. In 1994, she entered the Miss Florida pageant and won the title of first runner-up. She decided to try again the following year. She entered the same contest, and once again, won the prize as first runner-up. Tara was tempted to get down and discouraged, but she didn't do that. She stayed focused on her goal.

She decided she needed to change her environment, so she moved to Kansas, and in 1997, she entered the Miss Kansas pageant and won the title. That same year, she went on to be crowned Miss America. Tara Holland saw her dream come to pass.

In an interview after the pageant, someone asked Tara the secret to her success. She admitted that after she had lost twice in a row at the state-level competitions, she had been tempted to give up, but instead she went out and rented dozens of videos of local pageants, state pageants, Miss Teen, Miss Universe, Miss World—whatever she could find. She rented hundreds of videos of various pageants and watched them over and over again.

As Tara watched each young woman crowned a winner, she pictured herself in that situation. She pictured herself receiving the crown. She pictured herself walking down the runway in victory. Time and time again she envisioned herself winning. Seeing herself as a winner, said Tara, was the key to her success.

Another reporter asked her if she was nervous walking down the runway in front of millions of people watching on television and with the announcer singing the famous Miss America song.

Tara's response was interesting. "No, I wasn't nervous at all," she said. "You see, I had walked down that runway thousands of times before."

Have you ever walked down that runway? Have you ever seen yourself accomplishing your dreams? Do you keep that vision of victory in front of you? Tara Holland knew she would never be a winner until she first saw herself as a winner. She had to reprogram her mind, to rid herself as much as possible of the hurtful memories of losing. She had to replace that vision in her mind of herself as Miss Runner-up. She had to develop a can-do attitude. She saw herself stepping onto the winner's platform. She saw herself walking down that runway in victory. She created an environment of faith and success.

What you keep before your eyes will affect you. You will produce what you're continually seeing in your mind. If you foster an image of defeat and failure, then you're going to live that kind of life. But if you develop an image of victory, success, health, abundance, joy, peace, and happiness, nothing on earth will be able to hold those things from you.

Too many times we get stuck in a rut, thinking we've reached our limits. We don't really stretch our faith; we don't believe for anything bigger. But God wants us to constantly be increasing, to be rising to new heights. He wants to increase you in His wisdom and help you to make better decisions. God wants to increase you financially, by giving you promotions, fresh ideas, and creativity.

The Scripture says that God wants to pour out "His far and beyond favor."[1] God wants this to be the best time of your life. But if you are going to receive this favor, you must enlarge your vision. You can't go around thinking negative, defeated, limiting thoughts. *Well, I've gone as far as my education will allow.* Or, *I've had this sickness for years. I guess it's my lot in life.*

To experience this immeasurable favor, you must rid yourself of that small-minded thinking and start expecting God's blessings, start anticipating promotion and supernatural increase. You must conceive it in your heart and mind before you can receive it. In other words, you must make room for increase in your own thinking, then God will bring those things to pass. Until you learn how to enlarge your vision, seeing the future through your eyes of faith, your own wrong thinking will prevent good things from happening in your life. God will not pour fresh, creative ideas and blessings into old attitudes.

**You must conceive it in your heart and
mind before you can receive it.**

Get Rid of Those Old Wineskins

Centuries ago, wine was stored in leather wineskins rather than bottles. Animal skins were dried and cured until the leather could be shaped into containers to hold the wine. When the wineskins were new, they were soft and pliable, but as they aged, they often lost their elasticity; they wouldn't give anymore. They would become hardened and set, and they couldn't expand. If a person poured new wine in an old wineskin, the container would burst and the wine would be lost.

Interestingly, when Jesus wanted to encourage His followers to enlarge their visions, He reminded them, "You can't put new wine into old wineskins."[2] Jesus was saying that you cannot have a larger life with restricted attitudes. That lesson is still relevant today. We are set in our ways, bound by our perspectives, and stuck in our thinking. God is trying to do something new, but unless we're willing to change, unless we're willing to expand and enlarge our vision, we'll miss His opportunities for us.

The fact that you are reading this book, however, says that you are ready to go to a higher level; you want to reach your full potential. The good news is, God wants to show you His incredible favor. He wants to fill your life with "new wine," but are you willing to get rid of your old wineskins? Will you start thinking bigger? Will you enlarge your vision and get rid of those old negative mind-sets that hold you back?

One fellow whose marriage was on the verge of dissolution told me, "Joel, I've been this way for a long time. Nothing good ever happens to me. I don't see how my marriage could be restored. We've always had these problems."

"That kind of thinking will keep you from receiving the good things God wants to pour out in your life," I told him. "Those wrong attitudes will block the flow. You must stop dwelling on negative, destructive thoughts that keep you in a rut. Your life is not going to change until you first change your thinking."

Early in our marriage, Victoria and I were out walking through our neighborhood one day when we came upon a beautiful new home in the final stages of construction. The doors were open, so we stepped inside and looked around. It was a fabulous home, much prettier than any of the other homes in that community. Most of the other homes around us were one-story, ranch-style homes that were forty to fifty years old, but this house was a large two-story home, with high ceilings and oversized windows providing an appealing view of the backyard. It was a lovely, inspiring place.

When we came out of the house, Victoria was excited. She turned around, looked back at the home, and said, "Joel, one day we're going to live in a beautiful home just like that!" At the time, we were living in an extremely old house that had experienced some foundation problems, preventing all of our doors on the inside from closing properly. We had stretched our faith and spent everything we had just to buy that home and get into that neighborhood. Thinking of our bank account, and my income at the time, it seemed impossible to me that we'd ever work our way up to a home like the one we had toured.

Being the "great man of faith" that I am, I said, "Victoria, that home is so far beyond our reach, I don't see how we could ever afford something like that."

But Victoria had much more faith than I did, and she would not give up. We stood out in front of that house for thirty minutes and debated. She told me all the reasons why it could happen. I told her all the reasons why I doubted.

She said, "No, Joel; I feel it deep inside. It is going to happen."

She was so filled with joy, I didn't want to burst her bubble, so I let the matter drop. But Victoria didn't! Over the next several months, she kept speaking words of faith and victory, and she finally talked me into it. She convinced me that we could live in an elegant home like the one we saw. I got rid of my limited thinking and I started agreeing with her. I started believing that somehow, some way, God could bring it to pass. We kept on believing it, seeing it, and speaking it.

Several years later, we sold our property, and through another real estate deal, we were able to build a house just like the one we had viewed. We saw it come to pass. But I don't believe it ever would have happened had we not first conceived it on the inside. I don't believe it would have happened if Victoria had not talked me into enlarging my vision.

God has so much more in store for you, too. Start making room for it in your thinking. Conceive it on the inside. Start seeing yourself rising to a new level, doing something of significance, living in that home of your dreams. If you want to see God's "far and beyond" favor, then you must replace those old wineskins.

"I've gone as far as my parents were able to go," Steve said to me. "I've gone as far as anybody else in my family. That's good enough, isn't it?"

"No," I told him. "You don't have to be bound by the barriers of the past. God wants you to go further than your parents. I'm sure your parents were fine, hardworking people, but don't fall into that trap of just sitting back and accepting the status quo. You need to make a decision that you are not going to live an average, mediocre life. When you get up in the morning you need to have the attitude of: *I'm going to do something great. I'm going to excel in my career. I'm going to enthusiastically serve other people. I'm going to break out of this mold and rise to new heights.*

I tell my children all the time, "You're going to go much further than Daddy. You have so much potential. You're going to accomplish great things!"

I'm not simply trying to instill pride in our children; I want them to have a big vision. I want them to conceive great possibilities at an early age. I want them to grow up expecting God's favor, expecting to be leaders, expecting to excel in whatever they do. And I know they must have it on the inside before God can ever bring it to pass on the outside.

One day, I was driving through Houston with my eight-year-old son, Jonathan. As we drove down the freeway we came upon the Compaq Center, the sixteen-thousand-seat arena that was the former home of the Houston Rockets professional basketball team, and soon to be the home of Lakewood Church. I slowed down and pointed. "Jonathan, look over there. One day, that's where you're going to be preaching."

He said, "Oh, no, Daddy. When I get old enough, I'm going to preach in Reliant Stadium!" (Reliant Stadium is Houston's seventy-thousand-seat home of the Houston Texans football team.)

I thought, *I like the fact that he's got a big dream.* When I first told that story at Lakewood several years ago, after the service a lady came up and handed Jonathan a check for one hundred dollars toward that new stadium. He was so excited. He said, "Daddy, I wish you'd talk about me more often in your sermons!"

Even if you come from an extremely successful family, God still wants you to go further. My own father accomplished great things in his lifetime. He inspired people all over the world. But I'm not going to be satisfied to do merely what Daddy did. I don't want to simply hold my ground and maintain. No, I want to press on toward new heights.

If you look carefully, you will see that God has been trying to encourage you. He's allowed people to cross your path who are far more successful than you are, who have much stronger marriages, who are enjoying His favor in marvelous ways. When you see or hear about other people succeeding or doing what you want to do, be encouraged rather than jealous. Don't say, "That could never happen to me. I'm not that talented. I'll never get those kind of breaks. I'll never have that much money."

Get rid of those old wineskins. Change your thinking. Get beyond the barriers of the past and start expecting God to do great things in your life.

"Do You Not Perceive It?"

Understand, God is constantly trying to plant new seeds in your heart. He's constantly trying to get you to conceive, to give up antiquated ideas and spawn new bursts of creativity within. The key is to believe, to let the seed take root so it can grow.

What if Victoria had acquiesced concerning that new house, and said, "Yes, Joel; you're right. We're just young people. We'll never afford this. That house is way out of reach."

We'd probably still be living in our original crooked house. Thankfully, she enlarged her vision and conceived what God was saying to her. Perhaps God has been speaking to you, as well, trying to move you to a new level. He's put people in your life as examples to inspire you. When you see their accomplishments, their joys, their victories, something inside you should say, "Yes, God! I know You can bless me in a similar way. I know I can have a great marriage. I know I can be that happy. I know I can go to those new heights."

There is a seed within you trying to take root. That's God trying to get you to conceive. He's trying to fill you with so much hope and expectancy that the seed will grow and bring forth a tremendous harvest. It's your time. You may have been sick for a long time, but this is your time to get well. You may be bound by all kinds of addictions, all kinds of bad habits, but this is the time to be set free. You may be struggling financially, in all kinds of debt, but this is the time for promotion. This is your time for increase. Friend, if you will get in agreement with God, this can be the greatest time of your life. This can be the time that God pours out His immeasurable, far and beyond favor.

God says, "Behold, I am doing a new thing. Do you not perceive it?"[3] Notice, God is always ready to do new things in our lives. He's trying to promote us, to increase us, to give us more. Yet, it's interesting that God asked the question "Do you not perceive it?" In other words, are you making room for it in your own thinking? Are you believing for increase? Are you believing to excel at your job? Are you believing to be a more effective leader, or a better parent?

It's time to enlarge your vision.

Maybe God wants to improve your marriage, restore your family, or promote you at work. But that seed of opportunity can't take root because of your doubts.

"How could my business ever take off and begin to flourish? I've got so many obstacles. It's just impossible."

God is saying to you something similar to what He told the Virgin Mary and others throughout Scripture. It's not going to be by your might. It's not going to be by your power. God said it's going to be by His Spirit. The power of the Most High God shall come upon you and cause it to happen. With God on your side, you cannot possibly lose. He can make a way when it looks as though there is no way. He can open doors that no man can shut. He can cause you to be at the right place, at the right time. He can supernaturally turn your life around. Jesus said, "If you believe, then all things are possible."[4]

My question to you is: Will you believe? Will you allow that seed to take root? The angel told Mary that she would conceive without knowing a man. In other words, God was saying it could happen through supernatural means. It can happen without the bank loaning you the money. It can happen without having the right education. It can happen in spite of your past. It can happen despite what the critics are telling you. With God, all things are possible.

When we got the news that the Compaq Center might be coming available, some of my initial thoughts were similar to Mary's. *How could this be? How could we ever get that facility? It's going to be too expensive. The city will never let a church use that. It's much too prominent.* But this time, I expanded my vision. I let the seed take root. I conceived it on the inside. I began to "see" our congregation worshiping God in the Compaq Center in the heart of Houston.

Over the next few months, plenty of people told members of our congregation, staff, and me, "It's never going to happen. You don't have a chance. You're wasting your time."

That didn't matter. The seed was growing on the inside. When it looked impossible, and we faced all kinds of challenges, I just said, "Father, I thank You that You are fighting our battles for us. I thank You that You're going to show us some of that immeasurable, far and beyond favor." The seed kept growing, getting stronger and stronger. Sure enough, three and a half years later, against strong adversity, God turned the situation around, and He brought us out with the victory.

God wants to do big things in your life, as well. Don't settle for a small view of God. We serve the God that created the universe. We've got to eliminate this barely-get-by mentality. "God, if You'll just give me a fifty-cent raise, I think I'll make it this year." "God, if You'll just help me endure this marriage . . ." "God, all I want is a little happiness."

Get rid of those old wineskins. Get rid of that small-minded thinking and start thinking as God thinks. Think big. Think increase. Think abundance. Think more than enough.

Years ago, a famous golfer was invited by the king of Saudi Arabia to play in a golf tournament. He accepted the invitation, and the king flew his private jet over to the United States to pick up the pro. They played golf for several days, and enjoyed a good time. As the golfer was getting on the plane to return to the United States, the king stopped him and said, "I want to give you a gift for coming all this way and making this time so special. Anything you want. What could I get you?"

Ever the gentleman, the golfer replied, "Oh, please; don't get me anything. You've been a gracious host. I've had a wonderful time. I couldn't ask for anything more."

The king was adamant. He said, "No, I insist on giving you something so you will always remember your journey to our country."

When the golfer realized that the king was resolute, he said, "Okay, fine. I collect golf clubs. Why don't you give me a golf club?"

He boarded the plane, and on his flight back home, he couldn't help wondering what kind of golf club the king might give him. He imagined that it might be a solid gold putter with his name engraved on it. Or maybe it would be a sand wedge studded with diamonds and jewels. After all, this would be a gift from the oil-rich king of Saudi Arabia.

When the golfer got home, he watched the mail and the delivery services every day, to see if his golf club had come yet. Finally, several weeks later, he received a certified letter from the king of Saudi Arabia. The U.S. professional thought that rather strange. *Where's my golf club?* he wondered. He opened the envelope, and to his surprise, inside he discovered a deed to a five-hundred-acre golf course in America.

Sometimes kings think differently than you and I think. And friend, we serve the King of kings. We serve the Most High God, and His dream for your life is so much bigger and better than you can even imagine. It's time to enlarge your vision!

CHAPTER 2

Raising Your Level
of Expectancy

An old adage purports that if you want to be successful, you must follow your dreams. While I'd never suggest that anyone should abandon his or her dreams, the truth is, your life will follow your *expectations*. What you expect is what you will get. If you dwell on positive thoughts, your life will move in that direction; if you continually think negative thoughts, you will live a negative life. If you expect defeat, failure, or mediocrity, your subconscious mind will make sure that you lose, fail, or sabotage every attempt to push above average. That's why one of the key elements to enlarging your vision is *raising your level of expectancy*. You have to change your thinking before you can ever change your living.

Program Your Mind for Success

It's important that you program your mind for success. That won't happen automatically. Each day, you must choose to live with an attitude that expects good things to happen to you. The Bible says, "Set your mind and keep it set on the higher things."[1] When you get up in the morning, the first thing you should do is set your mind in the right direction. Say something such as "This is going to be a great day. God is guiding and directing my steps. His favor is surrounding me. Goodness and mercy are following me. I'm excited about today!" Start your day with faith and expectancy, and then go out anticipating good things. Expect circumstances to change in your favor. Expect people to go out of their way to help you. Expect to be at the right place at the right time.

Expect things to change in your favor.

Perhaps you work in sales, and you are scheduled to give an important presentation. You're really hoping to snag that big contract. Don't be surprised if you hear a voice whispering in your mind, *You don't have a chance. This is going to be a lousy day for you. Nothing good ever happens to you. You might as well not even get your hopes up. That way, when you don't get that great contract, you won't be too disappointed.*

Don't listen to such lies! God *wants* you to get your hopes up. We can't even have faith without hope. The Bible says, "Faith is the substance of things hoped for,"[2] and one definition of that sort of hope is "confident expectancy." We should get up in the morning confidently expecting the favor of God. Start expecting doors of opportunity to open for you. Expect to excel in your career. Expect to rise above life's challenges.

God usually meets us at our level of expectancy.

God usually meets us at our level of expectancy. If you don't develop the habit of expecting good things to come your way, then you're not likely to receive anything good. If you don't expect things to get better, they probably won't. If all you expect is more of the same, that's all you're going to have. Our expectations set the boundaries for our lives. Jesus said, "According to your faith . . . be it done to you."[3] In other words, "Have what your faith expects."

Some people tend to expect the worst. They go around with that "poor-old-me mentality," always negative, always depressed. "God, why don't You do something about my situation?" they grouse. "This is not fair!" They have what their faith expects.

Other people honestly feel so overwhelmed by their troubles, they have difficulty believing that anything good could happen to them. You hear them saying things such as, "Oh, I've got so many problems. My marriage is in trouble. My children won't do right. My business isn't doing well. My health is going downhill. How can I live with enthusiasm? How do you expect me to get up and say this is going to be a good day, when I have this big mess on my hands?"

Friend, that's what faith is all about. You have to start believing that good things are coming your way, and they will!

What are you expecting in life? Are you anticipating good things or bad things, significance or mediocrity? Are you expecting things to change in your favor? Are you expecting to experience the goodness of God? Or are you allowing your circumstances or feelings to dull your enthusiasm for life and imprison you in a negative frame of mind?

BREAK OUT OF YOUR SELF-IMPOSED PRISON!

One of the common slogans among men and women who are serving long sentences in federal prison is "You've got nothin' comin'." It's a sad, hopeless statement, robbing the inmates of what little hope they have left. "You've got no income; your kids are embarrassed to say they are related to you; your wife isn't coming to see you and will probably divorce you before too long; nothing is going to change in your life. Don't expect anything better. You're getting what you deserve. You've got nothing coming."

Sadly, many people "on the outside" are living behind self-imposed bars, in prisons of their own making, and have succumbed to the same type of thinking. *This is the best you can expect. It isn't going to get any better, so you might as well sit down, keep quiet, and endure it.*

No! You can break out of that prison! The door is unlocked. All you have to do is start expecting good things in your life and start believing God for a great future. You do have good things coming!

Eyes of Faith

You must look through your "eyes of faith" and start seeing yourself as happy, healthy, and whole. That means even when your situation looks bleak, when you're tempted to be discouraged or depressed, you must encourage yourself by praying, "God, I know that You are in control, and even though this looks impossible, I know today could be the day that things turn around. Today could be the day You restore my marriage. This could be the day You bring my child home. Today may be the day my business begins to prosper exponentially. This could be the day I see my miracle."

Then keep believing and watching for those good things to come to fruition in your life. You must make a conscious decision, an act of your will, to maintain an attitude of expectancy and keep your mind filled with thoughts of hope.

This could be the day I see my miracle.

"What if I do all that and it doesn't work?" you may be asking.

What if you do that, and it *does* work? Whom are we kidding here? What do you have to lose by keeping your hopes alive?

I can guarantee you that your difficult situation will never improve as long as you stay in a negative frame of mind. But if you'll develop an attitude of faith and expect events to change positively, then at the right time, that situation will turn around. Admittedly, sometimes good things don't happen as quickly as we would like, but instead of slouching into negative expectations, we must keep our minds set on God. Your attitude should be, "God I know that You are at work in my life. Although the miracle I've been watching for didn't happen today, I know I'm one day closer to it! I'm one day closer to my answered prayer, and I'm not going to get upset. I'll not allow myself to become discouraged. I know that Your timing is perfect, so I'm going to stay in an attitude of faith and keep trusting You to do what is best."

In his late forties, Brian felt as though everything in his world was falling apart and coming down on his shoulders. His business went bankrupt. He lost his family through divorce. His health was deteriorating. At one time, he had been an extremely successful man. But now, for many years he had been merely existing, living with no joy, no peace, no zest.

One day, a friend who cared enough to level with Brian told him, "I love ya, buddy, but you need to quit focusing on all the negative; stop looking at everything you've lost and start looking at all you have left." Brian's friend challenged him, "Start believing that things are going to change for the better, not because you deserve it, but simply because God loves you that much!"

The friend's words resonated with Brian's spirit and slowly but surely, he began to take the advice to heart. He established fresh patterns in his life. He decided that every morning before he got out of bed, he was going to write down ten things for which he could be thankful. All day long, he constantly thought about that list. He continued this habit day after day, week after week, month after month.

What was Brian doing? He was reprogramming his mind. He was breaking those old negative habits, and he was developing an attitude of faith.

Within a matter of months, his situation began to turn around. First, he got his joy back. Then his health and vitality returned. He soon got his job back and, eventually, many of his relationships were restored. Most important, he got his life back! Because he moved his expectations higher, he was able to escape that old negative mentality. He stopped focusing on what he didn't have, on what he had lost, on his past mistakes and failures. Instead, he started dwelling on the goodness of God. He filled his mind with thoughts of hope, faith, and victory. He developed a fresh vision, expecting things to change for the better. Sure enough, that's when his life turned around.

Many people sabotage their expectations by negative comments. You know the type:

"Well, nothing good ever happens to me."

"I don't think I'll ever get married. I haven't even had a date in ten years!"

"I might as well file bankruptcy; I'm so swamped with debt and bills, I can't see any other alternative."

"I don't see how I could ever be happy again. I've just been through too much pain in life."

Avoid such statements at all costs because your actions will follow your expectations. Low expectations will trap you in mediocrity. You must think positive thoughts of victory, thoughts of abundance, thoughts of favor, thoughts of hope; good, pure, excellent thoughts.

The career of the Old Testament prophet Elijah offers some fascinating insights. Elijah experienced numerous miracles, and his understudy, Elisha, witnessed many of them. As Elijah neared the end of his life, he asked Elisha what he would like to have from his mentor.

"I want a double portion of your spirit," Elisha replied boldly. "I want to be twice as powerful, twice as strong, twice as blessed. I want to see twice as many miracles."

Interestingly, Elijah didn't rebuke his underling. He simply responded, "Elisha, you've asked a very difficult thing. Nevertheless, if you can see me when I'm taken from you, it shall be done unto you. But if not, it shall not be so." Certainly, in a literal sense, Elijah was telling Elisha, "If God allows you to see it, you can count on your request being granted"; but we can't help but wonder if Elijah was also saying, "If you can see it, then you can be it. If you can visualize it in your heart and mind, seeing it through the screen of God's Word with your 'spiritual eyes,' it can become a reality in your life."

God is extremely interested in what you see through your "spiritual eyes." Seven times in the Scripture, He asks, "What do you see?" God is saying something similar to us today. If you have a vision of victory for your life, you can rise to a new level. But as long as you have your head down, with your gaze on the ground instead of on your possibilities, you run the risk of moving in the wrong direction and missing out on the great things God wants to do in and through you. It's a spiritual principle as well as a psychological fact: We move toward what we see in our minds. If you can't see it, it is not likely to come to pass in your life.

What about you? When you look into your future, what do you see? Do you see yourself getting stronger, healthier, happier, your life filled with God's blessings, favor, and victory? If you can see it, it can come to pass.

Bill and Cindy, some friends of mine, moved to a new city several years back. At the time, Bill worked two jobs to make ends meet while Cindy stayed at home with their young children. It was a difficult time in their lives, and they barely eked out enough money to pay the rent and buy food. Feeling like failures, they were tempted to give up and move back home. It would have been easy for them to allow attitudes of defeat to weigh them down, but they didn't do that. Instead, during that tough time they did something extremely unusual.

Many nights after Bill came home from work, rather than sitting around in their little apartment feeling sorry for themselves, they dressed up, got in the car, and drove down to one of the big fancy hotels in the city. They didn't have enough money to pay for parking at the hotel, so they parked far down the street and walked back to the hotel. They'd go inside the gorgeous facility and just sit in that elegant hotel lobby and dream. Bill later told me, "I wanted to expose myself to an atmosphere of success. I wanted to be in a place where I could keep my hopes up. I wanted to get into an environment where I could dream of victories."

What were they doing? They were expanding their vision, focusing on what they could be. They were looking beyond where they were to where they wanted to be, and in doing so, they let faith rise in their hearts. Cindy said, "Many times, we'd sit there in the lobby literally for hours at a time, talking and dreaming, and when we'd leave, our faith and vision were renewed."

Perhaps you, too, need to change your environment. Quit sitting around feeling sorry for yourself. Quit worrying about how nothing is ever going to get better in your life. Instead, go find somewhere you can dream. It may be in a church; it may be along the banks of a stream or at a park. Find someplace where you can dare to dream big dreams; a place where your faith will be elevated. Get out of that negative environment and get into an atmosphere of victory, where people build you up rather than tear you down. Find a place where people will encourage you and challenge you to be the best you can be. Find a place where people inspire you to reach for new heights. Friend, you have to envision good things happening to you before they ever will.

Find somewhere you can dream.

The Bible says, "If you walk with wise men, then you're going to become wise."[4] If you associate with successful people, before long you will become successful. Their enthusiasm will be contagious and you will catch that vision. If you stay in an atmosphere of victory, before long you're going to have an image of victory. If you hang around people of faith, before long you're going to be filled with faith. But you cannot soar with the eagles as long as you're pecking around with the chickens.

Let me encourage you to raise your expectations; start seeing yourself receiving good things. Expect the favor of God. Expect His blessings. Expect to increase. Expect promotion. Get up and face each day with enthusiasm, knowing that God has great things in store for you.

And even when circumstances don't go your way, don't let that get you down. Keep your mind set in the right direction.

If you'll do your part by continually contemplating the goodness of God, living with faith and expectancy, God will take you places you've never even dreamed of, and you'll live at a level you have never before dared to imagine. God has good things in store for you! Let me show you how to discover them.

CHAPTER 3

God Has More in Store!

Todd Jacobs dreamed of starting his own computer software business, but when he and Amy got married, he took a mundane job just to pay the bills. Then the baby came along and their budget went out the window, along with Todd's dreams.

At first, the shelving of his dreams didn't bother Todd, but before long, he and Amy both recognized the unspoken yet very real resentment seething just below the surface of every conversation about money and every decision about their future. Ironically, when an opportunity arose for Todd to develop software for a well-known, established company, working along with one of his best friends, he turned it down. "I'm not talented enough," he said. "I've been away from the business world too long."

"Todd, are you sure?" his best friend asked. "This is a tremendous opportunity. You can start your own company, help write software for the parent company, and you can even make some extra money from royalties. Are you sure you want to pass on this job?"

"Yes, I'm sure," Todd replied. "I can't afford to take a chance. My job doesn't pay a lot, but it's steady work. I'd better stay right where I am."

Like Todd, many people miss pivotal opportunities in their lives every day because they've grown accustomed to the status quo. They expect nothing better. God is opening a new door for them; all they have to do is step through it, yet regrettably they back away from God's blessings. Why? They refuse to make room in their own thinking for the new things God wants to do in their lives. When a great opportunity comes along, rather than latching onto it, launching out in faith, and believing for the best, they say, "Well, that could never happen to me. That's just too good to be true."

Unfortunately, what you will receive is directly connected to how you believe and what you expect. If you want God to do the extraordinary, then you must start believing Him for bigger things.

**What you will receive is directly
connected to how you believe.**

Like Todd, you may be thinking, *I'll just work at this same job, in this same position, for the rest of my life. After all, this is all I know how to do.*

No, quit limiting God. He may want to open another opportunity or a better position for you. God may intervene in your situation, replacing your supervisor so you can be promoted. One day, you may run that entire company! Once you begin expecting more, a second key element to enlarging your vision is *believing that God has more in store for you!*

There's an old story about a little frog that was born at the bottom of a small, circular well, similar to those you might see at a typical rural farm. He and his family lived there, and he was content to play in the water, swimming all around that little well. He thought, *Life doesn't get any better than this. I have all that I need.*

But one day, he looked up and noticed the light at the top of the well. The little frog became curious, wondering what was up there. He slowly climbed up the side of the well. When he got to the top, he cautiously peered out over the edge. Lo and behold, the first thing he saw was a pond. He couldn't believe it. It was a thousand times bigger than the well. He ventured farther and discovered a huge lake. He stood there gazing in amazement. Eventually, the little frog hopped a long way and came to the ocean, where everywhere he looked, all he could see was water. He was shocked beyond measure. He began to realize how limited his thinking had been. He thought he had it all back in the well, but all he really had was a drop in the bucket compared to what God wanted him to enjoy.

God's dream for your life is so much bigger and greater than you can imagine. If God showed you everything He had in store for you, it would boggle your mind. So many times we're like that little frog. We've been enclosed in our own little well. It's been our comfortable environment. It's how and where we were raised. It's all we've ever known, a certain level of living, a certain way of thinking. All the while, God has so much more in store for us.

Go a bit further than you've gone before. Dare to dream a little bigger. Look out over the edge like that little frog. God has oceans He wants you to enjoy.

ARE YOU LIMITING GOD?

When God puts a dream in your heart, when He brings opportunities across your path, do you step out boldly in faith, expecting the best, moving forward with confidence, knowing that you are well able to do what God wants you to do? Or do you shrink back in fear, and say, "That's too big for me. I'm not qualified. I'm not able. I could never do that."

God wants to do a new thing in your life. But you've got to do your part and get outside that little box. Start thinking big!

Many people settle for too little. "I've gone as far as my education will allow me to go."

"I've gone as far in my career as I can go. I've hit the peak. I'll never make any more money than I'm making right now."

Why? Your job is not your source. God is your source, and His creativity and resources are unlimited! God may give you an idea for an invention, a book, a song, or a movie. God can give you a dream. One idea from God can forever change the course of your life. God is not limited by your education or lack of it. He's not limited by what you have or what you don't have. God can do anything, if you believe. He can do anything, if you will simply stop limiting Him in your thinking.

A woman recently wrote to Victoria and me, telling us the story of how she received a check in the mail from a relative who had died and left her $90,000. She had never met this man and didn't even know they were related.

As she told us her story, I couldn't help smiling and thinking, *God, give me some relatives like that!*

Seriously, I was thrilled for the woman. She had believed for more, and the windfall was part of God's answer.

You can start expecting increase, as well. Not merely financial increase, but you can start expecting supernatural promotion in every area of your life.

Break the Curse

Too often, we get comfortable with where we are, and we use that as an excuse to remain in mediocrity. "My parents were poor," we say with a pout. "Before them, my grandparents were poor. Nobody in my family has ever amounted to much, so I guess I won't either."

Don't believe that lie. God is a progressive God. He wants you to go further than your parents ever went. He wants you to be the one to break out of that mold. Maybe you were raised in a negative environment. Everybody around you was negative and critical, depressed, down in the dumps, and discouraged. No doubt, you're tempted to use your negative upbringing as an excuse to live the same way. But you can be the person to change your family tree! Don't pass that junk down to your children and keep that negative cycle going. You can be the one to break the curse in your family. You can be the one to raise the bar. You can affect future generations by the decisions you make today.

My dad came from the poorest of the poor families. His parents were cotton farmers, and they lost everything they owned in the Great Depression. My grandmother worked fourteen to fifteen hours a day washing people's clothes, earning ten cents an hour. Many nights, they'd come home and not have enough food to eat. Daddy often went to school hungry, with holes in his pants and holes in his shoes.

They were good people, but nobody in our family line had ever amounted to much. They lived under a curse of poverty and defeat. But one day, at seventeen years of age, Daddy committed his life to Christ, and God put a dream in his heart to preach.

Certainly, the odds were against him. He came from the wrong family in the wrong part of town. He didn't have any money, and he had very little education. In the natural, he had no future, no hope. But God is not limited by environment, family background, or present circumstances. God is limited only by our lack of faith.

Daddy held that dream close to his heart. He had a hope that one day he was going to rise above that mentality of defeat and mediocrity. Not surprisingly, everybody around him tried to discourage him. They said, "John, you're never going to make it out there on your own. You better stay here with us and pick cotton. That's all you know how to do. Stay here where it's safe."

We affect generations to come with the decisions that we make today.

But I'm so thankful that Daddy didn't listen to all the naysayers. He wasn't satisfied with where he was. He didn't get stuck in that rut of defeat and mediocrity. He refused to limit God. He believed that God had more in store for him. And because he stayed focused on that dream and was willing to step out in faith, because he was willing to go beyond the barriers of the past, he broke that curse of poverty in our family. Now, my siblings and I, and our children, grandchildren, even our great-grandchildren, are all going to experience more of the goodness of God because of what one man did.

We affect generations to come with the decisions that we make today. If you're not experiencing God's abundant life, let me challenge you to believe for more. Don't merely sit back and accept the status quo. Don't travel the road for the next fifty years and end up at the same place you're at today. Make a decision to rise out of that rut. Don't simply settle for what your parents had. You can go further than that. You can do more, have more, be more.

I was blessed to be raised in a good family. I had great parents who were fine role models. My mom and dad touched people's lives all over the world. But as much as I respect what my parents have accomplished, I'm not going to be satisfied to simply inherit what they have, to do what they did. God wants each generation to go further than the previous generation. He wants each generation to be more blessed, to experience more of His love, goodness, and His influence in the world. He doesn't want you to stay where you are.

When Daddy passed away in 1999, and I took over as pastor of Lakewood Church in Houston, people often approached me and asked, "Joel, do you really think you can keep it going? Do you think you can hold down the fort? You've got some real big shoes to fill."

I understood what they meant, and I appreciated their comments because they loved my dad and he was a great leader. Beyond that, few other churches the size of Lakewood had ever survived for long after the loss of the founding senior pastor, and our local press was quick to point out the low chances of our success. But none of those matters worried me, because I knew God doesn't want one generation to shine, and then the next generation to fade into obscurity. God wants each generation to increase.

Furthermore, I knew I didn't have to fill my dad's shoes. I had only to fill my own shoes. I just had to be the person God made me to be. When I first became the leader, people sometimes asked me, "Joel, do you think that you will be able to do as much as your dad?"

I never answered arrogantly, but I always would say, "I believe I'm going to do more than my dad." That's just the way our God is. He's a progressive God. And I know my dad would be displeased and dishonored if I were to limit myself to what he had done, or to stay right where he was. My dad brought our family from nothing to where it is today. When he started ministering, he knew little about the Bible. Nobody in his family had ever been a church-attender, much less a Bible teacher. When Daddy first started out, he once preached an entire message on Samson, and at the end of his sermon, Daddy realized that he had been calling the hero of the story "Tarzan"!

But Daddy got better and, as a result, I have inherited a multitude of advantages. I have Daddy's life from which to draw inspiration, experience, and wisdom. Nevertheless, I say it humbly, but I believe I'm going to do far more than my dad was able to do. And I believe my son is going to do far more than I have, and his son will one day do far more than all of us combined.

Friend, don't ever get satisfied with where you are. Maybe you came from a family like my dad's, where they didn't have much materially. Or maybe you came from a family with tremendous wealth, prestige, and position. Regardless, you can experience more than the generation preceding you.

Maybe you hail from a long line of divorce, failure, depression, mediocrity, or other personal or family problems. You need to say, "Enough is enough. I'm not going to pass these negative attitudes down to my children. I'm going to break out of this cycle and change my expectations. I'm going to start believing God for bigger and better things."

That was the attitude of Phyllis, one of our members at Lakewood. When Phyllis was sixteen years old, she got pregnant and had to leave high school. Her dreams were shattered, and she was heartbroken. She rented a cramped, small apartment in which to live and raise her son. But she soon realized it was never going to work out. She didn't have enough money, and she was living off handouts. Eventually she had to go on public assistance—welfare. She was barely surviving in poverty, defeat, and despair.

But Phyllis refused to live in mediocrity. She said, "Enough is enough. I refuse to pass this lifestyle down to my children. I'm going to make a difference with my life. I'm going to fulfill my God-given destiny. I'm going to be the person God wants me to be." And she rose up and started believing for bigger and better things. She started expecting the supernatural favor of God. She got rid of her former thoughts of defeat and failure. She developed a "can-do" mentality. When times were tough, she didn't give up. She just kept on keeping on. She did her part, and God did His.

Phyllis got a job at a school cafeteria collecting meal tickets. The job paid minimum wage, and Phyllis was thankful for it. But Phyllis wasn't satisfied with that. She knew God had better things in store for her. She had a bigger dream for her life. She didn't just sit back and accept the status quo. She decided she wanted to go back to school, and she got her high school diploma. But she still wasn't satisfied.

She wanted to go to college. She worked all day at the school and then attended college classes at night. In just four years, she graduated from college with honors. But Phyllis still wasn't satisfied. She went back to school and got her master's degree.

Today, she's reaping the rewards of that effort. She's not on welfare anymore; she is a principal in that same school district where she used to collect meal tickets. She, too, broke the curse of poverty and lack in her family. Phyllis says, "I went from welfare to faring well!"

You can do something similar. Stop settling for mediocrity. Quit settling for the status quo. God has more in store for you. Much more! Dream bigger dreams. Enlarge your vision. Live with expectancy. Make room in your thinking for the great things God wants to do.

Your best days are ahead of you. God wants to do more than you can even ask or think, but remember, it's according to the power that works in you. Stir yourself up; step out of complacency; don't be satisfied with past glories.

God has more in store for you! But if you are going to believe for bigger and better things, you will have to break some barriers of your past. Come on; I'll show you what I mean. This is going to be exciting!

CHAPTER 4

Breaking the Barriers of the Past

Every four years, the world's attention turns to the summer Olympic games. For a few days, men and women from around the globe gather to compete against the best. Watching the summer games nowadays, it is almost difficult to remember that only a few decades ago, track-and-field experts pompously declared that no runner could break the four-minute-mile barrier. Ostensibly, a human being couldn't run that far, that fast, for that length of time. "Experts" conducted all sorts of profound studies to show it was impossible to beat the four-minute barrier. And for years, they were right. Nobody ever ran a mile in less than four minutes.

But one day a young man came along who didn't believe the experts' opinions. He didn't dwell on the impossibilities. He refused to let all those negative words form a stronghold in his mind. He began to train, believing he was going to break that record. Sure enough, he went out one day and broke the four-minute-mile barrier. He did what the experts said couldn't be done. His name was Roger Bannister, and he made sports history.

Now, here is what I find so interesting about the Roger Bannister story. Within ten years after Roger Bannister broke that record, 336 other runners had broken the four-minute-mile record as well! Think about that. For hundreds of years, as far back as statisticians kept track-and-field records, nobody ran a mile in less than four minutes; then, within a decade, more than three hundred people from various geographic locations were able to do it. What happened?

Simple. The barrier to running a four-minute mile was in the athletes' minds. For all those years, runners believed what the experts were saying. They were convinced that it was impossible to run a mile in less than four minutes.

The Battle in Your Mind

Here's the key point: You will never go beyond the barriers in your own mind. If you think you can't do something, then you never will. The battle is in your mind. If you are defeated in your mind, you've already lost the battle. If you don't think your dreams will ever come to pass, they never will. If you don't think you have what it takes to rise up and set that new standard, it's not going to happen. The barrier is in your mind.

That's what the Scripture calls a "stronghold."[1] It's a wrong thinking pattern that keeps us imprisoned in defeat. And that's why it is so important that we think positive thoughts of hope, faith, and victory.

Perhaps somebody has spoken negative words into your life. Maybe some so-called experts have told you that you're never going to be successful; you're never going to rise to the top; you just don't have what it takes to make it. Don't listen to those lies. If God is for you, who dares to be against you? Break through those limitations of the past and let your mind dwell on fresh, positive attitudes of faith. Breaking those barriers will change your life and the lives of your children.

Today, it's common for professional runners to break the four-minute-mile barrier. It's no big deal. Roger Bannister set a new standard. He cleared the path. Similarly, if you'll break through the barriers in your mind and start stepping out in faith, you will go beyond those old barriers, and the same thing will happen in your family. Your children, grandchildren, and future generations will continue to race past those barriers. They will continue to go further than people ever once thought possible. And it will be because you were willing to step out in faith, setting a new standard, paving the way for future generations.

If you fail to break through those barriers of the past, you run the risk of spinning your wheels, going around in circles. For instance, when God led the Hebrew people out of Egypt, where they had lived in slavery for four hundred years, they headed straight toward the Promised Land. It was an eleven-day journey, but it took them forty years to get there. Why? Why would they wander around in the wilderness, going around the same mountain, time after time, not making any progress?

After all, God had prepared the land flowing with milk and honey. It was a place of great abundance, a place of great freedom. But God's people had been beaten down by their oppressors for so long—mistreated, used, and taken advantage of—now, even though God wanted to do a new thing, they couldn't conceive it. They couldn't make room for it in their own thinking. Instead of moving forward with an attitude of faith, expecting good things, they insisted on going around with a poor, defeated mentality. Around and around they went, focusing on their problems, always complaining, fretting about the obstacles standing between them and their destiny.

God finally jolted them out of their complacency. He said to them, "You have dwelt long enough on this mountain."[2] I believe God is saying something similar to us. You've been wallowing where you are long enough. It's time to move on, to let go of past hurts, pains, or failures. It's time to believe for bigger things. It's time for increase, time for promotion, time for supernatural favor. But if that's going to happen, you can't keep going in circles, doing the same thing the same way year after year. The third key to developing a fresh vision for your life is *breaking the barriers of the past.*

Today Is a New Day

No matter what you've gone through in the past, no matter how many setbacks you've suffered or who or what has tried to thwart your progress, today is a new day, and God wants to do a new thing in your life. He has great things in store for you. Don't let your past determine your future.

Maybe you've lived in an abusive situation where somebody mistreated you, somebody walked out on you, somebody did you a great wrong. Please, don't inhibit the great future God has for you by dwelling on the pains in your past.

The Bible promises that God will give us "a twofold recompense for our former shame."[3] That means if you'll keep the right attitude, God will pay you back double for your trouble. He'll add up all the injustice, all the hurt and pain that people have caused you, the abuse and embarrassment, and He'll pay you back with twice as much joy, peace, and happiness. That is God's desire for you. But you must do your part and start expecting good things. Keep your mind moving in the right direction. You can't have a victim mentality and expect to live in victory. You can't live in a perpetual pity party and then wonder why situations aren't improving in your life.

If you will change your thinking, God can change your life.

God is just. He knows when people aren't treating us right. He knows when we're doing the right thing, yet the wrong thing keeps happening to us. He knows when we're operating with integrity, and yet somebody comes along and cheats us out of what should have been ours. God sees every time you've been taken advantage of. He sees every time you turn the other cheek and let an offense go by. He sees every time you forgive, or attempt to restore a broken relationship, even though it wasn't your fault. God sees all that; He's keeping a good record. And He's promised to take all the evil that's come into your life, turn it around, and use it for your good.

But here's the key question: Are you willing to change your thinking? Will you take the limits off what God can do in your life? Will you start believing Him for bigger and better things?

Change starts right here. If you will change your thinking, God can change your life. You can't go around thinking thoughts of defeat and failure and expect God to fill you with joy, power, and victory. You can't go around thinking thoughts of poverty and lack and expect God to fill you with abundance. The two concepts are incompatible. Surprisingly, many people have a narrow, limited mind-set. They think small, believe small, and expect small. And then they wonder why nothing big ever happens to them. It's their own thinking that's keeping them in defeat.

We often set our standards too low:

- *"I'm not really happy in my marriage, but we get along okay; I guess this is the best we can expect."*
- *"I'm not really healthy, but at least I can get out of bed in the morning."*

- *"I don't really have enough money, but with a little luck, I can pay a few of these bills."*

That is not the lifestyle God intends for you. God wants you to live an overcoming life of victory. He doesn't want you to barely get by. He's called *El Shaddai*, "the God of more than enough." He's not "El Cheapo," the God of barely enough!

Don't let anybody convince you that God wants you to barely get by in life. The Bible says, "Enlarge the place of your tent. Let the curtains of your habitation be stretched out. Spare not. Lengthen your cords and strengthen your stakes, for soon you will be bursting at the seams."[4] What a powerful picture of God's desire for you! God is saying get ready for more. Make room for increase. Enlarge your tents. He's saying expect more favor, more supernatural blessings. Don't become satisfied with where you are.

One fellow told me, "Joel, if God wants to bless me, then He'll bless me. After all, He's God. I'm not going to be too pushy. I'm not going to expect too much."

Unfortunately, that's just the opposite of how God operates. God works by faith. You must believe first, and then you'll receive. Maybe you've been waiting on God to make a move, but God is waiting on you to stretch your faith. Make room in your own thinking, and then you'll start experiencing some of His supernatural increase.

Notice the words God uses. He says to "enlarge, lengthen, stretch out." We ought always to be trusting God for more. You may have all you need, but don't be selfish. Why not stretch your faith and believe God for more so you can help somebody else in need? God is saying, "If you'll make room for more of My blessings, I won't disappoint you. Soon you'll be bursting at the seams."

If you have been going in circles long enough, dwelling long enough on that mountain, it's time to get moving. Don't be passive, sitting back and settling for a life of mediocrity. God wants you to be the one to rise up and put an end to that mind-set of defeat in your family. He wants you to be the one to set a new standard. Don't pass down an attitude of failure and defeat to the next generation.

Failure Begets Failure

Ten years ago, we had only a dozen or so prisons in my home state of Texas. Today, we have more than 140 prisons, with plans to build more. Each prison is filled with individuals who have had all sorts of defeat and failure passed down to them. Eighty-five percent of the inmates in Texas prisons have had either a parent or a close relative incarcerated at one time or another. Certainly, every person must accept the responsibility for his or her own actions, but we dare not ignore the fact that prisoners beget prisoners. Abused children often become abusive parents. Children of divorced parents are more likely to have a failed marriage. Failure begets failure.

A man recently came to my office seeking advice. He was contemplating his third divorce. After we talked for a while, I asked him, "Has anybody else in your family ever been divorced?"

"Oh, yes," he said. "My mom has been divorced four times, and my dad just ended his sixth marriage." That spirit of divorce, defeat, and failure has been perpetuated in their family line, and keeps getting passed down from generation to generation. We prayed together, and the man decided, "It stops here. I will not allow my marriage to fall apart." He went back home to his wife, determined to work on their relationship, and the couple stemmed the tide of divorce in their family.

Maybe you are living with things that have been in your family line for two or three or more generations. Alcoholism, drug addiction, poverty, depression, anger, low self-esteem, whatever the problem, the good news is that you have an opportunity to break the negative cycle. You can choose to rise up and say, "With God's help, I'm turning the tide. I'm trusting God and taking responsibility for my own actions. I'm setting a new standard."

God will help you break that curse in your family, but it will take perseverance and a willingness to change on your part. Beyond that, it's not enough to say a trite little prayer one time. You must change your thinking and start believing God for better things. Your attitude should be: *I don't care how defeated this family has been in the past. This is a new day. I boldly declare we are more than conquerors. It doesn't matter how broke we've been. I declare we're going to lend and not borrow. I don't care how big our obstacles are. I declare that no weapon formed against us is going to prosper. I don't care how pow-*

erful our enemies are. Greater is He who is in us than he who is in the world. We're not victims anymore. We are the victors. We are blessed and we cannot be cursed.

Have some determination; ask God to put some fire in your spirit. Begin speaking in terms of victory rather than defeat. Your words have amazing power, so quit talking about what you can't do, and start talking about what God *can* do. Keep your mind focused on God's goodness. Stay in an attitude of faith and victory, and you will no longer live under the bondage that's been passed down from previous generations. Take a stand and be the one to make a difference. Go beyond the old barriers of the past. Don't just accept whatever comes your way in life. You were born to win; you were born for greatness; you were created to be a champion in life.

Ask God to put some fire in your spirit.

You may say, "But nobody in my family has ever been successful. I don't see how I can do it."

Maybe nobody in your family ever really took God at His word. Break through those barriers of the past. This is a new day, and God wants to do a new thing. Enlarge your vision. Stretch your faith. You can be the first. You can be the one to "raise the bar." If you believe, all things are possible.

Many times, we pray almost as though we are inconveniencing God. We say, "God, would You please give me a bit bigger apartment? I don't want to bother You for too much."

No, God wants to give you your own house. God has a big dream for your life.

"How could that ever happen to me?" you ask. "I don't make enough money."

Perhaps not, but our God is well able. He's not having financial difficulties. He owns it all. Why not believe Him for bigger things?

We sometimes pray, "God, would You please show my one lonesome relative how much You love him? I'm not asking for much, just this one person."

No, God wants to have a relationship with the entire household. It's time to enlarge your vision.

We pray, "God, would You please give me this one new account so I can make my commission this month, so I can make ends meet?"

No, God wants to do more than you can ask or think. Perhaps God wants you to lead your company in sales.

Friend, God is saying you've dwelt long enough on that mountain. It's time to go to a new level. It's time to get a fresh vision. Go beyond the barriers of the past. Tear down those strongholds in your mind. Remember, you've got to change your thinking. No matter what anybody in your family has or hasn't done, don't let that impose limitations on you. Make up your mind that you are going to be the one to set the new standard. Be the one to affect generations to come.

CHAPTER 5

Increasing in Favor

A couple wanted to enroll their son in a particular private school, but his birthday fell four days after the cutoff date, necessitating a yearlong wait. They felt strongly that their child would do better by starting school with children his own age, so they called the school to see if they could make an exception.

"No way," the registrar told them. "I'm sorry; that's against the rules and we never make an exception. Your child will have to wait another year."

The couple remained kind; they weren't rude. They didn't jump down the registrar's throat or try to manipulate matters. They knew they had the favor of God, so they politely said, "That's fine, but we would like to speak with your boss."

The registrar referred them to the vice-principal of the school. My friends called him and explained the situation. He offered the same answer: "We'd love to help, but we just cannot bend the rules. You're going to have to wait until next year."

"Fine," the father said, "but we'd like to talk to *your* boss."

Eventually, they met with the principal of that school, but he responded similarly. "Rules are rules," he said. "I'm sorry. We can't change them. You're going to have to wait."

They said, "Fine. But we'd like to meet with *your* boss."

The principal said, "I report directly to the superintendent. I'll arrange a meeting for you."

The couple met with the superintendent of the private school and explained the situation. The man offered no comment. He didn't say yes; he didn't say no. He just listened. When they finished presenting their case, he said, "I'm going to have to get back with you." The couple left that meeting still declaring God's favor. They were expecting to get a good report, expecting things to turn around.

About a month after that conversation, they received a call from the school registrar, the first woman with whom they had spoken. She sounded perplexed as she said, "In the fifteen years I've been here, we have never done this before. We don't even know why we're doing it now, but we're going to make an exception and allow your child to attend school this term."

Friend, that is the favor of God. The school administrators may not have known why they were doing it, but we do. It's because God's favor surrounds us like a shield. It doesn't matter what the circumstances look like in your life. Regardless of how many people tell you that what you're attempting can't be done, if you'll persevere, declaring the favor of God and staying in an attitude of faith, God will open doors for you and change circumstances on your behalf.

If you'll persevere . . . God will open doors for you.

The fourth aspect—and one of the most important—to developing a fresh vision for your life is *discovering how to experience more of God's favor*. The Bible clearly states, "God has crowned us with glory and honor."[1] The word *honor* could also be translated as "favor," and *favor* means "to assist, to provide with special advantages and to receive preferential treatment." In other words, God wants to make your life easier. He wants to assist you, to promote you, to give you advantages. He wants you to have preferential treatment. But if we're going to experience more of God's favor, we must live more "favor-minded." To be favor-minded simply means that we expect God's special help, and we are releasing our faith, knowing that God wants to assist us.

All my life, I've been aware of God's favor. From the time my siblings and I were little kids, every day before we left for school, our mother would pray, "Father, I thank You that Your angels have charge over my children, and that Your hand of favor will always be upon them."

Consequently—and I say this humbly—I've come to expect to be treated differently. I've learned to expect people to want to help me.

My attitude is: I'm a child of the Most High God. My Father created the whole universe. He has crowned me with favor, therefore, I can expect preferential treatment. I can expect people to go out of their way to want to help me.

Please don't misinterpret what I'm saying. In no way should we ever be arrogant, thinking that we are better than somebody else, that everybody owes us a living or ought to bow down to us. But as God's children we can live with confidence and boldness, expecting good things. We can expect preferential treatment, not because of *who* we are, but because of *whose* we are. We can expect people to want to help us because of who our Father is.

I'm deeply aware that I've received tremendous favor simply because of who my earthly father was. John Osteen, my dad, was well respected and highly influential in our community. Many times people did good things for me simply because they loved my dad. One time as a teenager, I got pulled over by a policeman for speeding. I had just recently received my driver's license, and I was extremely nervous when I saw those flashing lights pull up behind me, and then the ominous-looking officer looming outside my window. But when that officer saw my license, he recognized that I was John Osteen's son. He smiled at me as though we were long-lost buddies, and he let me go with just a warning.

Another time I got pulled over by a policeman on Highway 59, right near Lakewood Church, where Daddy was the senior pastor. I had been driving much too fast, and this time, the officer wasn't quite as friendly. He looked mean and sounded gruff. He grunted as I handed him my driver's license. He simply stared at it for what seemed to be an eternity. (It was actually about a minute, but it seemed like an eternity to me!) I'll never forget what he said to me, and the way he said it. The officer groused, "Are you related to that ahh . . . , that ahhh, that *preacher*?"

By the way he spit out the words, I didn't know whether it was going to be a good thing to be related to Daddy. And I don't know why I answered him this way, but I think it was because I was nervous. I smiled and said, "Well, Officer, it all depends."

He glared at me and said, "Boy, what are you talking about?"

I said, "It all depends on whether you like him or not."

He looked up in the air for a long time, at least long enough for me to think, *Hmm, that's not a good sign, if he has to think about it.*

Then he looked back at me, cracked a hint of a smile, and said, "Yes, I like him. I like him a lot."

"Good!" I said. "Because that's my dad, and I'm sure he wouldn't want you to give me a ticket." Believe it or not, the officer let me go. I knew the day of miracles was not over! The point is, of course, that I received preferential treatment, not because of me, but because of my father.

A correlation exists in the spiritual realm. We do not receive favor because of who or what we are. It's not because we're something special on our own merit, or that we deserve to be treated so. Nor is it because we're better than anybody else. No, you will often receive preferential treatment simply because your Father is the King of kings, and His glory and honor spill over onto you.

Nevertheless, as odd as it may sound, when you live favor-minded, declaring God's goodness, you'll be amazed at how people will go out of their way to help you. They may not even know why they're doing it, but you'll know that it is because of the favor of God.

A young, successful businessman asked me to pray with him about a job interview that represented a chance for him to advance significantly in his career. An older gentleman had resigned, opening a prominent position in a large company. Numerous high-profile, highly touted executives were flying in from all over the world to interview for the position. Most of them, my friend admitted, had much more experience than he had and were much better qualified. On paper, at least, their résumés looked much better. Nevertheless, he had already interviewed several times with this company, and he was going back for his final evaluation later that week.

After we prayed, I encouraged him, "You have to get up every day and declare that you've got the favor of God. It doesn't matter how the situation appears, be bold and declare with confidence that you have God's favor. Throughout the day, declare, 'The favor of God is causing this company to want to hire me. The favor of God is causing me to stand out in the crowd. It's causing me to shine above the rest.'" I said, "Declare it day in and day out. Stay in an attitude of faith, and expect to get that position."

A few months later, I saw him at church, and he was beaming with joy. I could tell by his expression that he had gotten the job. Later, in describing his interview with the company executives, he said something extremely interesting. He said, "When I went in front of that board of directors, they were literally scratching their heads. They said, 'We don't really know why we're hiring you. You were not the most qualified. You were not the most experienced. You don't have the best résumé.' They said, 'There's just something about you that we like.' The board said, 'We can't quite put our finger on it. We don't know what it is, but there's something about you that makes you shine above the rest.'"

That is the favor of God.

Declare God's Favor

Let me encourage you to start expecting and declaring God's favor in your life. Every morning before you leave the house, say something like this: "Father, I thank You that I have Your favor. Your favor is opening doors of opportunity. Your favor is bringing success into my life. Your favor is causing people to want to help me." Then go out with confidence, expecting good things to happen, expecting doors to open for you that may not open for somebody else, knowing that you have an advantage. There's something special about you. You have the favor of God.

When you go to bed, continue thanking God and declaring His favor and goodness in your life. Anytime you get in a situation where you need favor, learn to declare it. You don't have to loudly broadcast it to the world. You can whisper it, if you prefer. The volume of your voice is irrelevant; it's your faith that makes the difference. Even in the mundane aspects of life, you will not be imposing on God's goodness by declaring His favor. He wants you to act on it. For example, maybe you'll find yourself in a crowded restaurant, with limited time, and you need to get a table as soon as possible. You can say, "Father, I thank You that I have favor with this hostess, and she's going to seat me soon."

Perhaps you're searching for a parking spot in a crowded lot. Say, "Father, I thank You for leading me and guiding me. Your favor will cause me to get a good spot."

"But what if I do all that, and I don't get a good parking spot?" you ask.

Then you get out and walk, and with every step, you thank God that you are strong and healthy and have the ability to walk. The Scripture promises, "All things work together for good to them that love the Lord."[2] If you love God, He's working life to your advantage, and it will all work out for your good.

Not long ago, Victoria and I and our two children drove down to Hermann Park near downtown Houston. But when we got there, the place was totally packed; people and cars everywhere! We hadn't realized it, but we had arrived right smack-dab in the middle of spring break.

At first, it didn't appear that we were going to be able to find a place to park. A half dozen cars were circling the parking lot, waiting for somebody to back out so they could pull in. I was having a good time, cutting up a bit with my family, so I said to everybody in the car, "You watch Daddy. I'm going to get a front-row parking spot. I can just feel it. I've got the favor of God all over me!"

On and on I went, really making a big deal about it. Then, to everyone's surprise, just as I steered our car past the front row of parked cars, another car backed out as I approached. It was almost as though we had timed it perfectly; he pulled out, and I pulled right into the open spot. I hardly had to slow down. Better yet, it was the premier spot in that parking lot.

I leaned over to Victoria and quipped, "Victoria, reach over here and get some of this favor off me. I can't stand it all!"

Victoria just rolled her eyes.

I turned around to our little boy and said, "Come on, Jonathan, touch Daddy. You need some of this favor. Just get it."

He looked at me and said, "Daddy, you are really strange."

Granted, life doesn't always work out quite so conveniently. You won't always get the best spot. A few months ago, I was in a similar situation. I pulled into a crowded parking lot, and I had a bunch of people in the car. I was hamming it up, telling them, "I've got the favor of God. I'm going to get a great parking space."

But this time, nobody pulled out for me. We drove around and around, and fifteen minutes later we all took the shuttle bus. But just because I didn't get what I wanted doesn't mean that I'm going to quit believing in the favor of God. No, I know God has my best interests at heart, that He is working everything for my good. A delay may spare me from an accident. Or a delay may cause me to bump into somebody that needs to be encouraged, somebody that needs to see a smile. No matter what does or doesn't happen, keep believing for the favor of God in your life.

Live favor-minded. Get up each day and expect it and declare it. Say, "I have the favor of God." Don't sit back passively. You do your part, and God will do His part. And you'll have everything you need.

You do your part, and God will do His part.

CHAPTER 6

Living Favor-Minded

God wants to help you in every area of your life, not just the big matters. When you live favor-minded, you'll begin to see God's goodness in the everyday, ordinary details at the grocery store, at the ball field, the mall, at work, or at home. You may be stuck in traffic. The lane next to you is moving well, but you just can't get over there. Then, suddenly, for no apparent reason, somebody slows down and waves you in. That's the favor of God.

You may be at a grocery store in an extremely long checkout line, and you're in a hurry. Another checker taps you on the shoulder and says, "Come with me. I'm opening this additional register over here." That's the favor of God assisting you. The favor of God causes other people to extend preferential treatment to you.

You may be out to lunch when you "just happen" to bump into somebody that you've been wanting to meet. Perhaps that person is somebody you admire or hope to learn from, or possibly he or she is someone with whom you have been hoping to do business, but you couldn't get to them. That is not a coincidence. That's the favor of God causing you to be at the right place at the right time.

When those kinds of things happen, be grateful. Don't take God's favor for granted. Say, "Father, thank You for Your favor. Thank You for assisting me."

Don't take God's favor for granted.

One day Victoria and I went to the mall together. I am not a shopper, but my wife loves to shop! She picked out a few items in a clothing store, and I took them over to the cashier to pay for them while she looked at something else. As I stood at the register, sort of daydreaming, the woman behind the counter smiled and said, "This blouse will be on sale later this week. I'm going to go ahead and give you the sale price."

"Really? Why, thank you very much," I said. "I really appreciate that."

As she began folding the blouse, she noticed something else. She said, "Look at that," she pointed to the bottom of the blouse. "It looks as though it has a mark on it. If it's defective, I'll have to give you a discount. What do you think?"

I said, "Oh, yeah, that looks terrible."

She said, "Well, if it's okay with you, I'm going to cut the price in half."

I said, "Well, that'll be fine with me!"

I later told Victoria, "I'm going to have to go shopping with you more often. It might save us some money!"

That's the favor of God. The clerk didn't have to give us that sale price. I wouldn't have known the difference. And she didn't have to discount the price of the garment based on that small defect. I hadn't even seen it until she brought it to my attention.

But when you are living favor-minded, the Bible says, "God's blessings are going to chase you down and overtake you." In other words, you won't be able to outrun the good things of God. Everywhere you go, things are going to change in your favor. Every time you turn around, somebody's going to want to do something good for you, to assist you in some manner. They may not even know why. But it's the favor of God that causes you to stand out in the crowd.

One time I was sitting on an airplane waiting at the gate, preparing to take off. Suddenly, I heard my name called over the plane's loudspeaker system and the flight attendant asked me to push my call button so she could locate me. At first I was startled. I thought that perhaps I'd left something at the security checkpoint or that something was wrong.

The flight attendant came back down the aisle, leaned over, and spoke quietly. "We would like you to come with us. We have a seat for you up in first class."

The people sitting around me stared, no doubt wondering, *Why is he getting singled out? What's up with him?*

I followed the flight attendant the length of the aircraft and sat down in the seat she indicated . . . in first class. Later during the flight, I asked her, "Why did you choose me?"

She waved her hand and said, "Oh, we needed the space in coach, so the computer just randomly picked somebody to bump up to first class."

I thought, *That's what you think!* I knew that it was my heavenly Father giving me preferential treatment. I knew it was the favor of God causing me to stand out above the rest.

That's the sort of thing that happens "naturally" when we live favor-minded. That's why we should get in the habit of consistently speaking God's favor over our lives. And not simply over our own lives, but over our businesses, our employees, our children, and our families.

If you work in sales, you ought to declare that you have favor with your clients. Every day you should say, "Father, I thank You that my clients are loyal to me and want to do business with me." If you work in real estate, you ought to speak God's favor over your property: "Father, I thank You that this property is going to sell. I thank You that Your favor is leading me to the right people. Your favor is causing people to want to buy this home." Learn to speak God's favor over every area of your life. If you're not experiencing as much favor as you would like, start declaring it more often. Become more diligent about speaking it out. And you don't even necessarily have to say it out loud; you can speak it under your breath. You can say it while you're driving to work. You can say it right before that big presentation. Remember, the more favor-minded you are, the more of God's favor you're going to experience.

Learn to speak God's favor over every area of your life.

The favor of God can cause people to make exceptions and change their policies, or do something unusual—even that which has never been done before. A few years ago, I was checking in at the airport for an overseas flight. I was carrying an expensive television camera, and I didn't really want to check it. I asked the woman at the check-in counter if there was any way I could take it on board with me.

"No, I'm sorry," she said. "Our policy is very strict. If a carry-on doesn't fit under the seat in front of you or in the overhead compartment, it must be checked."

I understood that. She was following the rules. But I also knew that the favor of God can make exceptions, so I respectfully asked her, "Is there anybody else I can talk to about taking my camera on board?"

She said, "No, I'm sorry; there's no use. There's no way you're going to take your camera on board."

About that time, a man dressed in a captain's uniform approached me. I didn't know him, had never seen him before, but he walked right up to me and asked, "How can I help you?"

"I'm trying to take my camera on board," I said, "so it doesn't get all beat up with the checked luggage."

"Where are you going?" he asked.

"I'm going to New Delhi, India, to meet my father," I replied.

"Really?" he said as he raised his eyebrows. "That's the flight I'm in charge of." He then said, "When you get on board, just bring the camera up to me, and I'll put it right behind the cockpit."

The woman behind the counter glared at me and shook her head, clearly aggravated. I just smiled and said, "Sorry, ma'am; it's the favor of God."

The favor of God can cause people to go out of their way to want to help you. The favor of God can cause people to make exceptions for you. Think about it. What caused that captain to come up to me in the midst of that busy airport? There were fifteen or twenty ticket counters and hundreds of people in lines. Why did he choose me?

The favor of God.

That was God giving me special advantages, giving me preferential treatment, not because I was a preacher's kid, or even a distinguished pastor's son, but because I am His child! God wants to do similar things for your life.

A young woman at Lakewood Church told me about an incident in which she had to have emergency surgery and, for some reason, it wasn't covered by her health insurance. Consequently, she owed the hospital $27,000. The hospital worked out a payment plan, and she was paying the bill little by little each month. But she was really struggling. As a single parent, she couldn't afford that extra payment. Nevertheless, she didn't get discouraged. She didn't go around complaining about how tough her life was, or how the hospital had the audacity to charge her so much. Instead she stayed in an attitude of faith and expectancy, declaring God's favor over her life. She was on the lookout for God's goodness.

Right before Christmas she received a letter from the hospital. The letter basically said, "Every year we like to choose a few families and do something good for them. And this year we've chosen you. We want to inform you that we are canceling your $27,000 debt." The letter went on to say, "Not only are we going to forgive your debt, but we are going to refund several thousand dollars that you've already paid us."

That is the favor of God.

You may say, "Joel, that sounds great, but you don't know my luck. You don't know the mistakes I've made. I've done a lot of things wrong. I can't imagine God ever wanting to bless me like that."

You're right. It won't ever happen—unless you change your thinking. You must become favor-minded. You have to start expecting God's blessings to overtake you, expecting God's goodness to show up in your life in a new way. We all have made mistakes and have had to ask for forgiveness. Once you've done that, move on, knowing that God still wants to pour out His favor in your life, to do great things in, through, and for you.

A New Start

Israel's second ruler, King David, made a lot of mistakes. He committed adultery and even ordered a man to be murdered. But when he repented and sought forgiveness, God forgave him and gave him a new start. The Bible compliments David, saying, "He was a man after God's own heart."[1] David didn't focus on his faults or on the things he had done wrong. No, he lived favor-minded. It was David who wrote, "Surely goodness and mercy shall follow me all the days of my life."[2] Notice, he was expecting goodness and mercy, not part of the time, but all the days of his life. I like the way *The Message* translation puts it: "God's kindness and goodness chases me down everywhere I go." David's attitude was, "I just can't get away from the good things of God!"

Instead of expecting to get the short end of the stick, why not start expecting God's blessings to chase you down? Instead of expecting to barely get by in life, start expecting the goodness of God to overtake you. You may say, "That's all great, but I have a lot of problems. I'm facing some difficult times. I have a lot of negative things going on in my life."

The favor of God can bring you out of your difficulties and turn your adversities around for good. David said, "The favor of God keeps my enemies from triumphing over me." The Bible is replete with examples of people who were in great need, but then the favor of God came on them in a new way, and their situations turned around.

Think about Noah facing the greatest challenge of his life. The whole earth was about to be destroyed by a flood, and God gave him the enormous job of building a huge boat, not to mention the gathering of the animals. No doubt, Noah was tempted to get discouraged. Yet amazingly, the Bible says, "Noah found favor in the sight of God."[3] In other words, God was pleased with Noah, so the favor of God came on him in a fresh, new way, giving him unusual ability. God assisted him, and he was able to build that ark to save his family, the animals, and himself.

Consider Ruth. Her husband had died, the land was in a severe famine, and she and her mother-in-law, Naomi, didn't have any food. They were practically starving to death. Ruth went out to the fields every day and followed behind the reapers, picking up whatever leftover grain they had missed. And the Bible indicates that in the midst of that adversity, Ruth found favor with the owner of the field.[4] That owner told his workers to leave handfuls of grain on purpose for Ruth. Notice again, the favor of God came during the crisis, and before long, Ruth and Naomi's circumstances turned around, and their needs were supplied in abundance.

Joseph is another biblical example of someone who found the favor of God in adversity. He was sold into slavery in Egypt, mistreated, and taken advantage of. But the Bible says, "The favor of God was upon Joseph."[5] No matter what other people did to him, no matter where they put him, he continued to prosper. Even when Potiphar's wife lied about him, unjustly accusing him of rape, and he was thrown into prison, he continued to thrive. The favor of God eventually caused him to be released, and he was put in charge of all Egypt's agricultural affairs.

In each of these examples, the favor of God came in the midst of a trial. The favor came in a flood. Favor came in the famine. Favor came when somebody was being mistreated. In other words, the favor came in the midst of life's challenges. When you are going through tough times—when, like Joseph, somebody is mistreating you, or like Ruth, you're having financial difficulty, or like Noah, your whole world is falling apart—instead of becoming discouraged and developing a sour attitude, more than ever, you must choose to be favor-minded. Start declaring God's favor. Start expecting God's favor.

Live with an Attitude of Faith

Is somebody mistreating you today? Start saying, "Father, I thank You that Your favor is coming on me in a new way, and it's going to turn this situation around. It's going to cause these people to start treating me well."

Similarly, if you are struggling financially, say something such as, "Father, I thank You that You're causing me to be at the right place at the right time. You are bringing wonderful financial opportunities my way."

If you will live with an attitude of faith, then, like the saints of old, before long God's favor is going to show up, and that situation will turn around to your benefit. Think about Job. He went through one of the most trying times any person could ever endure. In less than a year, he lost his family, his business, and his health. He had boils over his entire body and no doubt lived in perpetual pain. But in the midst of that dark hour, Job said, "God, I know that you have granted me favor."[6]

Now, here's the amazing part of the story: There are forty-two chapters in the book of Job. Job made this statement of faith in chapter 10. He was not delivered, healed, and set free until chapter 42! But at the very beginning, when his circumstances appeared darkest and most hopeless, Job looked up and declared, "God, I know You have granted me favor." Whew! That's real faith. Job was saying, "God, I don't care what the situation looks like. I don't care how badly I feel. I know You are a good God. And Your favor is going to turn this situation around."

Is it any wonder God restored to Job twice what he had before? Is it any wonder that his enemies could not triumph over him?

Friend, if you can learn to stay in an attitude of faith, and in your darkest hour boldly declare the favor of God, then nothing is going to be able to keep you down. You may be in a situation today that looks impossible, but don't rule out the favor of God. One touch of God's favor can turn everything around in your life.

Nothing is going to be able to keep you down.

The Bible says, "Hope to the end for the divine favor that is coming to you." In other words, don't give up. Keep on believing, expecting, declaring. Keep living favor-minded, and God promises that good things will come to you. If you will keep your hope in the Lord, God says divine favor is coming. You may not be able to see it right now. Things may not look good in the natural, but the good news is that if you keep expecting it and declaring it, God's favor will show up. And when God's favor shows up, things are going to change. The favor of God will cause you to rise up out of your problems. The favor of God will keep your enemies from defeating you. Regardless of your circumstances, keep boldly declaring, "God, I know Your favor is coming my way."

In 2001 we wanted to expand our television outreach on one particular network. I asked the man who represents us to contact the network and check into acquiring the Sunday-night eleven o'clock time slot.

He said, "Joel, there's just no way. That's a national network. That time is much too valuable. They'll never give it up."

I said, "Well, the Bible says, 'We have not because we ask not.' So let's give it a try."

Our agent flew to the network headquarters and met with the executives there. They responded just as predicted: "No, that time slot is too valuable. We can't let you have that. You'll have to try something else."

I said, "Fine. We'll just keep believing for the favor of God." Every day, I declared, "Father, I thank You that Your favor is coming in a new way. Your favor is opening doors that men say are impossible to open. I thank You that Your favor is causing this company to give us preferential treatment." Month after month went by and I never heard a word. But I didn't get discouraged. I didn't give up. I just kept hoping in faith. I knew that if I didn't give up, God promised that divine favor was coming. I may not have been able to see it, but I knew it was on its way.

About six months later I got a call from our representative. He said,

"Something must be happening, because the television network asked me to come back and meet with them again."

"Great," I said. "But I've got to tell you I've changed my mind. I don't want the eleven o'clock time slot anymore. I want the ten o'clock time period. I want to follow their number one show."

"Joel, are you kidding?" our agent said with a laugh. "Do you know what they're going to say to me when I ask them for that?"

"Listen," I said, "we've got the favor of God. God's opening doors that no man can shut. You go in there with confidence, with boldness, knowing that God's favor is all over you."

He laughed and said, "All right. I'll do it."

He met with the network officials and called me afterward. He said, "Joel, I did my best. I gave it my all, but they still turned us down."

I said, "That's fine. We'll just keep believing. I know the favor of God is coming. I know if I don't give up, divine favor will make a way."

About a month after that meeting, our representative called us. He was on cloud nine! He said, "You'll never believe what happened. The owner of that network just called me. Not the sales representative, but the owner, tracked me down in an airport. And he said, 'Listen, I know you've been interested in that Sunday night time period, and I really like that young minister. So I had them clear that slot especially for you. You can start whenever you want to.'"

Friend, that's the favor of God. Never give up on God. The Bible says, "If you will hope to the end, divine favor will come."[7]

When you really understand that you have this favor available to you, living with confidence comes much more easily. You can dare to be bold. You'll ask for things you normally don't ask for. And you'll view your adversities in a new way. Deep down inside you'll know you have an advantage in life. You've got an edge. You have the favor of God.

PART 2

DEVELOP A HEALTHY SELF-IMAGE

CHAPTER 7

Who Do You Think You Are?

By most standards, Carly should not have made it. Overweight, with one leg slightly shorter than the other as the result of a childhood accident, Carly was the lone woman employed in a largely male-dominated field. She had to earn her right to be heard nearly every day. Some people laughed at her appearance or her halting walk; some made snide remarks behind her back, some were inconsiderate to her face, but Carly paid little attention. She knew who she was, and she knew she was good at what she did, so when other people attempted to put her down, she regarded them as having the problem. "Emotionally challenged," she often quipped about her detractors.

Despite the factors working against her, Carly continued to receive one promotion after another, eventually becoming the CEO of her company and a highly-sought-after expert in her field. How did she do it?

Carly's secret is her incredibly positive self-image. A devout Christian, Carly believes that she has been made in the image of God, and that He gives her life intrinsic value. She doesn't strive for the approval of other people or depend on compliments from her superiors or peers to feel good about herself. Bright, friendly, articulate, and extremely competent at her work, Carly goes through life with a smile. While others shake their heads in amazement at her attitude, Carly is living her best life now!

A Healthy Self-Image

The second step to living *your* best life now is *developing a healthy self-image*. That means you must base your self-image on what God's Word says about you, rather than on false, fickle standards such as what neighborhood you live in, the style of car you drive, or the opinions of power-lunch groups. How you see yourself and how you feel about yourself will have a tremendous impact on how far you go in life and whether or not you fulfill your destiny. The truth is, you will never rise above the image you have of yourself in your own mind.

You will never rise above the image you have of yourself in your own mind.

What is your self-image? With the new interest in self-awareness these days, it is easy to become confused over terminology. Is my *self-image* the same thing as my *self-esteem* and *self-concept*? How do I measure my *self-worth*? Although clinical psychologists enjoy parsing the slight differentiations in actual meanings, most people use the words *self-image, self-esteem, self-concept,* and *self-worth* interchangeably. That's fine for our purposes.

Self-esteem, then, is that deep-down feeling you have about yourself. It's how you regard yourself, your opinion or judgment of your own value, the extent to which you think you matter in life. It's the feeling that says, "I like myself," or "I dislike myself." Similarly, your *self-image* is much like a self-portrait; it is who and what you picture yourself to be. Interestingly, your self-image may or may not be an accurate reflection of who you really are, but it is how you *perceive* yourself to be. Who do you think you are?

Unquestionably, a healthy self-image is one of the key factors in the success and happiness of any individual. The reason your self-concept is so important is: You will probably speak, act, and react as the person you *think* you are. Psychologists have proved that you will most consistently perform in a manner that is in harmony with the image you have of yourself. Oh, sure, even with a negative self-concept, you may occasionally break out of the pattern and land a big deal, win over a new friend, or belt a softball out of the park at the company picnic. Conversely, even those individuals with healthy self-images blow it from time to time. But usually, your mind will complete the picture you tell it to paint of yourself.

If you see yourself as unqualified, insignificant, unattractive, inferior, or inadequate, you will probably act in accordance with your thoughts. If your self-worth is low, you will imagine yourself as a born loser, a washout, unworthy of being loved and accepted.

"I can never do anything right."

"Why me?"

"I'll never amount to anything."

These are just a few of the phrases that dominate the conversations of a person with poor self-esteem. On the other hand, individuals who view themselves as God sees them are usually happy about who they are. They know that they have been created in God's image and He has crowned them with tremendous honor.[1] They feel good about themselves, because they know that God loves them and He feels good about them! They can honestly say, "Thank You, Father, for creating me the way You did. I know that You have a purpose and a plan for me, and I'd rather be me than any other person on earth. You have promised that You have good things in store for me, and I can't wait to discover them!"

Your self-image is not a physical part of your body. It is more a subconscious "governor" that controls your actions and performance. It functions similar to the cruise control on an automobile. Once the cruise mechanism is set at 70 miles per hour, the car may speed up or slow down as it encounters different terrains, but the cruise control will always bring the vehicle back to the set speed. Similarly, when you exceed your expectations or go a little too far, your self-image pulls you back in line. If you fall below the setting, your self-image will pull you back up.

Where did you get your self-esteem? Ironically, your current self-image may be the result of what other people have said about you, how your parents or peers regarded you, or it may stem from your own self-imposed images—portraits that you have painted of yourself in your own mind regarding your personality, your appearance, your abilities, or your accomplishments. Every person has an image of himself or herself. The question is, does your image of who you are line up correctly with who God says you are?

God wants us to have healthy, positive self-images, to see ourselves as priceless treasures. He wants us to feel good about ourselves. God knows we're not perfect, that we all have faults and weaknesses; that we all make mistakes. But the good news is, God loves us anyway. He created us in His image, and He is continually shaping us, conforming us to His character, helping us to become even more like the person He is. Consequently, we must learn to love ourselves, faults and all, not because we are egotists or because we want to excuse our shortcomings, but because that's how our heavenly Father loves us. You can hold your head up high and walk with confidence knowing that God loves you unconditionally. His love for you is based on what you are, not on what you do. He created you as a unique individual—there has never been, nor will there ever be, another person exactly like you, even if you are a twin—and He sees you as His special masterpiece!

Moreover, God sees you as a champion. He believes in you even more than you believe in yourself! So often, we sense God telling us that He has something big for us to do. But because of a poor self-image, we say, "God, I can't do that. I'm just a nobody. You've got to find somebody more qualified, somebody more educated. God, I don't have what it takes."

That's how a fellow named Gideon responded in Bible times. An angel appeared to Gideon and said, "The Lord is with you, you mighty man of valor." (The Amplified Bible says, "You mighty man of fearless courage.")

Believe it or not, that is how God sees you, too. He regards you as a strong, courageous, successful, overcoming person.

"Oh, Joel, He wouldn't say that about me," you may be saying. "I'm not any of those things. I'm not strong. I'm not successful. Courageous? Are you kidding? Me? God probably said those great things to Gideon because he was secure and confident, because he was a great leader."

Not so. When the angel went on to tell Gideon how God wanted him to save the people of Israel from the Midianites, a vicious, pagan people who had overrun their land, Gideon showed his true colors. He replied, "How do you expect me to save the people of Israel? I come from the poorest family in all of Manasseh. And I am the least one in my father's house."

Sound familiar?

But it's interesting to note the difference between the way Gideon saw himself and the way God regarded him. Although Gideon felt unqualified, full of fear, and lacking in confidence, God still addressed him as a mighty man of fearless courage. Gideon felt weak; God saw him as strong. Gideon felt unqualified; God saw him as competent to do the job. Gideon felt insecure; God saw him with enough confidence and boldness to lead His people into battle and come out with the victory. And Gideon did!

Similarly, God sees you as a champion. You may not see yourself that way, but that doesn't change God's image of you one bit. God still sees you exactly as His Word describes you. You may feel unqualified, insecure, or overwhelmed by life; you may feel weak, fearful, and insignificant, but God sees you as a victor!

Change Your Self-Image

Consider this: You can change the image you have of yourself. How? Start by agreeing with God. Remember, God sees you as strong and courageous, as a man or woman of great honor and valor. He sees you as being more than a conqueror. Start seeing yourself as God sees you. Quit making excuses and start stepping out in faith, doing what God has called you to do.

Are you allowing your weaknesses and insecurities to keep you from being your best? Are you making excuses as to why you can't take a new leadership position at work, get involved in some program in your church, serve in your community, or help a friend in need? Notice, God didn't disqualify Gideon, but He didn't excuse him from service either. You may be letting your feelings of inadequacy keep you from believing God for bigger things. God wants to use you in spite of your weaknesses. Don't focus on your weaknesses; focus on your God. If God chose to use perfect people only, He'd have no one to use.

Don't focus on your weaknesses; focus on your God.

God loves to use ordinary people just like you and me, faults and all, to do extraordinary things. You may not feel capable in your own strength, but that's okay. The apostle Paul said, "When we are weak, He is strong."[2] God's Word states that He always causes us to triumph. He expects us to live victoriously. He is not pleased when we mope around with a "poor me" attitude and a "weak worm of the dust" mentality. When you do that, you're allowing your self-image to be shaped by nonbiblical concepts that are contrary to God's opinion of you.

Yet many people do just that. Consequently, they suffer from low self-esteem; they feel insignificant and unworthy to receive God's attention, much less His blessings. This sort of poor self-image keeps them from exercising their God-given gifts and authority, and it robs them from experiencing the abundant lives their heavenly Father wants them to have. Most often, the lack of joy and meaning in their lives is a direct result of how those individuals see themselves.

Beware of associating with or adopting the attitudes of people who, through their negative outlook and lack of self-esteem, will rob you of the greatness that God has for you. A classic illustration of this is recorded in the Old Testament, after God supernaturally helped Moses deliver more than two million Hebrew people out of slavery in Egypt. They traveled all the way across the wilderness and made it to the border of Canaan, the land flowing with milk and honey. They camped right next door to the Promised Land, God's "Dreamland" for them. God had promised His people a rich possession and a fantastic future. There was only one problem: Their Dreamland was already inhabited.

Knowing they might be in for a tough fight, Moses sent twelve spies into Canaan to check out the opposition and get a feel for the land before launching the battle. After six weeks, the scouts came back with their report.

"It's just like we heard!" they excitedly shared with the welcoming party.

And all the people said, "Amen!"

"It *is* a land flowing with milk and honey," the spies continued. "Look at these grapes. Look at these pomegranates! Why, they're the biggest and best-tasting we've ever seen. And here—taste some of this honey. Is that not amazing?"

And the people said, "Amen!"

Then came the bad news. "But there are giants in the land, and compared to them, we look like a bunch of grasshoppers."

And all the people said, "Oh, me, oh, my!"

Ten of the twelve spies said, "It is indeed a land flowing with milk and honey, but we don't have a chance. We'll never defeat those people. They're too big and they're too strong." Moreover, they went on to say, "Moses, we were in our own sights as grasshoppers." Notice that phrase, "in our own sights." In other words, compared to the opposition and the obstacles in front of them, the mental image they had of themselves was as small, weak, defeated grasshoppers, ready to be squashed, helpless before the giants opposing them.

Those ten spies came back with a negative report because they were focused on their circumstances. They lost the battle before it even started. But the other two spies, Joshua and Caleb, had a totally different report. They possessed the same data as their ten colleagues, but it was almost as though they had gone to a different place.

"Moses, we are well able to possess the land," they said. "Yes, there are giants there, and the giants are formidable, but our God is much bigger. Yes, the people are strong, but our God is stronger. Because of Him, we are well able. Let's go in at once and possess the land."

What a tremendous truth! You and I are "well able" people. Not because *we* are so powerful, but because our God is so powerful! When we face adversity and hardships in life, we can rise up with boldness and confidence, knowing that because of God, we are well able to overcome them.

Joshua and Caleb were not naive. They faced the same facts as their fellow spies. They admitted the existence of the giants, the opposition, and the obstacles, but the difference was in their attitudes. They believed God. Their self-images were such that they refused to see themselves as grasshoppers ready to be stomped on. Instead, they saw themselves as God's men, led by God and empowered by God. Joshua and Caleb had the same data as the doubters, but they drew different conclusions.

Friend, God already has enough "grasshoppers." He wants you to be a "can do" person, someone who is willing, ready, and "well able" to do what He commands.

Sadly, of all the people who came out of Egypt, only two men, Joshua and Caleb, ever entered the land God intended for them. The others (except for Moses and Aaron) were a reproach to God; they dishonored Him and, as a result, spent the rest of their lives wandering around in circles throughout the wilderness, until they finally died. Their lack of faith and their lack of self-esteem robbed them of the fruitful future God had in store for them.

Remember, God had already guaranteed the Hebrews the victory, but because of their poor self-images, they never made it into the Promised Land. They never fulfilled their destiny, all because of the way they saw themselves.

How do you see yourself? Do you see yourself as successful? Healthy? Upbeat? Happy? Do you see yourself as being used by God? Do you see yourself as "well able" to do what God wants you to do, strong in the Lord and the power of His might? Or, have you allowed yourself to adopt a "grasshopper mentality"?

The grasshopper mentality says, "I'll never make it in life. My dreams will never come to pass. My marriage is too far gone; I'm too far in debt. I'll never get out of the hole I'm in."

You must learn how to cast down those negative thoughts and begin to see yourself as God sees you—as a winner, an overcomer. He sees you as being "well able." If you want the circumstances to change for the better in your life, you must first see them changing through your "eyes of faith." You must see yourself as happy, fulfilled, and successful, living an overcoming life.

See yourself as God sees you—as a winner, an overcomer.

Understand, you are not a cosmic accident, wandering randomly and aimlessly through life. God has a specific purpose for your life. He didn't intend for you to go through life miserable, depressed, lonely, sick, and defeated. You may be so beaten down by the struggles in your life that you've grown accustomed to being discouraged. Perhaps you've been deceived into accepting a life that is far less than God's best. Maybe at one time you had a good image of yourself, but now you see yourself as simply a survivor. The image God wants you to have of yourself has been distorted; the mirrors in which you have seen yourself—reflected in the words, actions, or opinions of your parents, your peers, or people who have hurt you—have become grossly cracked, delivering a contorted and distorted image of yourself. When you accept that warped image, you open yourself to depression, poverty, or worse. If you are not careful, before long you will begin thinking that the image you see in those cracked mirrors is a true reflection of the way life is supposed to be. You won't expect anything better. You won't expect God's blessings and victories. You will drift through life haphazardly, accepting whatever comes along, spinning your wheels until you die.

But friend, that is not God's intent for you! God is a good God, and He gives good things to His children. No matter who has denigrated you or how much pain you've experienced in life, no matter how many setbacks you have suffered, you cannot allow yourself to accept that as the way life is supposed to be. No, God has better things in store for you. You must reprogram your mind with God's Word; change that negative, defeated self-image, and start seeing yourself as winning, coming out on top. Start seeing that marriage as restored. See your business as flourishing. See your children as enjoying the good things of God. You must see it through your eyes of faith, and then it will begin to happen.

Learn to guard your mind, control your thought life, and begin to dwell on the good things of God. If you always think little, believe little, and expect little, then you will receive little. And if you're always thinking about defeat, failure, how weak you are, and about how impossible your circumstances look, then just as those ten spies in biblical times, you will develop a "grasshopper mentality."

One young man told me, "Joel, my grandparents were poor and my great-grandparents lived in poverty before them. And my parents never amounted to much either. I guess this is just my lot in life."

That's a grasshopper mentality.

"No, you must break out of that poverty mentality and change that negative self-image," I encouraged him. "Don't let your past determine your destiny or influence your self-image. See yourself the way God sees you. Picture yourself experiencing the wonderful things God has in store for you."

As I mentioned earlier, my dad was raised in one of the poorest of the poor cotton-picking families, who lost everything they owned when they went through the Great Depression in the late 1920s and early 1930s. But in 1939, at the age of seventeen, my dad gave his heart to God. Years later Daddy told me, "From that moment on, I made a quality decision that my children and my family would never have to experience the poverty and lack that I was raised in." And he began to see himself differently. He quit seeing himself as a poor, defeated farmer's child with no hope, no education, and no future. Instead, he started seeing himself as a child of the Most High God. He began to search the Scripture to see what God said about him.

Daddy realized that God had bigger and greater plans for his life. Over the years, he developed a better understanding of who he was as a child of God, and what rightfully belonged to him as a result of that relationship. He began to see himself as God saw him. He discovered that God was a God of increase. With that truth in mind, Daddy rose above the status quo of his day and broke the curse of poverty in our family. But it all started when he got a vision of who he was in God's sight. No wonder he held up his Bible every service and said, "This is my Bible. I am what it says I am. I have what it says I have."

You might be shocked if you really understood how much God wants to bless you. God wants you to accomplish great things in life. He wants you to leave your mark on this world. He's put incredible potential, gifts, and talents within you, ready for use as you start seeing yourself as God sees you, stepping out in faith and acting on the dreams and the desires that He's placed in your heart.

It's exciting, isn't it? You're beginning to see yourself as God sees you. You're getting rid of that grasshopper mentality. Yes, you may have some big obstacles in your path, but your God is much, much bigger. You are a "can do" person. You are developing a "well able to" attitude, seeing yourself as the champion God made you to be. Keep going; keep growing. God has much more in store for you!

CHAPTER 8

Understanding Your Value

My dad went to a high school football game with a dear friend of ours named Jesse. Jesse's son, Jeff, played on the defensive squad, so he rarely touched the ball during a game. But on one particular play, the punter kicked a short punt and Jeff fielded it. He ran over, caught the ball, took a half step to his right and a half step back to his left, his eyes darting in every direction, searching for some daylight. But there was no running room to be found. Just then, about ten guys from the opposing team clobbered him. I mean, he didn't advance the ball one inch.

For a long, awkward moment, Daddy sat silently staring out at the field as the referee untangled the pile of players climbing off Jeff. Daddy was feeling badly for Jesse, and he was trying to think of something good to say, but the play had been a disaster. Even Daddy couldn't come up with anything positive. About that time Jesse punched Daddy in the ribs. He had a big smile on his face as he nodded toward the field where Jeff was just getting to his feet. Jesse said, "Pastor, did you see those two good moves?" Only a loving father could see his son's two good moves, rather than the fact that his son just got tackled by everybody but the cheerleaders!

God Sees Our Two Good Moves

But friend, that's the way our heavenly Father looks at us. He's not dwelling on the times we get knocked down. He's not dwelling on our faults. No, God sees our two good moves. God focuses on the things you're doing right; He sees the best in you. You may not always control your temper as you know you should. Or you may slip and say things you wish you hadn't said. Seek forgiveness from God and from anyone you may have offended, but don't go around beating yourself up, living in condemnation. As long as you are pressing forward, you can hold your head up high, knowing that you are a "work in progress," and God is in the process of changing you. He's looking at your two good moves.

That's not to condone wrongdoing, but the truth is, we all have areas in which we need to improve. We can't become so focused on our faults that we cease to enjoy who God made us to be. You've got to be happy with who you are right now and accept yourself, faults and all.

An important factor in seeing yourself God's way is to understand your intrinsic sense of value, whether you make the right moves or the wrong moves. Too often we focus on our faults, weaknesses, past mistakes, and failures. Rejection and other painful experiences steal our self-esteem and make us feel unwanted and insecure.

Your sense of value cannot be based on your achievements, how well you perform, how somebody else treats you, or how popular or successful you are. Your sense of value should be based solely on the fact that you are a child of the Most High God. As His unique creation, you have something to offer this world that nobody else has, that nobody else can be.

It's vital that you accept yourself and learn to be happy with who God made you to be. If you want to truly enjoy your life, you must be at peace with yourself. Many people constantly feel badly about themselves. They are overly critical of themselves, living with all sorts of self-imposed guilt and condemnation. No wonder they're not happy; they have a war going on inside. They're not at peace with themselves. And if you can't get along with yourself, you will never get along with other people. The place to start is by being happy with who God made you to be.

Learn to be happy with who God made you to be.

You may not be perfect—nobody is! Sure, you've got some flaws— we all do! But to be truly free, you must have a healthy respect for yourself in spite of those "imperfections."

Some people are always putting themselves down. "I'm so slow."

"I'll never break these bad habits." "I'm unattractive. Look at my nose; what am I ever going to do with my hair?"

Don't be so hard on yourself! Certainly, there may be some things in your life that you aren't happy about; you may have some habits you need to break. But remember, God is not finished with you. He's in the process of changing you.

The Scripture says we are God's workmanship.[1] The word *work-manship* implies that you are not yet a finished product; you are a "work in process." Throughout our lives, God is continually shaping and molding us into the people He wants us to be. The key to future success is to not be discouraged about your past or present while you are in the process of being "completed." The Bible indicates that we go from glory to glory as we are being transformed into God's image.[2] Whether you realize it or not, right now God is moving you onward toward greater things. The path of the righteous gets brighter and brighter.[3]

When you are tempted to get discouraged, remind yourself that according to God's Word, your future is getting brighter; you are on your way to a new level of glory. You may think you've got a long way to go, but you need to look back at how far you've already come. You may not be everything you want to be, but at least you can thank God that you're not what you used to be.

Our value is intrinsic. It is not something you or I have earned; indeed, we cannot earn it. God built value into us when He created us. To God, we are His ultimate creations. That means you can stop obsessing about all your faults and give yourself a break. Every person has weaknesses. Even the great men and women of the Bible made mistakes. They all had shortcomings, but that didn't stop God from loving them, blessing them, and using them to accomplish great deeds. Besides, we need to learn how to keep our flaws in perspective. You may think there is a lot wrong with you, but there is also a lot right with you.

The great news is that God knows everything about you, both good and bad, and He still loves you and values you unconditionally. God does not always approve of our behavior. He is not pleased when we go against His will, and when we do, we always suffer the consequences and have to work with Him to correct our thoughts, words, actions, or attitudes. And while you should work to improve in the areas where you fall short, nothing you do will ever cause God to love you less . . . or more. His love is a constant you can depend on.

Understand, your value in God's eyes never changes. Some people want us to think that the moment we do something wrong or get off course, God gets His big marker out, crosses our name off His list, and says, "I knew they couldn't do it. I knew they didn't have what it takes." No, God is a forgiving God. He is a God of second chances. No matter how many times you fail Him or how many mistakes you make, your value in God's eyes remains exactly the same.

Imagine that I am handing you a new, crisp one-hundred-dollar bill. Would you want it? Probably so! Suppose I crumpled it up so it wasn't quite as good-looking as it was the day it came from the mint. Would you still want it? Sure! But wait, what if I took it out in the parking lot, threw it on the ground, and stomped on it until the picture on the bill was barely perceptible? It's now dirty, stained, and soiled. Would you still want it?

Of course. Why? Because it is still valuable despite the rough treatment it has experienced. A hundred dollars is a hundred dollars (forgetting about exchange rates, inflation, and other factors, for the moment). It doesn't lose its value simply because it has aged, is not as pretty as it once was, or has taken some bumps and bruises in life.

That's the way God sees each one of us. We all go through challenges and struggles. Sometimes we feel like that hundred-dollar bill, all crumpled and soiled. But just as that hundred-dollar bill still has value, we do, too! In fact, we will never, ever lose our value. Our value has been placed in us by the Creator of the universe, and nobody can take it away from us.

Don't let other people, systems, or circumstances influence your estimation of your value. You may have gone through some traumatic, painful experiences in which somebody mistreated you, used you, or rejected you. Maybe your husband or wife walked out on you and you went through a bitter divorce. Maybe a good friend turned on you for no reason, and you now feel alone and worthless. Or, maybe you felt rejected as a child, and you are living with feelings of guilt and shame. Perhaps you've even convinced yourself that the negative things that happened in your past are all your fault, that you deserve nothing but heartache, pain, guilt, and condemnation.

Friend, nothing could be farther from the truth.

God Knows Your Value

I recall talking to Steve, a young man who had suffered severe rejection as a child. Steve's parents continually beat him down verbally, telling him that he was never going to make it in life, that he'd never amount to anything. Day after day, those destructive words pounded into his thoughts and his subconscious mind, destroying his self-image and his sense of value. Steve told me later how he discovered the root cause of the problem was the fact that his parents had hoped for a baby girl. They had been sorely disappointed when he was born. Seventeen years later, he was still living with tremendous guilt and shame. And for what? *Being born!* Sadly, Steve was convinced that he was to blame for all the heartache in his family, that he was the reason his parents were so unhappy, that he'd done something wrong, that his life was one horrible mistake.

I told him, "Steve, you cannot allow your self-esteem and your sense of value to be determined by how other people treat you. The Bible tells us that God accepts us even if everybody else in this world rejects us."

I could see a glimmer of hope reflected in Steve's eyes, so I continued to encourage him. "I love what the psalmist said in Psalm 27:10: 'Although my mother and my father have rejected me, the Lord will take me in and adopt me as His very own child.' God will never reject you, Steve. He always accepts you. Don't allow the rejection of other people to cause you to reject yourself." It took a while for Steve to accept the truth of what I was telling him, but today he is well on his way to living a happy, productive life.

Maybe you live or work with somebody who is emotionally abusive, always putting you down and criticizing you, telling you what a terrible person you are. Let that misinformation go in one ear and out the other. Constantly remind yourself that you are made in the image of Almighty God. Remind yourself that He has crowned you with glory and honor, that you are God's own masterpiece. Don't let other people play games with your mind, deceiving you into thinking that your value has diminished.

You may feel that your great aspirations have been dashed by the choices you have made or the choices imposed on you by others. You may feel that you are trapped in a rut, but there's hope! God wants to restore your sense of value. David wrote, "God has lifted me out of the horrible pit and He set my feet upon a rock and He put a new song in my mouth."4 God wants to put a new song in your heart; He wants to fill you with hope. He wants you to know that He loves you more than you can imagine and He can turn your dashed dreams into something beautiful.

I recently read a retelling of the timeless story *The Tale of Three Trees*. This fictitious children's book relates the lofty aspirations of an olive tree, an oak tree, and a pine tree. Each of these trees had a great dream to become something special in life. The olive tree dreamed of becoming a finely crafted treasure chest. It wanted to hold gold, silver, and precious jewels. One day a woodsman chose the one olive tree, out of all the trees in the forest, and cut it down. The olive tree was so thrilled. But as the craftsmen began working on him, the tree realized they weren't making him into a beautiful treasure chest; they were making him into a manger to hold food for dirty, smelly animals. Heartbroken, his dreams were shattered. He felt worthless and demeaned.

Similarly, the oak tree dreamed of becoming part of a huge ship that would carry important kings across the ocean. When the woodsman cut down the oak, he was so excited. But as time went on, he realized the craftsmen weren't making him into a huge ship. They were making him into a tiny fishing boat. He was so discouraged, so disappointed.

The pine tree lived on top of a high mountain. Its only dream was to always stand tall and remind people of God's great creation. But in a split second, a bolt of lightning sent it tumbling to the ground, destroying its dreams. The woodsman came and picked it up and carried it off to the scrap pile.

All three of these trees felt they had lost their value and their worth; they were so discouraged, so disappointed. Not one of their dreams had come to pass. But God had other plans for these trees. Many years later, Mary and Joseph couldn't find any place to give birth to their little baby boy. They finally found a stable, and when Jesus was born they placed Him in a manger made from—you guessed it—the olive tree. The olive tree had wanted to hold precious jewels, but God had better plans, and it now held the greatest treasure of all time, the Son of God.

A few years went by and Jesus grew up. One day He needed a boat to cross to the other side of the lake. He didn't choose a large, fancy ship; He chose a small, simple fishing boat made from—you guessed it—the oak tree. The oak tree wanted to carry important kings across the ocean, but God had better plans. The oak now carried the King of kings.

A few more years went by, and one day some Roman soldiers were rummaging around in the pile of scrap wood where the discarded pine tree lay. That pine tree just knew they were coming to cut him up for firewood. But much to its surprise, they cut only two small pieces out of it and formed them into a cross. And it was on this pine tree that Jesus was crucified. That tree is still pointing people to God's love and God's compassion to this day.

The point of the classic story is clear: All three trees thought they had lost their value, that their stories were over, yet they became integral parts of the greatest story ever told.

God knows your value; He sees your potential. You may not understand everything you are going through right now. But hold your head up high, knowing that God is in control and He has a great plan and purpose for your life. Your dreams may not have turned out exactly as you'd hoped, but the Bible says that God's ways are better and higher than our ways. Even when everybody else rejects you, remember, God stands before you with His arms open wide. He always accepts you. He always confirms your value. God sees your two good moves! You are His prized possession. No matter what you go through in life, no matter how many disappointments you suffer, your value in God's eyes always remains the same. You will always be the apple of His eye. He will never give up on you, so don't give up on yourself.

CHAPTER 9

Become What You Believe

Our thoughts and expectations wield tremendous power and influence in our lives. We don't always get what we deserve in life, but we usually get no more than we expect; we receive what we believe. Unfortunately, this principle works as strongly in the negative as it does in the positive.

We receive what we believe.

Nick was a big, strong, tough man who worked in the railroad yards for many years. He was one of his company's best employees—always there on time, a reliable, hard worker who got along well with the other employees. But Nick had one major problem. His attitude was chronically negative. He was known around the railroad yards as the most pessimistic man on the job. He perpetually feared the worst and constantly worried, fretting that something bad might happen.

One summer day, the crews were told that they could go home an hour early in order to celebrate the birthday of one of the foremen. All the workers left, but somehow Nick accidentally locked himself in a refrigerated boxcar that had been brought into the yard for maintenance. The boxcar was empty and not connected to any of the trains.

When Nick realized that he was locked inside the refrigerated boxcar, he panicked. Nick began beating on the doors so hard that his arms and fists became bloody. He screamed and screamed, but his coworkers had already gone home to get ready for the party. Nobody could hear Nick's desperate calls for help. Again and again he called out, until finally his voice was a raspy whisper.

Aware that he was in a refrigerated boxcar, Nick guessed that the temperature in the unit was well below freezing, maybe as low as five or ten degrees Fahrenheit. Nick feared the worst. He thought, *What am I going to do? If I don't get out of here, I'm going to freeze to death. There's no way I can stay in here all night.* The more he thought about his circumstances, the colder he became. With the door shut tightly, and no apparent way of escape, he sat down to await his inevitable death by freezing or suffocation, whichever came first.

To pass the time, he decided to chronicle his demise. He found a pen in his shirt pocket and noticed an old piece of cardboard in the corner of the car. Shivering almost uncontrollably, he scribbled a message to his family. In it Nick noted his dire prospects: "Getting so cold. Body numb. If I don't get out soon, these will probably be my last words."

And they were.

The next morning, when the crews came to work, they opened the boxcar and found Nick's body crumpled over in the corner. When the autopsy was completed, it revealed that Nick had indeed frozen to death.

Now, here's a fascinating enigma: The investigators discovered that the refrigeration unit for the car in which Nick had been trapped was not even on! In fact, it had been out of order for some time and was not functioning at the time of the man's death. The temperature in the car that night—the night Nick froze to death—was sixty-one degrees. Nick froze to death in slightly less than normal room temperatures because he believed that he was in a freezing boxcar. He expected to die! He was convinced that he didn't have a chance. He expected the worst. He saw himself as doomed with no way out. He lost the battle in his own mind.[1]

For Nick, the thing he feared and expected to happen came to pass. The old adage "Life is a self-fulfilling prophecy" held true for him. It will usually be true in your life as well. Many people today are similar to Nick. They're always expecting the worst. They expect defeat. They expect failure. They expect mediocrity. And they usually get what they expect; they become what they believe.

Believe for Good Things

But you can believe for good things. Drawing on the improvements you are making in your self-image, it is possible to believe for more, to see yourself performing at increasingly higher levels in every area of life. When you encounter tough times, don't expect to stay there. Expect to come out of that trouble. Expect God to supernaturally turn it around. When business gets a bit slow, don't expect to go bankrupt; don't make plans for failure. Pray and expect God to bring you customers.

If you go through difficulties in your marriage, don't simply give up in frustration and say, "I should have known that this marriage was doomed from the start."

No, if you do that, you're responding as Nick did. Your low expectations will destroy your marriage; your own wrong thinking will bring you down. You've got to change your thinking. Change what you expect. Quit expecting to fail. Start believing that you are going to succeed.

Even if the bottom falls out of your life, your attitude should be: "God, I know that You are going to turn this around and use it for my good. God, I believe that You're going to bring me out stronger than ever before."

As we have already established, here is where self-image really comes into play. It is crucial that we see ourselves as God sees us, since we will never rise above the image we have of ourselves. If we see ourselves as barely making it, always having problems, never happy, we will subconsciously move toward that sort of life. To move forward in life, we must change our focus. We must believe.

Understand this: God will help you, but you cast the deciding vote. If you choose to stay focused on negative elements in your life, if you focus on what you can't do and what you don't have, then by your own choice you are agreeing to be defeated. You are conspiring with the enemy by opening the door and allowing destructive thoughts, words, actions, and attitudes to dominate your life.

On the other hand, if you'll get into agreement with God, if you'll focus on your possibilities, your faith can cause God to show up and work supernaturally in your life. Your faith will help you overcome your obstacles and allow you to reach new levels of victory. But it's up to you. It depends on your outlook. Are you focused on your problems, or are you focused on your God?

In the New Testament, there's a fascinating account of two blind men who heard that Jesus was passing by, and faith began to rise in their hearts. They must have thought, *We don't have to stay like this. God can turn this situation around. There's hope for a better future.* So they began to cry out, "Jesus, Son of David, have mercy on us and heal us."

When Jesus heard their cries, He stopped in His tracks. He walked over to them and posed a most intriguing question. "Do you believe that I am able to do this?"[2] He asked. Jesus knew what they wanted; He wanted to know what they believed, whether they had genuine faith. The blind men answered back with great confidence. They said, "Yes, Lord; we believe. We know beyond a shadow of a doubt that You can heal us. We know You are able. We have trust and confidence in You."

The Bible says, "When Jesus heard their faith, He touched their eyes and said unto them, 'According to your faith be it done unto you.' And their eyes were immediately opened."[3] Those men believed God could do something spectacular in their lives . . . and they received their sight!

Notice, it was their faith that turned the situation around. It was their believing that brought them the healing. Nobody can have faith for you. Certainly, other people can pray for you, they can believe for you, they can quote the Scripture to you, but you must exercise faith for yourself. If you are always depending on somebody else to keep you happy, somebody else to encourage you or to get you out of trouble, you will live in perpetual weakness and disappointment. You must make a decision that you are going to be a believer. Take charge of your life and decide, "No matter what comes against me, I believe in God. I'm going to have a positive outlook for my life." Other people's faith can indeed bolster yours. But your own faith will bring you a miracle much faster than anybody else's. What *you* believe has a much greater impact on your life than what anybody else believes.

What *you* believe has a much greater impact on your life than what anybody else believes.

The modern-day biblical paraphrase *The Message* relates the story about the blind men with an interesting twist: "[Jesus] touched their eyes and said, 'Become what you believe.'"

What a powerful statement! *Become what you believe!* What are you believing? Are you believing to go higher in life, to rise above your obstacles, to live in health, abundance, healing, and victory? You will become what you believe. The truth is, I am what I am today because of what I believed about myself yesterday. And I will be tomorrow what I believe about myself right now.

Be careful what you believe. If you go around with a poor-old-me mentality, thinking that you don't deserve God's blessings, focused on your faults, always feeling badly about yourself, you will live a dismal life at best. But if you change your believing and start seeing yourself as God sees you—as more than a conqueror, well able to succeed, strong in the Lord, the head not the tail, the victor not the victim—you will rise to a new level of fulfillment. It's up to you. According to your faith, let it be done to you.

Dare to Believe for Greater Things

Will you dare to start believing God for greater things? God doesn't want you to drag through life, barely making it. He doesn't want you to have to scrimp and scrape, trying to come up with enough money to pay for food, shelter, transportation, to pay your bills, or to worry about how you are going to send your children to college. He doesn't want you to be unhappy in your marriage. It is not His preference for you to live in perpetual pain.

God wants you to have a good life, a life filled with love, joy, peace, and fulfillment. That doesn't mean it will always be easy, but it does mean that it will always be *good*. God causes all things to work together for good to those who love Him.[4] You can dare to start believing Him for a better marriage. Start believing Him for better health. Believe for joy and peace and happiness. Start believing for increase and abundance. Become a true believer, knowing that you will become what you believe.

God said to Abraham, "I'm going to bless you so that you can be a blessing."[5] God is saying that same thing to you. He wants to bless you with abundance, so you can turn around and be a blessing to other people.

Maybe you have endured terrible disappointments. Unspeakable negative things may have happened to you, to the point that you have ceased believing for anything good to occur in your life. You've lost your dreams. You are drifting through life, taking whatever comes your way. You may be tempted to tell yourself, "I've been living this way too long. I'm never going to get any better. I've prayed, I've believed, I've done everything I know how to do. Nothing's changed. Nothing's worked. I might as well give up."

I've had people tell me, "Joel, I don't want to get my hopes up. I've been through so many hurts in the past. If I don't get my hopes up and nothing good happens to me, at least I won't be disappointed."

Friend, that attitude is contrary to God's desires for you. No matter how many setbacks you've suffered, God still has a great plan for your life. You *must* get your hopes up. If you don't have hope, you won't have faith. And if you don't have faith, you can't please God, and you won't see His power revealed in your life. Keep hope alive in your heart. Don't ever give up on your dreams. Don't allow discouragement or other setbacks to keep you from believing what God says about you.

DOUBLE FOR YOUR TROUBLE

If you will keep the right attitude, God will take all your disappointments, broken dreams, the hurts and pains, and He'll add up all the trouble and sorrow that's been inflicted on you, and He will pay you back with twice as much peace, joy, happiness, and success. The Bible says, "God will give us a twofold recompense for our former shame."[6] If you'll just believe, if you'll put your trust and confidence in God, He will give you double for your trouble.

God wants the latter part of your life to be better than the first part of your life. You are never too far gone with God. Some people say, "Yes, but you can't unscramble eggs," and that is true. But God can take scrambled eggs and make an amazing omelet. Nothing is too hard for our God.

The Bible says about God: "Be confident of this: He that began a good work in you will continue to perform it until it's perfectly complete."[7] This means that God wants to finish the course with you. God will not get tired and quit halfway through the process; nor will He renege on His promises. He will continue until you get to where He is taking you. God doesn't want you to be "a little" happy. He doesn't want you to be slightly blessed. He doesn't want you to be partially healed. God wants your life to be characterized by joy, and He wants your joy to be full. He wants you to live in abundance. He wants to give you the desires of your heart. He wants you to be complete and content.

When times get tough or things don't go your way, keep your confidence up. When discouragements come or when people tell you that your dreams are never going to come to pass, you're never going to be happy, and you can never change, boldly remind yourself who is at work in your life. God is turning things around in your favor. God is opening doors of opportunity for you. He is restoring relationships; He is softening people's hearts toward you. God is completing what He started. You may not see anything happening with your natural eyes, but you must believe that in the unseen world, God is at work on your behalf.

Remember, no weapon formed against you is going to prosper. That doesn't mean that there will not be opposition in your life; there will be weapons formed against you, and they may be formidable and frightening. But they cannot ultimately hurt you. Your future is intact with God. You will not go under, you will go through. The Scripture says, "Many are the afflictions of the righteous, but the LORD delivers him out of them all."[8]

The Bible says when you've done all you know how to do, just keep on standing strong.[9] You've got to show your enemy you are more determined than he is. Keep praying, keep believing, keep singing songs of praise. Keep fighting the good fight of faith. If you do that, God promises to bring you out with the victory.

I like the way *The Message* translates Philippians 1:6: "There has never been the slightest doubt in my mind that the God who started the great work in you would keep at it and bring it to a flourishing finish on the very day Christ Jesus appears." The best is yet to come. You can get up each morning expecting things to turn in your favor. Start expecting the goodness of God. Start expecting His blessings. If you believe, Jesus said, "all things are possible." Let me challenge you to be a believer. Let faith rise in your heart. Get into agreement with God, and He'll do more than you can ask or think.

You've got to believe good things are on their way. You must believe that God is at work in your life, that He is restoring you to your rightful place. In other words, you've got to see those things coming to pass. You've got to see your marriage being restored. You have to see that wayward child coming home. You need to see that business turning around. It has to be conceived in your heart. Look at life through your eyes of faith into that invisible world and see your dreams coming to pass.

Remember, "Faith is the substance of things hoped for, the evidence of things not seen."[10] Notice, faith has to do with the unseen world. You may not be able to perceive anything positive happening in your life with your natural eyes today. In fact, everything may be falling apart—your finances, your health, your business, your children. You may have all kinds of problems, and in the natural order, it doesn't look as though anything is turning around. But don't be discouraged. Look into that invisible world, into the supernatural world, and through your eyes of faith, see that situation turning around. See your joy and peace being restored.

The world tells you, "You need to see it to believe it." But God says just the opposite. Only as you believe it will you ever see it. You've got to look out through your eyes of faith and see it. Once you see it by faith, it can come into existence in the physical world.

What do you believe about yourself? Do you see things getting better in your life? Or are you just drifting along, accepting whatever comes your way? "I knew I wasn't going to get that promotion. Nothing good ever happens to me. This is just my lot in life. I knew I'd never get married. I knew I'd never be blessed."

Friend, God wants to do a new thing in your life. Don't limit Him with your small thinking. Have a big vision for your life. Dream bigger dreams. Live with faith and expectancy. You will become what you believe.

I love the Old Testament account of when God told Abraham that he and his wife, Sarah, were going to have a child—even though they were close to one hundred years old. When Sarah heard the news, she laughed. She probably said, "Abraham, you've got to be kidding. I'm not going to have a baby. I'm too old. That's never going to happen to me. And besides, look at you. You're no spring chicken either!"

Sarah didn't have the correct vision. The condition of her heart wasn't right. She couldn't see herself having that child; she couldn't conceive it in her heart.

And you probably recall the story: Year after year went by, and Abraham and Sarah had no children. After a while, they decided to "help" God fulfill His promise. Sarah told Abraham to sleep with her maid, Hagar. The two of them conceived and gave birth to a child named Ishmael. But that wasn't God's best. God wanted to give Sarah a baby, one that she gave birth to herself.

Still more years went by, and no child. Finally, Sarah became pregnant. What changed? God's promise was the same all along. I'm convinced that the key to the promise coming to pass was that Sarah had to conceive it in her heart before she was able to conceive it in her physical body. She had to believe she could become pregnant before she actually became with child.

Nearly twenty years after God spoke the promise, little Isaac was born to Abraham and Sarah. And I believe the main reason he wasn't born sooner, one of the major delays in the fulfillment of the promise for year after year, was simply the fact that Sarah couldn't conceive it in her heart. She couldn't see it through her eyes of faith. I wonder how many great things God is trying to do in your life. We're just like Sarah. We can't conceive it. We're not in agreement with God, so we're missing out on His blessings. Jesus said, "I want you to live life to the full, till it overflows."[11] Many times, when we read passages of Scripture such as that, the first thing we think of is why it can't happen to us. "God, I could never be healthy. I've got too many things wrong with me. I just received a bad report from the doctor." "God, I could never be prosperous. I just don't have what it takes. I've never been to college." On and on, we tell God all the reasons why good things can't happen to us. "I'm too old. I'm too young. I'm the wrong gender. My skin is the wrong color. I'm not educated enough." All that time, God is trying to plant the new seed of victory inside us. He's trying to get us to conceive. He knows if we don't conceive in our hearts through faith, it will never come to pass.

Too many times, like Sarah, we delay God's promise. We delay His favor because of our limited thinking. The condition of our hearts is not right. We're filled with doubt and unbelief. The tragedy is, if we don't change our believing, we could go through our entire lifetimes missing out on the great things God has in store for us.

Friend, please stop limiting God with your narrow-minded thinking. Learn how to conceive. Keep the image of what you want to become in front of you. You're going to become what you believe. Maybe God has told you something, and in the natural, it seems totally impossible. When you look at your situation, just as Sarah looked at her physical body, you're tempted to think, *God, I don't see how You're going to bring this to pass. I don't see how You'll ever get my child off drugs. I don't see how I'll ever get healed. I don't see how You can bless my career.*

Stop focusing on what you can't do, and start focusing on what God can do. The Bible says, "The things which are impossible with men are possible with God."[12] Let that seed take root inside you. You don't have to figure out how God is going to solve your problems. You don't have to see how He's going to bring it to pass. That's His responsibility; that's not your job. Your job is to be a believer. Your job is to live with faith and expectancy. Just turn that situation over to God and trust Him to take care of it. God is a supernatural God. The Bible says, "God's ways are not our ways. They are higher and better than our ways."[13] God can do what human beings cannot or will not do. He is not limited to the laws of nature. And if you'll let that seed take root so it can grow, put your trust and confidence in the Lord, God will surely bring it to pass. If you can see the invisible, God will do the impossible.

Don't restrict your vision; instead, begin seeing yourself as God's child. See yourself as receiving good things from your heavenly Father. Friend, if you'll do your part by believing, having a big vision for your life, living with faith and expectancy, and seeing yourself as God sees you, God will take you places that other people said were impossible to experience this side of heaven. You will become what you believe!

CHAPTER 10

Developing a Prosperous Mind-Set

One of the most important aspects of seeing ourselves God's way involves developing a prosperous mind-set. As we've already established, how we see ourselves will make or break us.

Understand, God has already equipped you with everything you need to live a prosperous life. He planted "seeds" inside you filled with possibilities, incredible potential, creative ideas, and dreams. But just because those things are within you doesn't mean they will do you any good. You have to start tapping into them. In other words, you've got to believe beyond a shadow of a doubt that you have what it takes. You must keep in mind that you are a child of the Most High God and you were created for great things. God didn't make you to be average. God created you to excel, and He's given you ability, insight, talent, wisdom, and His supernatural power to do so. You have everything you need right now to fulfill your God-given destiny.

God didn't make you to be average.

The Bible says that "God has blessed us with every spiritual blessing." Notice, that description is in the past tense. God has already done it. He's already deposited within us everything we need to succeed. Now it's up to us to start acting on what we already possess.

Remember, that is what Abraham had to do. Twenty years before he ever had a child, God spoke to him and said, "Abraham, I have made you the father of many nations."

Abraham could have said, "Who, me? I'm not a father. I don't have any children." Instead, Abraham chose to believe what God said about him. His attitude was, "God, it doesn't seem possible in any natural sense, but I'm not going to doubt Your word. I'm not going to try to figure it out rationally. I'm just going to agree with You. If You say that Sarah and I can have a baby at our age, as outlandish as it may seem, I'm going to believe You."

Interestingly, God's promise came to Abraham in the past tense, and although it carried a present-tense reality as well as a future fulfillment, God regarded it as if it had already happened. "I have made you a father of many nations." Obviously, God planned to give Abraham a son, but as far as He was concerned, it was already a done deal. Nevertheless, Abraham had a responsibility to trust God and to believe. Sure enough, some twenty years later, Abraham and Sarah had a son, whom they named Isaac.

Similarly, throughout the Bible, God has said great things about you. But those blessings will not happen automatically. You have to do your part, believing that you are blessed, seeing yourself as blessed, acting as though you are blessed. When you do, the promise will become a reality in your life.

For instance, the Bible says, "We are more than conquerors."[1] It doesn't say that we will be more than conquerors when we grow stronger, get older, or achieve some superspiritual level. Scripture says we are more than conquerors *right now*.

"Well, Joel, that couldn't be true in my life," I hear you saying. "I've got so many problems, so many things coming against me. Maybe when I get out of this mess, then I'll be more than a conqueror."

No, God declares you are more than a conqueror right now. If you will start acting like it, talking like it, seeing yourself as more than a conqueror, you will live a prosperous and victorious life. You must understand that the price has already been paid for you to have joy, peace, and happiness. That's part of the package that God has made available to you.

Don't Miss Out on God's Best

Years ago, before transatlantic flight was common, a man wanted to travel to the United States from Europe. The man worked hard, saved every extra penny he could, and finally had just enough money to purchase a ticket aboard a cruise ship. The trip at that time required about two or three weeks to cross the ocean. He went out and bought a suitcase and filled it full of cheese and crackers. That's all he could afford.

Once on board, all the other passengers went to the large, ornate dining room to eat their gourmet meals. Meanwhile, the poor man would go over in the corner and eat his cheese and crackers. This went on day after day. He could smell the delicious food being served in the dining room. He heard the other passengers speak of it in glowing terms as they rubbed their bellies and complained about how full they were, and how they would have to go on a diet after this trip. The poor traveler wanted to join the other guests in the dining room, but he had no extra money. Sometimes he'd lie awake at night, dreaming of the sumptuous meals the other guests described.

Toward the end of the trip, another man came up to him and said, "Sir, I can't help but notice that you are always over there eating those cheese and crackers at mealtimes. Why don't you come into the banquet hall and eat with us?"

The traveler's face flushed with embarrassment. "Well, to tell you the truth, I had only enough money to buy the ticket. I don't have any extra money to purchase fancy meals."

The other passenger raised his eyebrows in surprise. He shook his head and said, "Sir, don't you realize the meals are included in the price of the ticket? Your meals have already been paid for!"

When I first heard that story, I couldn't help but think of how many people are similar to that naive traveler. They are missing out on God's best because they don't realize that the good things in life have already been paid for. They may be on their way to heaven, but they don't know what has been included in the price of their ticket.

Every moment that we go around with that weak worm-of-the-dust mentality, we're eating more cheese and crackers. Every time we shrink back and say, "Well, I can't do it; I don't have what it takes," we're eating more cheese and crackers. Every time we go around full of fear, worry, anxiety, or we are uptight about something, we're over there eating more cheese and crackers. Friend, I don't know about you, but I'm tired of those cheese and crackers! It's time to step up to God's dining table. God has prepared a fabulous banquet for you, complete with every good thing imaginable. And it has already been paid for. God has everything you need there—joy, forgiveness, restoration, peace, healing—whatever you need, it's waiting for you at God's banquet table if you'll pull up your chair and take the place He has prepared for you.

You may have gone through some great disappointments in life or faced some serious setbacks. Welcome to the real world! But you must remember, you are a child of the Most High God. Just because something didn't work out your way or somebody disappointed you, that does not change who you are. If one dream dies, dream another dream. If you get knocked down, get back up and go again. When one door closes, God will always open up a bigger and better door. Hold your head high, and be on the lookout for the new thing that God wants to do in your life. But don't go off in the corner of life and start eating cheese and crackers.

If one dream dies, dream another dream.

You may have gotten off to a rough start in life. Perhaps you experienced horrible poverty, despair, abuse, or other negative things during your childhood. You may be tempted to let those negative experiences set the course for the rest of your life. But just because you started life that way doesn't mean you have to finish that way. You need to get a fresh vision of what God can do in your life and develop a prosperous mind-set.

My dad had to do something similar. As I mentioned earlier, Daddy grew up with a "poverty mentality." That's all he had ever known. When he first started pastoring, the church could pay him only $115 a week. Daddy and Mother could hardly survive on that little amount of money, especially once my siblings and I came along. The most dangerous aspect of their life, however, was that Daddy had come to expect poverty. For a number of years, he wasn't even able to accept a blessing when it came.

During a time of special services at the church, although our family barely had enough food to get along, my parents hosted the guest minister in their home that entire week. The following Sunday, a businessman in the church said, "Pastor, I know you cared for our guest speaker in your home all week. Things are tight, and I realize you can't afford those extra expenses. I want you to have this money to use personally, just to help you out." He handed my dad a check for a thousand dollars, tantamount to ten thousand dollars today!

Daddy was overwhelmed by the man's generosity, but he was so limited in his thinking at that time, he held that check by the edge of the corner, as though it might contaminate him if he clutched it any tighter, and he said, "Oh, no, brother, I could never receive this money. We must put it in the church offering."

Daddy later admitted that deep down inside, he really preferred to keep the money. He knew that he and Mother needed that money, but he had a false sense of humility. He couldn't receive the blessing. He thought he was doing God a favor by staying poor.

Daddy later said, "With every step I took as I walked to the front of the church to put that check in the offering, something inside was saying, *Don't do it. Receive God's blessings. Receive God's goodness.*"

But he didn't listen. He reluctantly dropped the check into the offering. He later said, "When I did, I felt sick to my stomach."

God was trying to increase my dad. He was trying to prosper him, but because of Daddy's deeply imbedded poverty mentality, he couldn't receive it. What was Daddy doing? He was eating more cheese and crackers. God was trying to get him to step up to the banquet table, but because of Daddy's limited mind-set, he couldn't see himself having an extra thousand dollars.

I'm so glad that Daddy later learned that as God's children, we are able to live an abundant life, that it is okay to prosper; that we should even expect to be blessed. Indeed, it is as important to learn how to receive a blessing as it is to be willing to give one.

Maybe you have come from a poor environment, or maybe you don't have a lot of material possessions right now. That's okay; God has good things ahead for you. But let me caution you; don't allow that poverty image to become ingrained inside you. Don't grow accustomed to living with less, doing less, and being less to the point that you eventually sit back and accept it. "We've always been poor. This is the way it's got to be."

No, start looking through eyes of faith, seeing yourself rising to new levels. See yourself prospering, and keep that image in your heart and mind. You may be living in poverty at the moment, but don't ever let poverty live in you.

The Bible says, "God takes pleasure in prospering His children." As His children prosper spiritually, physically, and materially, their increase brings God pleasure.

What would you think if I introduced our two children to you and they had holes in their clothes, uncombed hair, no shoes, and dirt under their fingernails? You'd probably say, "That man is not a good father. He doesn't take good care of his children." Indeed, my children's poverty would be a direct reflection on me as their dad.

Similarly, when we go through life with a poverty mentality, it is not glorifying to God. It does not honor His great name. God is not pleased when we drag through life, defeated, depressed, perpetually discouraged by our circumstances. No, God is pleased when we develop a prosperous mind-set.

Too often we become satisfied and complacent, accepting whatever comes our way. "I've gone as far as I can go. I'll never get any more promotions. This is just my lot in life."

That's not true! Your "lot in life" is to continually increase. Your lot in life is to be an overcomer, to live prosperously in every area. Quit eating the cheese and crackers and step into the banquet hall. God created you for great things.

What a tragedy it would be to go through life as a child of the King in God's eyes, yet as a lowly pauper in our own eyes. That is precisely what happened to a young man in the Old Testament by the name of Mephibosheth. (I don't know why they couldn't have named him Bob!)

Don't Settle for Mediocrity

Mephibosheth was the grandson of King Saul and the son of Jonathan. You may recall that Saul's son, Jonathan, and David were best friends. They actually entered into a covenant relationship, similar to the ancient covenant of being "blood brothers." That means whatever one had, it belonged to the other. If Jonathan needed food, clothing, or money, he could go over to David's house and get whatever he needed. Moreover, in the covenant relationship, if something were to happen to one of these two men, the remaining "brother" would be obligated to take care of the other's family.

King Saul and Jonathan were killed in battle on the same day, and when word got back to the palace, a servant grabbed Mephibosheth,

Jonathan's little son, picked him up, and took off running. Going out of Jerusalem in such haste, the servant tripped and fell while carrying the child. Mephibosheth became crippled as a result of the fall. The servant transported Jonathan's son all the way to a city called Lodebar, one of the most poverty-stricken, desolate cities in that entire region. That is where Mephibosheth, grandson of the king, lived almost his entire life. Think about that. He was the grandson of the king, yet he was living in those terrible conditions.

David succeeded Saul as king, and years later, long after Saul and Jonathan were mere memories in the minds of most people, David asked his staff the question, "Is there anyone left from the house of Saul that I could show kindness to for Jonathan's sake?" Remember, that was part of the covenant Jonathan and David had entered: If something happens to me, you will take care of my family. But by now, most of Saul's family was dead, and thus David's question.

One of David's staff members replied, "Yes, David. Jonathan has a son that's still alive, but he's crippled. He lives in Lodebar."

David said, "Go get him and bring him to the palace."

When Mephibosheth arrived, he was no doubt fearful. After all, his grandfather had chased David throughout the country trying to kill him. Now that Saul's family had been decimated and was no longer a threat to David, Mephibosheth may have felt that David planned to execute him as well.

But David said to him, "Don't be afraid. I'm going to show kindness to you because of your father, Jonathan. I'm going to give you back all the land that once belonged to your grandfather Saul. And from this day forward, you will eat at my table as though you are one of my sons." David treated Mephibosheth as royalty. After all, he was the grandson of the king. And David was in a covenant relationship with his father.

Mephibosheth's life was transformed instantly—that's the good news—but think of all the years that he lived in that dirty city of Lodebar. All the while, he knew he was royalty; beyond that, it was commonly known that David and Jonathan were in a covenant relationship; based on that alone, Mephibosheth knew he had rights. Why didn't he just go into the palace and say, "King David, I'm Jonathan's son. I'm living in poverty down in Lodebar, and I know that I'm made for more than that. I'm here to claim what belongs to me through my father's covenant relationship with you."

Why did Mephibosheth settle for mediocrity? We catch a clue from his initial response to David. When David told him that he was going to take care of him, the Bible says, "Mephibosheth bowed his head low and he said, 'Who am I that you should notice such a dead dog like me?'" Do you see his self-image? He saw himself as defeated, as a loser, as a dead dog. He saw himself as an outcast. Yes, he was the grandson of the king, but his image of himself kept him from receiving the privileges that rightfully belonged to him.

How many times do we do the same thing? Our self-image is so contrary to the way God sees us that we miss out on God's best. God sees us as champions. We see ourselves as dead dogs.

But just as Mephibosheth had to cast off that "dead dog mentality," replacing it with a prosperous mind-set, you and I must do something similar. You may have made some mistakes in life, but if you have honestly repented and done your best to do right since then, you no longer have to live with guilt and shame. You may not be everything you want to be. You may be crippled physically, spiritually, or emotionally. That does not change God's covenant with you. You are still a child of the Most High God. He still has great things in store for you. You need to be bold and claim what belongs to you. It brings God no pleasure for you to live in your own personal "Lodebar," in poverty, with low self-esteem, with that dead-dog mentality.

How would you feel if your children had that kind of attitude toward you? Imagine it's dinnertime and you have worked diligently to prepare a delicious dinner. The food is spread out on the table; you are ready to eat. But one of your children comes in with his head down, and he refuses to sit at the table with the family. He crawls around on the ground, waiting for some scraps or crumbs to fall. You'd say, "Son, daughter, what in the world are you doing? Get up here and take your place. I've prepared all this for you. You are a part of the family. You insult me when you act like a dog, begging for scraps."

God is saying something similar: "You are part of the family. Put down the cheese and crackers. Rise up and receive what rightfully belongs to you."

In Victoria's and my home, we have two big La-Z-Boy chairs in our bedroom. The chairs are delightfully comfortable and, every once in a while when I want to watch a ball game, read, or simply be alone to think or pray, I'll go in the bedroom, shut the door, and sink into one of those chairs. It's a great place to just relax.

I came home one day and couldn't find my little boy, Jonathan, anywhere. He was about four years old at the time, so I was concerned. I looked in all the usual places—he wasn't in his bedroom, the playroom, or the kitchen. I even went outside and looked around the garage, but I couldn't find him. I finally went to my bedroom, and I saw the door was closed. When I opened it, there was little Jonathan in my favorite chair. He had his legs propped up, and he was lying back comfortably. He had a bowl of popcorn in one hand and the television remote control in the other. I looked at him and smiled, relieved that I had found him.

Jonathan looked at me and said, "Daddy, this is the life."

I tried not to laugh, but Jonathan's remark made me feel good as a father. I was glad that he felt confident enough to go right into my room and sit in my favorite chair. I was glad he knew he was part of the family and everything I had was his.

Friend, do you want to make your heavenly Father happy? Then start stepping up to the dinner table. Start enjoying His blessings. Put down the cheese and crackers and come into the banquet hall. You don't have to live in guilt and condemnation any longer; you don't have to go through life worried and full of fear. The price has been paid. Your freedom is included in your ticket if you'll just rise up and take your place. Crawl up in your "Daddy's chair" and develop a prosperous mind-set, seeing yourself as the royalty God made you to be.

CHAPTER 11

Be Happy with Who You Are

You can dare to be happy with who you are right now and accept yourself, faults and all. A lot of us don't realize it, but the root cause of many social, physical, and emotional problems is simply the fact that people don't like themselves. They are uncomfortable with how they look, how they talk, or how they act. They don't like their personality. They are always comparing themselves with other people, wishing they were something different. "If I just had his personality . . ." "If I looked like she looks . . ." "If my thighs just weren't so big . . ." "If I had less here and more somewhere else, then I'd be happy."

No, you can be happy with who God made you to be, and quit wishing you were something different. If God had wanted you to look like a fashion model, a movie star, a famous athlete, or anyone else, He would have made you look like them. If God had wanted you to have a different personality, He would have given you that personality. Don't compare yourself to other people; learn to be happy with who God made you to be.

Many people are insecure about who they are, so they constantly try to gain the approval of everybody around them so they can feel better about themselves. They end up living to please other people, trying to fit into their molds so they can be accepted. They act one way for their boss, another way for their spouse, and another way for their friends. They live a life of pretense, wearing various masks, and hoping to please everybody. In essence, they are not being true to anyone, especially themselves.

But if you are going to enjoy your life to the full, you must learn to be confident as the individual God made you to be. Understand this: You were not created to mimic somebody else. You were created to be you. When you go around copying and trying to be like somebody else, not only does it demean you, it steals your diversity, your creativity, and your uniqueness.

God doesn't want a bunch of clones. He likes variety, and you should not let people pressure you or make you feel badly about yourself because you don't fit their image of who you should be. Some people spend three-fourths of their time trying to be somebody else. How foolish!

Be an original, not a copycat. Dare to be different; be secure in who God made you to be and then go out and be the best you that you can be. You don't have to look or act like anyone else. God has given us all different gifts, talents, and personalities on purpose. You don't really need anybody else's approval to do what you know God wants you to do.

Certainly, you should always be open to wise counsel. I'm not suggesting that you be foolish or rebellious. Nor am I suggesting that you move from liberty to license in your spiritual life. We never have permission to live an ungodly life. But we do have God's blessing to be confident, not letting outside pressures mold us into something or someone we're not. If you want to wear your hair a certain way, that's your prerogative. You don't have to check with all your friends to make sure it's okay. Be secure in who you are. If you want to join the choir at church or start a new business or buy a new car or home, you don't need anyone's approval before you can do what you know God wants you to do. Your attitude should be: *I am confident in who I am. I'm not going to go around pretending, wishing I was something else, trying to fit into everybody's mold. I am free to run my own race.*

It's okay to be you! God made you the way you are on purpose. He went to great lengths to make sure that each of us is an original. We should not feel badly because our personality, tastes, hobbies, or even spiritual tendencies are not the same as another person's. Some people are outgoing and energetic. Other people are more timid and laid back. Some people like to wear suits and ties. Other people are more comfortable wearing blue jeans. Some people close their eyes and lift their hands when they worship God. Others worship God in a more subdued manner. And guess what? God likes it all! God loves variety.

Don't think that you have to fit into somebody else's mold and, similarly, don't be upset when other people don't fit into your molds. Just be the person God made you to be.

Interestingly, Victoria and I are totally opposite in many respects. I'm a very routine person, extremely structured and organized. I get up at the same time every day. I do the same things, maintain the same schedule from week to week. I go to the same restaurants and eat the same food. In most cases, I don't even have to look at the menu, because I know I'm going to order the same things I always order. Victoria, on the other hand, does not like routine. She likes variety. She's outgoing, energetic, fun, adventurous, and daring. There's no telling what she's going to do next! My prayer is always, "Please, God, just don't let her get arrested!"

And here is the wonderful part: God made her that way! One of the reasons why we have a good relationship is because I don't spend my time trying to change her, and she doesn't make me feel badly about being myself, or nag me because I'm not just like her. We've learned to appreciate our differences. We've learned to enjoy the person God made each of us to be.

In the process, we balance each other. I'm structured and routine; she's fun and adventurous. Without her, my life would be boring; without me, she would be in prison! (Just kidding.)

Learn to Appreciate the Differences

The truth is, we all must learn to appreciate our differences. Don't try to squeeze everybody into your little box. And don't allow anyone else to cramp your style. Certainly, we can always learn from other people, and sometimes we need to be open to change. But you need not feel insecure because you don't have the same physical, emotional, or intellectual traits that someone else has. Be happy with who God made you to be.

The reason many people are discontented today is because they compare themselves with other people. You know how it goes. You start out in a perfectly good mood, happy as can be, but then you see one of your coworkers drive up in a brand-new car. You start thinking,

I wish I had a new car. Here I am, driving this old clunker. Before long, your good mood is gone, and you are discouraged and discontented. Or maybe you see a friend walk into the room and she is being escorted by her handsome husband who looks as though he just stepped out of *GQ* magazine. Then you look over at your husband . . . and . . . well, you get my point.

But it's as silly to compare your spouse to somebody else's spouse as it is to compare your talent, abilities, or education to somebody else's. Such comparisons are almost always counterproductive, causing you to lose your joy. Just run your race. Don't worry about anyone else.

Not long ago, I heard a minister on television tell how he got out of bed every day at four o'clock in the morning and prayed for two hours. My first thought was, *Oh, my. I don't pray for two hours a day, and I surely don't get up that early.* The more I thought about it, the worse I felt!

Finally, I had to get a hold of myself, and say, "That's great for him, but thank God, it's not great for me! I'm going to run my race, and I'm not going to feel guilty or badly about myself just because I'm not doing what he's doing."

God has an individual plan for each of our lives. Just because something works for somebody else doesn't necessarily mean it's going to work for you. God gives each of us special grace to do what He's called us to do. If we make the mistake of trying to copy other people, we're going to be frequently frustrated, and we're going to waste a lot of time and energy. Worse yet, we may miss the good things God has for us to do!

I've seen mothers who are always running their children here and there, investing a lot of time in their kids. Their children are involved in every club and sport, and usually that's great. But some moms simply try to copy another person, or they enroll their children in all sorts of activities out of a sense of guilt and condemnation. Some frantic, frazzled parents are so desperately trying to keep up with their peers (*their* peers, not their children's!), they are missing the entire point of the horizon-expanding programs in the first place. Not only that, but all that running around is wearing out Mom and Dad!

Here's some good news: You don't have to keep up with anyone else. You can run your own race and be an individual. God has given you the grace to do what He's called you to do. He has not given you the grace to do what everybody else is doing. You don't have to be the best mother in the world, just be the best mother that you can be.

I may not ever be the world's greatest pastor. I may not be the best husband or the best father, but I'm determined to be the best *I* can be. And I'm not going to feel bad about myself. If somebody can do what I do better, fine. I'm not in a contest; I'm not comparing myself with anyone else. As far as I'm concerned, I'm number one! I know I'm doing the best I can do.

That is what the Scripture teaches. It says, "Let each one examine his own work."[1] In other words, quit looking at what everybody else is doing and run your own race. You can take pride in yourself without comparing yourself to anybody else. If you run your race and be the best that *you* can be, then you can feel good about yourself.

Be the best that *you* can be, then you can feel good about yourself.

Granted, you will face enormous pressure to do what everybody else is doing, to try to please everybody and meet all their expectations. If you're not careful, though, your life can become a blur, a pale imitation rather than an original. But you don't have to please everyone else; you need to please only God. The truth is, if you're going to run your own race, you may not be able to meet other people's expectations. You can't be everything to everybody. You'll have to accept the fact that some people may not like you. Everybody's not going to agree with every decision you make. You probably will not be able to keep every person in your life happy. But you can't let the demands, pressures, and expectations from others stop you from doing what you know God wants you to do.

Melanie is a bright young woman who does a marvelous job of balancing her responsibilities as wife and mother with her desires for a career outside the home. But she felt pressured to keep moving up the ladder in her company. When a new position opened, her boss urged her to accept a promotion. Her husband approved, and Melanie knew it was a great opportunity. But something inside caused her to take pause. She didn't feel good about accepting the new position. She didn't want to work in that stressful an environment, and besides, she was fulfilled and contented in her current position. She was highly competent at her job, enjoyed her career, and was able to work flexible hours, which allowed her to spend plenty of time with her family.

"I'm honored that my employer wants to promote me," Melanie said, "but I'm happy with the way things are. I'm afraid, though, that I will let everybody down if I don't take the new job. I feel that I won't be living up to their expectations if I turn down the new opportunity. What do you think I should do?"

"Melanie, you can't live to please everybody else," I told her. "And although those people may mean well and may want the best for you, only you know deep down inside what is right for you. You have to learn to follow your heart. You can't let other people pressure you into being something that you're not. If you want God's favor in your life, you must be the person He made you to be, not the person your boss wants you to be, not the person your friends want you to be, not even the person your parents or your husband wants you to be. You can't let outside expectations keep you from following your own heart."

Melanie declined the offer for the new position, and she and her family are thriving. In her case, a promotion would have been a step backward.

Seek Good Counsel

When you face difficult decisions or uncertain choices, it helps to seek counsel from someone you respect. Certainly, as the Bible says, "there's safety in a multitude of counselors," and we should never be hardheaded and stubborn. We should always stay open and be willing to take advice. But after you've prayed about something and looked at all the options, if you still don't feel good about it, be bold enough to make a decision that is right for you. If you're trying to please everybody else by doing things you don't really want to do, so you won't hurt somebody's feelings, or you are trying to keep everybody happy, you will be cheating yourself. You can run yourself in circles trying to be something that you're not, and you'll run the risk of missing out on God's best for your own life.

Sometimes you can even get too much advice. If you're not careful, conflicting opinions will simply cause confusion. Sometimes the friends who are giving you advice can't even run their own lives. But they sure are good at telling you how to run yours! Be careful about whom you allow to influence your decision-making process. Make sure the people who are giving you advice know what they're talking about and are people who have earned your respect as a source of wisdom. Besides, secure people rely on their inner direction 75 percent of the time and on their outer direction only 25 percent of the time. That means for most of the decisions you make, you should not have to seek everybody else's opinions and approval. You need to follow your own heart in light of God's Word and do what you feel is right and good for you.

Similarly, parents, you should not put pressure on your children to fulfill your dreams. You should allow them to fulfill the dreams God has placed in their own hearts. Of course it's good to give our children direction and guidance, but don't be a controller or a manipulator. Don't put unrealistic expectations on your children.

One of the things I appreciated about my mom and dad's parenting style was that they never planned my siblings' lives or my life. Certainly, they pointed us in the right direction, offering advice and wise counsel. They helped us see where our gifts and talents were, even those that were buried. But they always let us fulfill our own dreams. From the time I was a little boy, I knew my dad wanted me to preach, but I never had that desire. Despite his disappointment, Daddy never once tried to cram preaching down my throat. He never tried to make me feel guilty or that I was less of a person because I wasn't doing exactly what he wanted me to do. In fact, he often told me, "Joel, I want you to fulfill your dreams for your life, not my dreams for your life." Today, I can preach with the freedom of knowing I'm not doing just what pleases my dad or other family members; I'm doing what pleases God.

Are you being the person God made you to be?

Are you being the person God made you to be? Or are you just going around pretending, trying to be what everybody else wants you to be, living up to their expectations and following their dreams for your life? When my dad went to be with the Lord and I first started pastoring at Lakewood Church, one of my biggest concerns was "How is everybody going to accept me?" After all, Daddy had been there for forty years, and everyone was accustomed to him. His style and personality were much different from mine. My dad was a fireball of a preacher, always energetic and exciting. I'm a bit more laid back.

One night I was praying, asking God what I should do. "Should I try to be more like my dad? Should I copy his style? Should I preach his messages?" On and on I went. I was just so concerned about it. But the Lord spoke to me, not out loud, but deep down in my heart, saying, *Joel, don't copy anybody. Just be yourself. Be who I created you to be. I don't want a duplicate of your dad. I want an original.*

That truth set me free!

I love the reminder in the book of Joshua. Moses had just died, and God wanted Joshua to take over as leader of His people. God said to Joshua, "As I was with Moses, I will be with you." Notice He didn't say, "Joshua, you need to try to be just like Moses, then you'll be okay." No, God said to Joshua, "Be an original. Be who I made you to be, and then you'll be successful."

One of the secrets of any success I've had at Lakewood—and I know it all comes from God—would be that I have walked in my own shoes. I haven't tried to fill Daddy's shoes or anyone else's. I have not tried to be something that I'm not or tried to copy somebody else. I don't step up on the platform and act one way, then go home and act another way. No, with me, what you see is who I am. That's all God requires me to be.

And that's all He expects of you, as well. If you will learn to be the original God made you to be, God will take you places you've never even dreamed of. You may have some faults, some areas you and God are refining. But remember, God is in the process of changing you. And if you'll just be happy with who God made you to be and make a decision that you're going to be the best you can be, God will pour out His favor in your life, and you'll live that life of victory He has in store for you.

PART 3

DISCOVER THE POWER OF YOUR THOUGHTS AND WORDS

CHAPTER 12

Choosing the Right Thoughts

A war is raging all around you, yet, amazingly, you may not even be aware of it. The battle is not for a piece of land or for natural resources such as gas, oil, gold, or water. The prize in this war is much more valuable. The battle is for your mind.

The third step you must take if you want to live at your full potential is to *discover the power of your thoughts and words*. Let's think about your thoughts first of all.

Your enemy's number one target is the arena of your thoughts.[1] He knows if he can control and manipulate how you think, he'll be able to control and manipulate your entire life. Indeed, thoughts determine actions, attitude, and self-image. Really, thoughts determine destiny. That's why the Bible warns us to guard our minds. We must be extremely careful not only about what we ingest through our eyes and ears, but what we think about. If you dwell on depressing thoughts, you will live a depressing life. If you continually gravitate toward negative thoughts, you will gravitate toward negative people, activities, philosophies, and lifestyles. Your life will always follow your thoughts.

Almost like a magnet, we draw in what we constantly think about. If you're always thinking positive, happy, joyful thoughts, you're going to be a positive, happy, joyful person, and you will attract other happy, upbeat, positive people.

Our thoughts also affect our emotions. We will feel exactly the way we think. You will never be happy unless you first think happy thoughts. Conversely, it's impossible to remain discouraged unless you first think discouraging thoughts. So much of success or failure in life begins in our minds and is influenced by what we allow ourselves to dwell on.

Set Your Mind on Higher Things

Many don't realize it, but we can choose our thoughts. Nobody can make us think about something. God won't do it, and the enemy can't do it. You decide what you will entertain in your mind. Simply because the enemy plants a negative, discouraging thought in your brain doesn't mean you have to "water" it, nurture it, coddle it, and help it to grow.

No, you can choose to cast it down and dismiss it from your mind. Granted, your mind is similar to a giant computer in that your brain stores every thought you've ever had. That's encouraging when you're trying to find your car keys, but it's not such good news when you consider the amount of smut, foul language, ungodly concepts, and other negative input with which we are inundated every day of our lives. Nevertheless, simply because a destructive thought is stored in your mental computer does not mean you have to pull it up and run it on the main screen of your mind.

If you make that mistake and start dwelling on it, that thought will affect your emotions, your attitudes, and—if you continue to give it free rein in your mind—it will inevitably affect your actions. You will be much more prone to discouragement and depression, and if you continue pondering that negative thought, it holds the potential to sap the energy and strength right out of you. You will lose your motivation to move forward in a positive direction.

The more we dwell on the enemy's lies, the more garbage we willingly allow him to dump into our minds. It's as though we have flung the door wide open and put up a sign that reads: "Trash goes here!"

Anyone can be temporarily discouraged and depressed. Life is tough, and it sometimes takes a toll on us. We all get knocked down occasionally. But you need not remain down. If you are depressed, you must understand, nobody is *making* you depressed.[2] If you're not happy, nobody is forcing you to be unhappy. If you're negative and you have a bad attitude, nobody's coercing you to be bored, uncooperative, sarcastic, or sullen. You are choosing to remain in that condition, and the first step out of that mess is to recognize that the only person who can improve the situation is you!

We must take responsibility for our own actions. As long as we keep making excuses and blaming the family tree, our environment, past relationships with other people, our circumstances, and attributing blame to God, Satan, *anyone*, or *anything*, we will never be truly free and emotionally healthy. We must realize that to a large extent, we can control our own destinies.

Some people say, "Well, my circumstances have me down. You just don't know what I'm going through."

Actually, your circumstances don't have you down. Your *thoughts* about your circumstances have you down. On the other hand, you can be in one of the biggest battles of your life and still be filled with joy and peace and victory—if you simply learn how to choose the right thoughts. It's time to think about what you're thinking about.

It's time to think about what you're thinking about.

What are you allowing your mind to dwell on? Are you focused on your problems? Are you constantly dwelling on negative things? How you view life makes all the difference in the world—especially for you!

Obviously, we can't ignore problems and live in denial, pretending that nothing bad ever happens to us. That is unrealistic. Bad things do sometimes happen to good people, just as good things often happen to bad people. Pretense is not the answer; nor is playing semantic games to make yourself sound more spiritual. If you are sick, it's okay to admit it; but keep your thoughts on your Healer. If your body is tired, if your spirit is weary, fine; we all understand that. Sometimes the most spiritual thing you can do is to get some rest. But focus your thoughts on the One who has promised, "Those who wait on the LORD shall renew their strength."[3]

Tough times come to all of us. Jesus said, "In this life you will have trouble, but be of good cheer for I have overcome the world."[4] He wasn't saying that troublesome times wouldn't come; He was saying that when they do, we can choose our attitudes. We can choose to believe that He is greater than our problems; we can choose the right thoughts.

As you dwell on the promises of God's Word, you will be filled with hope. You will develop a positive attitude of faith, and you will draw in the victory. Like metal filings being pulled across a desk by a magnet, you will draw in the good things of God.

A lot of people say, "Well, as soon as my situation turns around, I'll cheer up. As soon as I get out of this mess, I'll have a better attitude."

Unfortunately, that's not going to happen. You have the process backward. You must cheer up first, then God will turn your situation around. As long as you harbor that poor, defeated outlook, you will continue to live a poor, defeated life.

Interestingly, the Scripture says, "Strip off the old nature and put on the new man." It says, "Be constantly renewed in the spirit of your mind, having a fresh mental and spiritual attitude."[5] You can't sit back passively and expect this new person to suddenly appear; nor can you go through life in a negative frame of mind and expect anything to change for the better. No, you need to strip off those old negative thoughts and "put on" a fresh new attitude. In other words, you must change your thought patterns and start dwelling on the good things of God. When you lose focus and start dwelling on negative thoughts, it becomes easy to get discouraged.

The first place we must win the victory is in our own minds. If you don't think you can be successful, then you never will be. If you don't think your body can be healed, it never will be. If you don't think God can turn your situation around, then He probably won't. Remember, "As a person thinks in his heart, so he will become."[6] When you think thoughts of failure, you are destined to fail. When you think thoughts of mediocrity, you are destined to live an average, just-get-by life. But friend, when you align your thoughts with God's thoughts and you start dwelling on the promises of His Word, when you constantly dwell on thoughts of His victory, favor, faith, power, and strength, nothing can hold you back. When you think positive, excellent thoughts, you will be propelled toward greatness, inevitably bound for increase, promotion, and God's supernatural blessings.

When you think positive, excellent thoughts, you will be propelled toward greatness.

We must continually choose to keep our minds set on the higher things. The Bible says, "Set your minds on the things which are above."[7] Notice again there is something that we are to do—we must continually choose, day in and day out, twenty-four hours a day, to keep our minds set on the higher things. What are the things that are above, the higher things? Quite simply, they are the positive things of God. The apostle Paul provides a great list by which we can evaluate our thoughts: "whatever things are true, whatever things are noble, whatever things are just, whatever things are pure, whatever things are lovely, whatever things are of good report, if there is any virtue and if there is anything praiseworthy—meditate on these things."[8]

People sometimes tease me, "Joel, you talk so much about being positive." But God is positive! There is nothing negative about Him. If you are going to live God's way and be the person He wants you to be, you must line up your vision with His and learn to live in a positive frame of mind. Learn to look for the best in every situation.

No matter what you're going through, if you look hard enough and keep the right attitude, you can find something good about the experience. If you get laid off at work, you can choose to be negative and bitter and blame God. Or, you can say, "God, I know You are in control of my life, and when one door closes, You always open a bigger and better door. So, Father, I can't wait to see what You have in store for me."

When you get stuck in traffic, you can choose to be mad and frustrated, or you can choose to say, "Father, You said that all things work together for good to them that love the Lord. So I thank You for guiding me and protecting me and keeping me in Your perfect will."

You must make a choice to keep your mind focused on the higher things. It's not going to automatically happen. You must be determined and put forth some effort if you're going to keep your mind set on the good things of God and experience His best.

We must be especially on guard during times of adversity, in times of personal challenge. When troubles strike, often the first thoughts that come to mind are not higher thoughts; they're not positive thoughts. Negative thoughts bombard us from every possible angle. Right there, we must choose to trust God for good things and not allow ourselves to be down and discouraged or just give up.

Our mind is similar to the transmission in a car. We have a forward gear, and we have a reverse gear; we can choose which way we want to go. It doesn't take any more effort to go forward than it does to go backward. It's all in the decision process. Similarly, we determine, by our own choices, which way our lives are going to go. If you choose to stay focused on the positive and keep your mind set on the good things of God, all the forces of darkness are not going to be able to keep you from moving forward and fulfilling your destiny. But if you make the mistake of dwelling on the negative, focusing on your problems and your impossibilities, it's similar to putting that car in reverse and backing away from the victory God has in store for you. You must decide which way you want to go.

Focus on the Positive

I heard a story about a positive farmer and a negative farmer. When rain fell on the land, the positive farmer would say, "Thank You, Lord, for watering our crops."

The negative farmer said, "Yeah, but if this rain keeps up, it's going to rot the roots away, and we're never going to have a harvest."

The sun came out and the positive farmer said, "Thank You, Lord, for the sunshine. Our crops are getting the vitamins and minerals they need. We're going to have a great harvest this year."

The negative farmer said, "Yeah, but if it keeps this up, it's going to scorch those plants. We're never going to make a living."

One day the two farmers went goose hunting together, and the positive farmer brought along his new bird dog. He was so proud of that dog, he couldn't wait to show him off. They went out in a small boat and waited. Before long, a big goose flew overhead. *Boom!* The positive farmer brought the bird down in the middle of the lake. He turned to his friend and said, "Now watch what this dog can do." That dog jumped out of the boat and ran *on top of the water*, picked up the goose, ran back all the way on top of the water, and put the bird down perfectly in the boat. The positive farmer was beaming from ear to ear. He turned to his friend, and said, "What did you think of that?"

The negative farmer shook his head in disgust. "Just what I thought," he said. "That dog can't even swim!"

Of course, that story is just a joke, but don't you know people like that? They are always focused on the negative. If you must be around a pessimist, be sure to guard against their negative attitudes infecting your thinking!

Stay focused on the positive things in life. Psychologists are convinced that our lives move in the direction of our most dominant thoughts. If thoughts of joy, peace, victory, abundance, and blessings dominate your thoughts throughout the day, you will move toward those things, drawing them to yourself at the same time. Your life will follow your thoughts.

When your thoughts have been running in a certain pattern for a long period of time, it's as though you have been digging a deep riverbed, and the water can flow in only one direction. Imagine a person who habitually leans toward negative thinking month after month, year after year. With every pessimistic thought, they dig that riverbed a bit deeper. The flow accelerates, growing stronger as it goes. After a period of time, the water is flowing so strongly, every thought that comes out of the river is negative; that's the only way the water is flowing. The person has programmed his or her mind into a negative thinking pattern.

Fortunately, we can dig a new river, one going in a positive direction. The way we do so is one thought at a time. When you dwell on God's Word and start seeing the best in situations, little by little, one thought at a time, you are redirecting the flow of that river. At first, just a little water will be redirected out of the negative stream and trickle over into that positive stream. It may not look like much at first, but as you continue to reject negative thoughts and redirect the flow, as you choose faith instead of fear, expecting good things and taking control of your thought life, then little by little that negative stream will dwindle and the positive river will flow with much greater force. If you'll keep it up, that old negative river eventually will dry up, and you will discover a whole new river flowing with positive, faith-filled thoughts of victory.

Occasionally, you may be tempted to think discouraging thoughts, such as, "You're never going to make it; your problems are just too big, they're insurmountable."

In the old days, you'd go back to the same old negative river and you'd think, *Oh, my. What in the world am I going to do? God, how am I going to get out of this mess?*

But not this time; you have a new river flowing. You can rise up and say, "No, greater is He that is in me than he that's in the world. I can do all things through Christ, and I'm coming out of this."

You can start tapping into that new river, and every time you do, you're digging that new positive river a little deeper, and that water flows more freely.

Negative thoughts assail you: *You're never going to get out of debt. You're never going to be successful. You're always going to live in poverty and lack.*

In the old days, you'd go back to that depressing river and say, "Well, yes, my family has always been poor. Nobody has ever amounted to anything. I guess it's just my lot in life."

But not this time. Now, you go back to that positive river of faith. You say, "I thank You, Father, that You called me to be the head, not the tail. I'm above and not beneath. You said that I will be able to lend money and not have to borrow. You said that whatever I put my hands to do shall prosper. So Father, I thank You that I am blessed, and I cannot be cursed."

What are you doing? You are reprogramming your mind.

Friend, don't be passive, sitting back and allowing negative, critical, pessimistic thoughts to influence your life. Learn to dwell on the good; reprogram your thinking. The Bible tells us that we need to be "transformed by the renewing of our mind."[9] If you will transform your mind, God will transform your life.

**If you will transform your mind,
God will transform your life.**

Let's be real, though. You may have dug a deep river of negativity, and it's going to take a strong will to change. That river wasn't formed overnight, nor will it be redirected without some conscious, strenuous effort on your part. God will help you, but you are going to have to make quality decisions every day, choosing the good, rejecting the bad. Determine to keep your mind set on the good things of God. Start expecting good things. Get up each day knowing that God has great things in store for you. When you get out of bed, say, "Father, I'm excited about today. This is a day You have made; I'm going to rejoice and be glad in it. God, I know You reward those who seek You, so I thank You in advance for Your blessings, favor, and victory in my life today." Then go out and live with expectancy; live with faith.

Our thoughts contain tremendous power. Remember, we draw into our lives that which we constantly think about. If we're always dwelling on the negative, we will attract negative people, experiences, and attitudes. If we're always dwelling on our fears, we will draw in more fear. You are setting the direction of your life with your thoughts.

The choice is up to you. You don't have to dwell on every thought that comes to your mind. The first thing you need to do is ascertain where that thought is coming from. Is that thought from God, is it your own thought, or is it a destructive thought from the enemy?

How can you tell? Easy. If it's a negative thought, it's from the enemy. If it's a discouraging, destructive thought; if it brings fear, worry, doubt, or unbelief; if the thought makes you feel weak, inadequate, or insecure, I can guarantee you that thought is not from God. You need to deal with it immediately.

The Bible says, "We should cast down every wrong imagination and take into captivity every wrong thought."[10] That simply means: Don't dwell on it. Get rid of it immediately. Choose to think on something positive. If you make the mistake of dwelling on the enemy's lies, you allow the negative seed to take root. And the more you think about it, the more it's going to grow, creating an enemy stronghold in your mind from which attacks can be launched. Night and day, the enemy will pummel your mind with notions such as: *You're never going to be successful. Nobody in your family has ever amounted to much. You're not smart enough. Your parents were poor. Your grandmother was always depressed. Your grandfather couldn't keep a job. Even your pet dog was always sick! You were just born into the wrong family.*

If you believe those kinds of lies, you will set limits in your life that will be nearly impossible to rise above. You must get in the habit of casting down the thoughts of the enemy and start believing what God says about you. God is not limited by your family tree. He is not limited by your education, your social standing, economic status, or your race. No, the only thing that limits God is your lack of faith.

There is no such thing as the wrong side of the tracks with our God. If you will put your trust in Him, God will make your life significant.

God longs to make something great out of your life. He'll take a nobody and shape that person into a somebody. But you must cooperate with God's plan; you must start thinking of yourself as the champion God made you to be.

**There is no such thing as the wrong side
of the tracks with our God.**

God Has Confidence in You

If you can catch a glimpse of how much confidence God has in you, you will never again shrink back into an inferiority complex. You will rise up with boldness. When we know that somebody we respect has confidence in us, it often inspires us to believe better of ourselves. More often than not, we'll rise to the occasion and meet that person's expectations.

One time I was playing basketball with a group of players that were a lot better than I am. Most of them had played in college; I had not. We were in a heated game, rough, and competitive. Toward the end of the game, the score was tied, and we called time out. As we huddled for one last play, one of my teammates whispered in my ear, "Joel, we want you to take the final shot. We're being guarded too closely."

Now, that was quite a vote of confidence, but to tell the truth, I hadn't taken a shot that entire game! The guy that was guarding me was about a foot and a half taller than I am.

At first, I thought, *This is not a good idea.* But then, I got to thinking, *If my teammates have that much confidence in me, if they believe in me enough to want me to take the most critical shot in the game, then I must be able to do it.*

We took the ball out, came down court, and sure enough, I worked myself into an open position, and my teammates fed me the ball. The guy guarding me towered above me, but I took a dribble and arched the ball high above his outstretched arms—I couldn't even see the basket—and that ball went way up in the air like a rainbow, much higher than I'd normally shoot it. I watched the ball soar through the air, almost as if I were watching myself in slow motion. I think I even had time to pray, "Oh, God, please help that ball to go in!" The ball came down, swished right through the center of the hoop, and we won that game! (I knew then that God still answers prayer!)

When somebody has confidence in you and believes in you, things once thought impossible become possible. My wife, Victoria, thinks I can do anything. She has so much confidence in me. I wouldn't be where I am today if she hadn't constantly been telling me, "Joel, you can do it. You have what it takes." Years ago, when she and I attended church services at Lakewood, Victoria used to tell me, "Joel, one day you're going to be up there leading this church. One day that's going to be you."

I said, "Victoria, please quit saying that. That makes me nervous just thinking about it. Besides, I don't even know how to preach."

"Sure you do," she'd say with a mischievous twinkle in her eyes. "Just preach to the people like you preach to me!"

Year after year, Victoria encouraged me, "Joel, you've got so much to offer. God is going to use you. You're going to be the pastor of Lakewood Church." That seed was being planted inside me. And when Daddy went to be with the Lord, I believe one of the main reasons I was able to step up to the plate so quickly was the fact that Victoria believed in me, and she had helped instill that confidence in me.

Victoria's belief in me has not only helped me to enlarge my vision, it's helped me to understand how much confidence Almighty God has in me. Immediately after Daddy passed away, one of the first things I did was cancel our national television broadcast. We were on the Family Channel on Sunday nights at that time. I thought, *I'm not a national TV preacher. I don't even know if I can preach. Who is going to want to listen to me?* I called our representative and explained to him that my dad had died, and we were going to have to let go of that television time.

When I told Victoria what I had done, she said, "Joel, I think you should call him back and tell him we want our time back. We're not going to go backward. We're not going to shrink back in fear. There are people all over the world who are watching to see what's going to happen to Lakewood, and we need that TV time."

I knew Victoria was right. Something just clicked in my spirit. That was a Friday afternoon, so I called the man, but I couldn't get him. I left him a message, and we also sent him some faxes and e-mails. We knew that time was of the essence if we wanted to rescue our television program. That program slot was extremely valuable; the cable network would be able to sell it easily and quickly to another programmer.

Monday was a holiday, but first thing Tuesday morning, we got a call back from the sales representative. He said, "Joel, I had already sold your time slot last week. But when I went to sign the contract on Friday, something inside me said, *Don't do it until next week*." He continued, "When I got here this morning, I knew what that something was. God wanted you to have that time period back." He told me he'd torn up the other contract, and then he said, "You can have your original slot." I believe that decision was providential. Today, we are on more than two hundred television stations in various parts of the world. God has done more than we can even ask or think.

But the point I want you to see is that a key part of that process happened when somebody instilled confidence in me. Victoria helped me to enlarge my vision, to change my thinking. She believed in me more than I believed in myself. It's one thing for people we love and respect to believe in us, but when we comprehend how much God believes in us, nothing can stop us from fulfilling our destinies.

The enemy in your mind says you don't have what it takes; God says you do have what it takes. Whom are you going to believe? The enemy says you're not able to succeed; God says you can do all things through Christ. The enemy says you'll never get out of debt; God says not only are you going to get out of debt, you will lend and not borrow. The enemy says you're never going to get well; God says He will restore your health. The enemy says you'll never amount to anything; God says He will raise you up and make your life significant. The enemy says your problems are too big, there's no hope; God says He will solve those problems; moreover, He will turn those problems around and use them for your good. Friend, start believing what God says about you, and start thinking God's thoughts. God's thoughts will fill you with faith and hope and victory. God's thoughts will build you up and encourage you. They will give you the strength you need to keep on keeping on. God's thoughts will give you that can-do mentality.

CHAPTER 13

Reprogramming Your Mental Computer

A little boy went out to the backyard to play with a baseball bat and a ball. He said to himself, "I am the best hitter in the world." Then he threw the ball up in the air and took a swing at it, but he missed. Without a moment's hesitation, he picked up the ball and tossed it in the air again, saying as he swung the bat, "I'm the best hitter in all the world." He swung and missed. Strike two. He tossed the ball up again, concentrating more intensely, even more determined, saying, "I am the best hitter in all the world!" He swung the bat with all his might. *Whiff!* Strike three. The little boy laid down his bat and smiled real big. "What do you know?" he said. "I'm the best pitcher in all the world!"

Now that's a good attitude! Sometimes you simply have to choose to see the bright side of situations. When things don't work out as you planned, rather than complaining, look for something good in your circumstances. Fill your mind with good thoughts.

Your mind is similar to a computer. What you program into it dictates how it will function. How foolish it would be to complain, "I hate this computer! It never gives me the right answer; it never does what I want it to do." Think about it: You can have the most powerful computer in the world, but if you program it with the wrong software or with misinformation, it will never function as the manufacturer intended.

Beyond that, we now have a myriad of computer viruses lurking in cyberspace, waiting for an opportunity to destroy your hard drive and the information stored in your computer. Such viruses can get into a perfectly good computer and contaminate the software. Before long the computer will develop a sluggishness; it will malfunction. You may not be able to get to the programs you need or retrieve important documents. All too often, you unwittingly pass along the virus to a friend, family member, or business associate, exacerbating the problem by contaminating their systems with the same virus that infected yours. Usually these problems occur not because the computer is defective, but because somebody has reprogrammed the software or contaminated good, valuable programs or information within.

Similarly, too often we allow negative thoughts, words, and other devious viruses to access our minds, subtly changing our software, or corrupting our information and values. We were created in the image of God. Before we were ever formed, He programmed us to live abundant lives, to be happy, healthy, and whole. But when our thinking becomes contaminated, it is no longer in line with God's Word. We make serious mistakes and wrong choices. We go through life with low self-esteem, worries, fears, feelings of inadequacy and insecurity. Making matters worse, we pass on our negative attitudes to others.

When you recognize these things happening, you must reprogram your computer. You must change your thinking. Understand, *you* are not defective. God made you, and He has programmed you for victory. But until you get your thinking in line with your owner's manual, God's Word, you will never operate to your full potential.

God made you, and He has programmed you for victory.

It's a Thinking Problem

I talked to a man recently who said, "Joel, I've been watching your messages on television about being happy and enjoying your life, but it just doesn't seem to work for me." He explained that five or six years ago, he went through a very painful breakup in a relationship. He was heartbroken and devastated. He said, "I just can't seem to get past those emotions. I get up every morning depressed. I go through the day, and I can't shake the sadness. I come back home, and I go to bed depressed." He informed me that he had been through several counseling sessions, but he was not seeing any progress.

"Do you think you can help me solve these emotional problems?" he asked.

"Sir, I don't really believe you have an emotional problem," I answered straightforwardly. "I believe you have a thinking problem."

"What do you mean?"

"What is the first thing you think about when you get up in the morning?"

"I think about how lonely I am and how hurt I've been," he replied.

"What do you think most about as you go through the workday?"

"I think about how messed up my life is, how many mistakes I've made, and how I wish I could do it all over again."

"So what do you think about when you go to bed?"

"Same thing."

"Sir, I'm not a psychologist or a psychiatrist, but I think your emotions are working just fine. They are working just the way God intended them to. Our emotions simply respond to what we're thinking about. They are neither positive or negative. They merely allow us to feel what we're thinking. If you go around thinking sad thoughts all the time, you're going to feel sad. If you go around thinking angry thoughts, you're going to be angry. But if you go around thinking happy thoughts, thoughts of victory, you're going to be happy. You're going to be victorious. You cannot go around all day long thinking about the people who have hurt you and all the mistakes you've made, and expect to live any kind of happy, positive life. You've got to let go of the past and start dwelling on the fact that God has a great future in store for you. He has a new beginning for you. Start dwelling on the fact that God has promised He will turn this situation around and use it to your advantage. Choose to think on good things. You have to reprogram your mental computer, and when you do, your emotions will follow."

The Bible says, "I have set before you life and death, blessings and curses, positive and negative; therefore God says choose life."[1] This is not a once-and-for-all matter. It's a choice we have to make on a moment-by-moment basis. We must choose to dwell on the positive, choose to dwell on the good. The negative is always going to be around us. We have to choose to dwell on what's right, rather than on what's wrong. Choose to dwell on what you have, not on what you don't have. Choose to think the right thoughts.

You cannot prevent negative thoughts from knocking at your door, but you can control whether or not you're going to open the door and allow them to come in. If you will stand guard over that doorway and keep your mind focused on the good things of God, the Bible says that "God will keep you in perfect peace."[2] You can have peace in the midst of your storms if you'll simply learn to choose the right thoughts. That means in the tough times of life, instead of dwelling on your problems, you must decide that you will dwell on your God. Dwell on the fact that Almighty God is on your side. Dwell on the fact that He's promised to fight your battles for you. Dwell on the fact that no weapon formed against you can prosper. If you start thinking these kinds of thoughts, you will be filled with faith and confidence, no matter what comes against you in life.

You may have gone through some disappointments, and things in your life may not have turned out as you had hoped. People may have treated you wrong. You may have suffered some major setbacks. But you never come to a dead end with God. He always has a new beginning available for you. Start dwelling on the solution. Dwell on the fact that God still has a great plan in store for your life. When one door closes, God will always open up a bigger and better door. But you have to do your part and stay in an attitude of faith, stay filled with hope.

Understand, this is an ongoing battle. We never get to a place where we don't have to deal with negative, destructive thoughts. So the sooner we learn how to guard our minds and control our thought lives, the better off we will be.

No matter how many years we have trusted in God, or how positively we live, we all will occasionally be susceptible to discouragement. That's part of the price we pay for living in a sinful world. As much as I attempt to keep my attitude positive, I am not immune from such attacks.

Stand Still

In December 2001, when Lakewood Church decided to lease the Compaq Center in Houston, we signed a sixty-year lease with the city to move into the Rockets' sixteen-thousand-seat basketball arena. Our congregation was excited and couldn't wait to get started on renovations of the arena.

But another company that wanted the property filed a lawsuit to keep us from moving in. Naturally, we were disappointed about the delay, but after we prayed about it, we knew that God wanted us to continue forward with our plans. In March 2002, our congregation made a major commitment toward that end.

Unfortunately, in the fall of that year, the lawsuit started heating up. Throughout the winter, legal wrangling dragged on and on. Finally, we got word that we were scheduled to go to trial in the spring of 2003. Our attorneys had already warned us that there wasn't a chance in the world our opponent would settle with us. They just had too much to lose. We discussed our options, laying out the various possibilities, with the attorneys clearly spelling out our chances of winning or losing, the enormous amounts of money it might cost, and how much time it could take. When I looked at the bleak reports, it seemed to be an impossible situation. Even if we were to win the lawsuit, it could be tied up for years in the court system through appeals. All the while, large sums of our money remained at risk.

During that long, drawn-out period, I'd often wake up in the middle of the night, my mind bombarded by all sorts of disturbing thoughts: *Man, you have made a terrible mistake. You told all those people you're going to get the Compaq Center. You showed them the plans. You had them give money. What's going to happen if you lose the lawsuit? You're going to look like a fool. Worse yet, what's going to happen if it's tied up for eight or nine years in the court system? You've got all that money at risk. You can't make any plans. What are you going to do then?*

Thoughts of failure and loss pelted my mind: *It's impossible. It's never going to work out. You'd better just get your money back and move on.* And I was tempted to try to figure it out in my own reasoning. I was tempted to lose my joy. But during that time, I had to make a decision whether I was going to dwell on the lies of the enemy, get depressed, and stop God from working, or keep my trust and believe that God was fighting our battles for us. Was I going to dwell on the fact that God was in control, and that He was guiding and directing our steps?

I made the decision to go with God. When those thoughts of doubt and unbelief assailed me, I did my best to cast them down, to reject them. I made a conscious decision not to focus on the problem, but to focus on God.

When that thought came saying, *It's impossible*, I rejected it and reminded myself that with God all things are possible. When thoughts came saying, *This was a poor decision; it's never going to work out*, I cast them down and reminded myself that all things work together for good to those who love the Lord. When thoughts came saying, *The opposing company is too powerful. You'll never defeat them*, I rejected that and reminded myself that no man—or company—can stand against our God. If God is for us, who dares to be against us? When thoughts threatened, *This is going to be a mess. You're going to drag the church through all kinds of mud, and it's going to end in a big disappointment*, I learned to lift my hands and declare, "Father, You said when we walk in integrity, You would keep our feet from stumbling. So Father, I thank You that You are preventing us from making a mistake."

Every time those negative, discouraging thoughts popped into my mind, I used that as an opportunity to thank God that victory was on the way. I knew that if we entertained doubt and unbelief, God could not work in that situation. And I didn't want anything I was doing to keep God from bringing that victory to pass.

God works where there's an attitude of faith.

When we're always worried, upset, or depressed, all we're really doing is delaying God in bringing the victory. God works where there's an attitude of faith. Jesus said, "If you believe, all things are possible," and the opposite of that is true as well. If you don't believe, if you're negative, fretting, worried, or upset, then supernatural changes will not be possible for you. When you are going through a tough time in your life, even if you don't feel like keeping a positive attitude—which, at times, you probably won't—you should do it anyway, knowing that every minute you allow yourself to lapse into a negative attitude is a minute that God cannot work in that situation.

In the midst of the Compaq Center lawsuit, one night I awakened and picked up my Bible. The Lord seemed to be prompting me toward a passage of Scripture in which the people of Judah were facing a formidable foe, an impossible situation, really. God said to them, "You don't have to fight this battle. Stand still and you will see the deliverance of the Lord."[3] And when I read that, two words jumped off the page—*stand still*. That means to stay calm, to stay at peace. Don't get all frustrated. Don't try to figure it out in your own reasoning. Instead, stand still. Be confident. Keep a good attitude. God says, "I'll fight your battles for you."

A few weeks later, we received a phone call from our attorneys—the same attorneys who told us our opponents would never settle. The company that had filed the lawsuit wanted to sit down and talk with us that next morning. In less than forty-eight hours, we came to an agreement and totally settled that lawsuit!

The Bible says, "When a man's ways are pleasing to the LORD, He makes even his enemies to be at peace with him."[4] And that's just what God did for us. Not only did we settle the lawsuit, but the company that was once so adamantly opposed to our church leasing the arena agreed to lease us nearly ten thousand covered parking spaces at the Compaq Center for the next sixty years. Not only did that save us millions of dollars, but it allowed us to move into that new facility approximately a year sooner than we would have otherwise.

If you'll keep your trust in God, He'll fight your battles for you. If you'll stand still, you'll see the deliverance of the Lord. It doesn't matter what you're going through, or how big your opponents are. Keep an attitude of faith. Stay calm. Stay at peace. Stay in that positive frame of mind. And don't try to do it all your own way. Let God do it His way. If you will simply obey His commands, He will change things in your favor.

You may be going through great difficulties, and you're tempted to think, *I'm never going to get out of this. This is never going to change. I'm never going to win in this situation.*

No, the Bible says, "Don't get weary and faint in your mind."[5] Remember, you must first win the battle in your mind. Stand strong. When negative thoughts come, reject them and replace them with God's thoughts. When you're in that attitude of faith, you are opening the door for God to work in your situation. You may not see anything happening with your natural eyes, but don't let that discourage you. In the unseen realm, in the spiritual world, God is at work. He is changing things in your favor. And if you'll just do your part and keep believing, in due season, at the right time, God will bring you out with the victory.

The key is to choose the right thoughts, to keep your mind set. Not just when you feel good, not just when things are going your way, not just when you don't have any problems, but even in the tough times of life—especially in the difficult times—you must keep your mind set on the good things of God. Stay focused. Stay full of faith. Stay full of joy. Stay full of hope. Make a conscious decision that you are going to stay in a positive frame of mind.

Some people take one step forward and then two steps backward. They are happy and in a good attitude one day, then the next day they are negative and depressed. They make a little progress, then they back up. Because of their vacillating faith, they never really get to the place God wants them to be. They never experience the victories He has in store for them. Friend, you must be consistent. Set your mind for success, victory, and progress. Cast down anything negative, any thought that brings fear, worry, doubt, or unbelief. Your attitude should be: *I refuse to go backward. I am going forward with God. I'm going to be the person He wants me to be. I'm going to fulfill my destiny.*

If you will do that, God will continually work in your life. He'll fight your battles for you. He'll give you peace in the midst of a storm, and He'll help you live that life of victory that He has in store for you.

CHAPTER 14

The Power in Your Words

Jose Lima starred as a pitcher for the Houston Astros for several years in the late 1990s. Jose is an outgoing, energetic, likable young ballplayer who usually exudes a positive attitude. But when the Astros built their new ballpark, now known as Minute Maid Park, Jose was upset. The fence in left field was much closer than the fence at the Astrodome. In fact, Minute Maid Park has one of the shortest distances from home plate to the left-field fence of any ballpark in Major League Baseball. The hitters love it, but the short left field makes it tougher on the pitchers, especially when they are working against right-handed batters who tend to hit to left field.

The first time Jose Lima stepped onto the new diamond, he walked out to the pitcher's mound, and when he looked into the outfield, he immediately noticed the close proximity of that left-field fence. "I'll never be able to pitch in here," he said.

The next season, despite the enthusiasm of the fans and the excitement of playing in that brand-new ballpark, Jose had the worst year of his career. He plummeted from being a twenty-game winner to being a sixteen-game loser in back-to-back seasons. Never in the history of the Astros franchise had any pitcher experienced such a pronounced negative turnaround.

Self-Fulfilling Prophecies

What happened to Jose? The same thing that happens to many of us every day—we get what we say. Our words become self-fulfilling prophecies. If you allow your thoughts to defeat you and then give birth to negative ideas through your words, your actions will follow suit. That's why we need to be extremely careful about what we think and especially careful about what we say. Our words have tremendous power, and whether we want to or not, we will give life to what we're saying, either good or bad.

Sadly, many people are living discouraged lives because of their words. They say things such as:

- *"Nothing good ever happens to me."*
- *"I'll never be successful."*
- *"I don't have what it takes. I can't do it."*
- *"I'll never get out of this mess."*

Some people even call themselves names! "What an idiot! You never can do anything right." They don't realize it, but their own words are paving the way for failure.

Words are similar to seeds. By speaking them aloud, they are planted in our subconscious minds, and they take on a life of their own; they take root, grow, and produce fruit of the same kind. If we speak positive words, our lives will move in that direction. Similarly, negative words will produce poor results. We can't speak words of defeat and failure yet expect to live in victory. We will reap exactly what we sow.

The Bible compares the tongue to the rudder of a huge ship.[1] Although that rudder is small, it controls the direction of the entire ship, and, in a similar manner, your tongue will control the direction of your life. If you habitually speak words of failure, you are going to move in the direction of a defeated, discouraged life. If your conversation regularly includes phrases such as "I can't. I'm not able to. I don't have what it takes," or other negative comments, you are setting yourself up for defeat. Those negative words will keep you from being the person God wants you to be.

I heard about a doctor who understood the power of words. One prescription he gave to all his patients was for them to say at least once every hour, "I'm getting better and better every day, in every way." The doctor's patients experienced amazing results, much better than the patients treated by many of his colleagues.

When you say something often enough, with enthusiasm and passion, before long your subconscious mind begins to act on what you are saying, doing whatever is necessary to bring those thoughts and words to pass. Sadly, most people insist on saying negative things over their lives. They continually denigrate themselves with their own words. They don't realize that their own words will decimate their confidence and destroy their self-esteem. In fact, if you are struggling with low self-esteem, you need to go overboard in speaking positive, faith-filled words of victory about your life. Get up each morning and look in the mirror and say, "I am valuable. I am loved. God has a great plan for my life. I have favor wherever I go. God's blessings are chasing me down and overtaking me. Everything I touch prospers and succeeds. I'm excited about my future!" Start speaking those kinds of words, and before long, you will rise to a new level of well-being, success, and victory. There truly is power in your words.

We have to be particularly careful about what we say during times of adversity or hardship, when things aren't going our way. How you respond in the adversities of life and what you say in the midst of your difficulties will have a great impact on how long you stay in those situations. As a rule, the more positive your thoughts and words, the stronger you will be and the sooner you will get over whatever ails you. Admittedly, when times get tough, our human nature tends to want to complain, to talk about the problem, to tell everybody who will listen how badly life is treating us. But such conversations are self-defeating. To get through a tough time quicker and with better results, we must learn to speak as positively as possible.

What you say in the midst of your difficulties will have a great impact on how long you stay in those situations.

Too often, we make the mistake of adopting negative attitudes and complaining.

"I knew my marriage wasn't going to work out."

"I don't think I'll ever get out of debt."

"I guess I'll just have to put up with this health problem for the rest of my life."

When you start talking like that, you become your own worst enemy. If there's ever a time you must guard what you say, it's in times of trouble. When you feel overwhelmed, when you're stressed out, when everything in the world has come against you, when that left-field fence looms largely over your shoulder, that's when you need to be on high alert. That's when you are the most vulnerable and the most likely to slip into a negative attitude, speaking negative comments. Your subconscious mind picks up your words, treats them as true, valid statements, and then sets about trying to fulfill them. When that happens, you have nobody else to blame but yourself; you've been undermined by your own thoughts and words.

Guard What You Say

If you're in a storm today, now more than ever you need to guard what you say and not allow any negative, destructive words to come out of your mouth. Scripture says, "Death and life are in the power of the tongue; and you will eat the fruit thereof."[2] In other words, you create an environment for either good or evil with your words, and you are going to have to live in that world you've created. If you're always murmuring, complaining, and talking about how bad life is treating you, you're going to live in a pretty miserable, depressing world. You may be tempted to merely use your words to describe negative situations, but God wants us to use our words to *change* our negative situations. Don't talk about the problem, talk about the solution.

The Bible clearly tells us to speak to our mountains.[3] Maybe your mountain is a sickness; perhaps your mountain is a troubled relationship; maybe your mountain is a floundering business. Whatever your mountain is, you must do more than think about it, more than pray about it; you must speak to that obstacle. The Bible says, "Let the weak say I'm strong. Let the oppressed say I'm free. Let the sick say I'm healed. Let the poor say I'm well off."[4]

Start calling yourself healed, happy, whole, blessed, and prosperous. Stop talking to God about how big your mountains are, and start talking to your mountains about how big your God is!

Stop talking to God about how big your mountains are, and start talking to your mountains about how big your God is!

I love what David did when he faced the giant Goliath. He didn't murmur and complain and say, "God, why do I always have these huge problems?" No, he changed his whole atmosphere through the words that came out of his mouth. He didn't dwell on the fact that Goliath was three times his size. Nor did he dwell on the fact that Goliath was a skilled warrior and he was just a shepherd boy. No, he didn't focus on the magnitude of the obstacle before him. He chose instead to focus on the greatness of his God.

When Goliath saw how young and small David was, he began to laugh. He jeered, "Am I a dog that you'd come at me with a stick?"

But David looked him right in the eyes, and with great determination, he said, "Listen, Goliath, you come against me with a sword and a shield, but I come against you in the name of the Lord God of Israel."[5]

Now, those are words of faith! Notice, too, that he spoke the words aloud. He didn't merely *think* them; he didn't simply *pray* them. He spoke directly to the mountain of a man in front of him, and said, "I will defeat you and feed your flesh to the birds of the air this very day." And with God's help, he did exactly that!

Those are the kinds of words you must learn to speak in your everyday circumstances, and especially in times of crisis and adversity. When you're facing obstacles in your path, you must boldly say, "Greater is He who is in me than he who is in the world.[6] No weapon formed against me is going to prosper.[7] God always causes me to triumph." Quit worrying and complaining about the obstacle, and start speaking to it. Quit complaining about poverty and lack and start declaring, "God supplies all of my needs in abundance." Quit nagging that friend or family member who is not serving God and start declaring, "As for me and my house, we will serve the Lord." Quit complaining that nothing good ever happens to you and start declaring, "Everything I touch prospers and succeeds." We must stop cursing the darkness. Let's start commanding the light to come.

Friend, there is a miracle in your mouth. If you want to change your world, start by changing your words. When times get tough, don't give in to murmuring, disputing, and complaining. Speak to those problems. If you'll learn how to speak the right words and keep the right attitude, God will turn that situation around.

You may be thinking, *This sounds too good to be true, Joel.* I know it's true! I saw the power of our thoughts and words turn an impossible situation in my own family into a modern-day medical miracle. Come on, let me tell you about it.

CHAPTER 15

Speaking Life-Changing Words

In 1981, my mother was diagnosed with cancer and given just a few weeks to live. I'll never forget what a shock that news was to our family. I had never seen my mother sick one day in all my life. She was extremely healthy and active. She loved being outdoors, working in the yard, working in her flowerbeds.

I was away at college when the doctor's report came. My brother, Paul, called me and said, "Joel, Mother is very, very sick."

"What do you mean, Paul? Does she have the flu or something like that?"

"No, Joel," Paul replied. "She's losing weight. Her skin is yellow, and she's extremely weak; something is seriously wrong with her."

Mother was hospitalized for twenty-one days, while the doctors ran test after test. They sent her lab work all over the country, hoping to find some key to help her. Finally, they came back with the dreaded report that she had metastatic cancer of the liver. They called my dad out into the hallway and said, "Pastor, we hate to tell you this, but your wife has only a few weeks to live. Not months, weeks . . ."

Medical science had reached the limits of what they could do. The best and brightest doctors in the world had exhausted their efforts, so they basically sent our mom home to die.

We expressed our sincere appreciation to the doctors and hospital staff for their hard work, but we refused to accept their opinions. I'm grateful for doctors, hospitals, medicine, and science, but the medical professionals can present only what their medical charts tell them.

Thank God, you and I can appeal to a higher Authority. We can always have another report. God's report says, "I will restore health to you and heal your wounds."

We serve a supernatural God. He is not limited to the laws of nature. He can do what human beings cannot do. He can make a way in our lives where it looks as if there is no way. That's what we prayed that He would do in Mother's life.

And my mother never gave up. She refused to speak words of defeat. She didn't complain about how sick or weak she felt, or how awful her life was, or how hopeless her situation looked. She chose to put God's words in her mind and in her mouth.

She started speaking faith-filled words. She started calling in health and calling in healing. All during the day, we'd hear her going through the house speaking aloud, "I will live and not die, and I will declare the works of the Lord." She was like a walking Bible!

I'd say, "Mother, how are you doing?"

She'd say, "Joel, I'm strong in the Lord and the power of His might." She pored over her Bible and found about thirty or forty favorite passages of Scripture concerning healing. She wrote them down, and every day, she'd read over them and boldly declare them aloud. We'd see her walking up and down the driveway, saying, "With long life, He satisfies me and shows me His salvation."

Mother mixed her words with God's Words, and something powerful began to happen. Her circumstances began to change. Not overnight, but little by little, she began to feel better. She got her appetite back and started gaining weight. Slowly but surely, her strength returned.

What was happening? God was watching over His Word to perform it. God was restoring health to her and healing her of her wounds. A few weeks went by and Mother got a little better. A few months went by, and she was even better. A few years went by, and she just kept on confessing God's Word. Today, it has been more than twenty years since we received the report that Mother had just a few weeks to live, and as I write these words, Mother is totally free from that cancer, healed by the power of God's Word!

And she is still confessing God's Word. She gets up every morning and reviews those same Scriptures on the subject of healing. She still speaks those words of faith, victory, and health over her life. She won't leave the house until she does it. Beyond that, she loves to remind "Mr. Death" that he has no hold on her life. Every time my mother passes a graveyard, she literally shouts out loud, "With long life He satisfies me and shows me His salvation!" The first time she did that when I was riding in the car with her, I nearly jumped out of my seat!

But Mother refuses to give the enemy a foothold.

Boldly Confess God's Word

Mother used her words to change her world, and you can do the same thing. Maybe you are facing a "hopeless" situation. Don't give up. God is a miracle-working God. He knows what you're going through, and He will not let you down. He is a friend that sticks closer than a brother. If you will trust in Him and start speaking words of faith, your circumstances will begin to change.

God is a miracle-working God.

Of course, we don't have to be in life-threatening situations to use God's Word. We can speak God's Word in our everyday lives. Parents, you ought to speak God's Word over your children every day before they go to school. Just say, "Father, You promised me in Psalm 91 that You will give Your angels charge over us and that no evil would come near our household. So I thank You that my children are supernaturally protected, and You are guiding them and watching after them. Father, You said that we're the head and not the tail, and You will surround us with favor. So I thank You that my children are blessed, and they will excel at whatever they put their hands to do."

Speaking God's Word over your children can make an enormous difference in their lives. I know my mother prayed over my siblings and me every day before we went to school. She prayed specifically that we'd never break any bones. She raised five healthy, very active children. We all played sports and did a lot of crazy things, but to this day, as far as I know, not one of us has ever broken a bone.

Just as it is imperative that we see ourselves as God sees us and think about ourselves as God regards us, it is equally important that we say about ourselves what God says about us. Our words are vital in bringing our dreams to pass. It's not enough to simply see it by faith or in your imagination. You have to begin speaking words of faith over your life. Your words have enormous creative power. The moment you speak something out, you give birth to it. This is a spiritual principle, and it works whether what you are saying is good or bad, positive or negative.

In that regard, many times we are our own worst enemies. We blame everybody and everything else, but the truth is, we are profoundly influenced by what we say about ourselves. Scripture says, "We are snared by the words of our mouth."[1]

"Nothing good ever happens to me. My dreams never come to pass. I knew I wouldn't get promoted." Statements such as these will literally prevent you from moving ahead in life. That's why you must learn to guard your tongue and speak only faith-filled words over your life. This is one of the most important principles you can ever grab hold of. Simply put, your words can either make you or break you.

God never commanded us to repeatedly verbalize our pain and suffering. He didn't instruct us to go around discussing our negative situations, airing our "dirty laundry" with all our friends and neighbors. Instead, God told us to speak constantly of His goodness, to speak of His promises in the morning at the breakfast table, in the evenings around the dinner table, at night before bedtime, continually dwelling on the good things of God.

You could experience a new sense of joy in your home, if you'd simply stop talking about the negative things in your life and begin talking about God's Word.

If you are always talking about your problems, don't be surprised if you live in perpetual defeat. If you're in the habit of saying, "Nothing good ever happens to me," guess what? Nothing good is going to happen to you! You must stop talking about the problem and start talking about the solution. Quit speaking words of defeat, and start speaking words of victory. Don't use your words to describe your situation; use your words to *change* your situation.

Every morning, when I get out of bed, I say, "Father, I thank You that I am strong in the Lord and the power of Your might. I am well able to do what You have called me to do." I quote several other passages of Scripture regarding God's favor in my life. What am I doing? I am starting off my day on a positive note, aligning my thoughts and words with His.

Set the tone for the entire day as soon as you get out of bed. If you wait until you have read the morning newspaper, you'll start your day with all sorts of sad, dreary news. Try starting your day with some good news by speaking God's Word over your life! Don't wait till you've checked the stock report, or you'll be up one day and down the next. The moment you wake up, begin to give new life to your dreams by speaking words of faith and victory.

Understand, avoiding negative talk is not enough. That's similar to a football team having a good defense but no offense. If your team is constantly playing defense, you stand little chance of scoring. You must get the ball and move it down the field; you must get on the offense. You have to be aggressive.

**Avoiding negative talk is not enough . . .
You must get on the offense.**

Similarly, you must start boldly confessing God's Word, using your words to move forward in life, to bring to life the great things God has in store for you. The Scripture says, "With the heart one believes unto righteousness, and with the mouth confession is made unto salvation."[2] This same principle is true in other areas. When you believe God's Word and begin to speak it, mixing it with your faith, you are actually confirming that truth and making it valid in your own life.

If you are facing sickness today, you should confirm God's Word concerning healing. Say something such as, "Father, I thank You that You promised me in Psalms that I will live and not die and I will declare the works of the Lord." As you boldly declare it, you are confirming that truth in your own life.

If you are struggling financially, instead of talking about the problem, you need to boldly declare, "Everything I put my hands to prospers and succeeds!"

Friend, when you make those kinds of bold declarations, all heaven comes to attention to back up God's Word.

God has not given us hundreds of promises simply for us to read and enjoy. God has given us His promises so we might boldly declare them to bring us victory, health, hope, and abundant life.

In 1997, Victoria and I had the opportunity to develop the last full power television station available in Houston, channel 55. It was a tremendous opportunity but also an enormous undertaking. All we had was a construction permit, basically, a piece of paper giving us the right to build the station. We didn't have a studio, we didn't have a transmitter or a tower to put it on; oh, and we had no programming! We were starting totally from scratch. And we had less than a year to get the station on the air or we'd lose the license. We really needed God's supernatural wisdom to deal with the day-to-day details of building a television station.

I decided to do what my mother did, and every morning when I read my Bible, I wrote down any verse or passage of Scripture that had to do with wisdom or guidance. After a couple of weeks, I had recorded twenty or thirty passages, and every day, before we would leave the house, Victoria and I would read those Scriptures and boldly declare them.

One of my favorite passages was: "For the Lord grants wisdom! His every word is a treasure of knowledge and understanding. He grants good sense to the godly—his saints. He is their shield, protecting them and guarding their pathway. He shows how to distinguish right from wrong, how to make the right decision every time."[3] We'd say, "Father, we thank You that we have Your supernatural wisdom, and we do have the ability to make the right decision every time. Father, You said the steps of a good man are ordered by the Lord, so we thank You that You are guiding and directing our steps." And I cannot tell you how many times during the development of that television station God supernaturally protected us and kept us from making mistakes.

For instance, I was just about to pick up the phone and order an extremely expensive and critical piece of equipment, probably the most important piece of equipment in a television station. Just before I did, a man called me out of the clear blue, and we discussed numerous issues. Toward the end of our conversation, he said something that gave me insight and totally changed the decision I was about to make.

What was happening? God was using that man to help guide us;

God was protecting us from making a poor decision, and He was giving us good sense to make the correct decision. God was watching over His Word to perform it.

God wants to do something similar for you, but you can't be lazy. Search the Scriptures and highlight those that particularly apply to your life situation. Write them down and get in the habit of declaring them.

God has already done everything He's going to do. The ball is now in your court. If you want success, if you want wisdom, if you want to be prosperous and healthy, you're going to have to do more than meditate and believe; you must boldly declare words of faith and victory over yourself and your family.

In the next chapter, we'll discover how you can do just that!

CHAPTER 16

Speaking a Blessing

As parents, we can profoundly influence the direction of our children's lives by the words we say to them. I believe as husbands and wives we can set the direction for our entire family. As a business owner, you can help set the direction for your employees. With our words, we have the ability to help mold and shape the future of anyone over whom we have influence.

And each of us has influence over somebody. You may not consider yourself a leader, but you have a sphere of influence nonetheless—somebody or some group that looks up to you. Even if you're a teenager, somebody values your opinion. It is vital that we speak "good things" into the lives of those over whom we have influence. That doesn't mean we will never disagree with them or have to confront and correct them. But the general tenor of our words to them and about them should be positive.

A well-meaning mother was constantly nagging her teenage son. "You're so lazy; you're never going to amount to anything! If you don't shape up, you're never going to get into college. You'll probably wind up getting into trouble."

Those kinds of negative words will destroy a person quicker than you can imagine. You cannot speak negatively about someone on one hand, then turn around and expect that person to be blessed. If you want your son or daughter to be productive and successful, you need to begin declaring words of life over your children rather than predictions of doom and despair. The Scripture reminds us that with our words we can bless people or we can curse them.

In the Old Testament, the people clearly understood the power of the blessing. As the family patriarch approached senility or death, the oldest sons gathered alongside their father. The father would then lay his hands on each son's head and speak loving, faith-filled words over them about their future. These pronouncements comprised what was known ever after as "the blessing." The family realized that these were more than Dad's dying wishes; these words carried spiritual authority and had the ability to bring success, prosperity, and health into their future.

Many times, children even fought over the father's blessing. They weren't fighting over money that they might inherit. Nor were they arguing over the family business. No, they were fighting over faith-filled words. They realized that if they received the father's blessing, wealth and success would be a natural by-product. Beyond that, they deeply desired the blessing from somebody they loved and respected.

One of the most amazing biblical records concerning the power of the blessing comes out of the lives of Jacob and Esau, the two sons of Isaac.[1] Jacob wanted his father's blessing—not just any blessing, but the blessing that rightfully belonged to the firstborn son in the family. Isaac was old, near death, and he was practically blind. One day he called in his son Esau and said, "Esau, go kill some game, and prepare me a meal and I will give you the blessing that belongs to the firstborn son." But Jacob's mother, Rachel, overheard this conversation. Rachel loved Jacob more than she loved Esau, so she told Jacob to put on Esau's clothes in an attempt to trick Isaac into giving him the blessing. Then she prepared one of Isaac's favorite meals.

While Esau was out in the field hunting, she said to Jacob, "Go to your father and present him this food. And he'll give you the blessing that really belongs to your brother."

Jacob recognized the seriousness of this duplicity. He said, "But Mother, what if he finds out that I'm lying, and he curses me instead of blesses me? I'll be cursed for the rest of my life!"

Think about that. Jacob understood that he was risking his entire future on this gambit. He recognized that the words his father spoke over him would impact him, for either good or evil, the rest of his life.

Declare God's Favor

Whether we realize it or not, our words affect our children's future for either good or evil. Our words have the same kind of power that

Isaac's words had. We need to speak loving words of approval and acceptance, words that encourage, inspire, and motivate our children to reach for new heights. When we do that, we are speaking blessings into their lives. We are speaking abundance and increase. We're declaring God's favor in their lives.

**Our words affect our children's future,
for either good or evil.**

But too often, we slip into being harsh and critical with our children, constantly finding fault in something our children are doing. "Why can't you make better grades? You didn't mow the lawn right. Go clean your room—it looks like a pigpen! You can't do anything right, can you?"

Such negative words will cause our children to lose the sense of value God has placed within them. As parents, we do have a responsibility before God and society to train our children, to discipline them when they disobey, to lovingly correct them when they make wrong choices. But we should not constantly harp on our kids. If you continually speak words that discourage and dishearten, before long you will destroy your child's self-image. And with your negative words, you will open a door, allowing the enemy to bring all kinds of insecurity and inferiority into your child's life. Millions of adults today are still suffering as a result of the negative words their parents spoke over them as children.

Remember, if you make the mistake of constantly speaking negative words over your children, you are cursing their future. Moreover, God will hold you responsible for destroying their destiny. With authority comes responsibility, and you have the responsibility as the spiritual authority over your child to make sure that he feels loved, accepted, and approved. You have the responsibility to bless your children.

Beyond that, most children get their concepts of who God is and what He is like from their fathers. If their father is mean, critical, and harsh, inevitably the children will grow up with a distorted view of God. If the father is loving, kind, compassionate, and just, the child will better understand God's character.

One of the reasons I talk so much about the goodness of God is because I saw it modeled by my dad. Nobody could have represented God any better to us Osteen kids than my dad did. Even when we made mistakes or got off track, while Daddy was firm, he was also loving and kind. He nurtured us back to the right course. He never beat us into line; he loved us into line. Although he was very busy, he always took time for us. He encouraged us to do great things, to fulfill our dreams. He used to say, "Joel, don't do what I want you to do. Do what you want to do. Follow your own dreams."

Daddy believed in my brother and sisters and me. He told us we were great, even when we knew we weren't. He referred to us as blessings when we knew we weren't acting as blessings. Sometimes we'd make him mad, and he'd say, "I'm about to beat a little blessing to death!"

Mother and Daddy raised five children in our home. When we were growing up, we didn't have children's church programs such as many churches now have. We all met in the same auditorium. My little sister, April, and I used to sit on the front row of that little feed store that held about two hundred people. We'd play tic-tac-toe the whole service. (I'm confessing to let you know there's still hope for your children. I didn't pay attention, and God made me a pastor. Who knows what God is going to do with your children!)

Daddy would be up on the platform, and Mother would have all five of us kids lined up in a row. She'd have her hands raised in the air, worshiping God with her eyes completely closed. Yet she had an incredible ability, even with her eyes closed, to know when we kids were cutting up. That amazed me. I think that was my first experience with the supernatural power of God! I'd watch Mother to make sure that her eyes were closed before I'd do something to aggravate my brother, Paul. Without missing a beat, Mother would slowly bring one hand down, very gracefully grab my arm, and pinch the fire out of me! I wanted to scream, but I knew better. And then she'd lift that arm back up and continue worshiping the Lord.

I used to think, *Mama, you have a gift. That's supernatural!*

I'm joking (a little), but the point is my siblings and I were not perfect kids. We made plenty of mistakes. But my parents never focused on our weaknesses or on the problems. They always focused on the solutions. They constantly told us we were the best kids in the world. And we grew up secure, knowing that our parents not only loved each other, but they loved us and believed in us. They were going to stand behind us through thick and thin. We knew they were never going to criticize or condemn us, but would always believe the best in us.

Because I grew up with acceptance and approval from my parents, now, as a father myself, I'm practicing the same sort of things with my children. I'm speaking words of blessing into their lives that will be passed down to another generation. And I know my children will pass down the goodness of God to their children, and on and on.

One of the first things I do when I see my little boy, Jonathan, in the morning is to say, "Jonathan, you're the best." I'm constantly telling him, "Jonathan, you are God's gift to Mother and me. We love you. We're proud of you. We'll always stand behind you." I tell our daughter, Alexandra, the same sort of things.

Before they go to bed, I tell both of our children, "Daddy will always be your best friend." Victoria and I constantly tell them, "There's nothing you can't do. You have a bright future in front of you. You're surrounded by God's favor. Everything you touch is going to prosper."

Victoria and I believe that we have an opportunity and a responsibility to speak God's blessings into our children now, while they are young. Why should we wait till they are teenagers, or in their twenties and about to get married, to begin praying for God's blessings in their lives? No, we're declaring God's blessings over them all the days of their lives. And we are convinced that our words will impact our children long after they are grown and have children of their own.

What are you passing down to the next generation? It's not enough to think it; you must vocalize it. A blessing is not a blessing until it is spoken. Your children need to hear you say words such as, "I love you. I believe in you. I think you're great. There's nobody else like you. You are one of a kind." They need to hear your approval. They need to feel your love. They need your blessing.

A blessing is not a blessing until it is spoken.

Your children may be grown and gone, but that shouldn't stop you from picking up the phone to call and encourage them, to tell them you are proud of them. Maybe you didn't do well at blessing your children as they were growing up. It's not too late. Start to do it now.

Words Can't Be Taken Back

Jacob stood before his nearly blind father, Isaac, pretending to be his brother, Esau. Although Isaac's eyesight was dim, his intellect was not. He questioned, "Esau, is that really you?"

"Yes, Father; it's me," Jacob lied.

Isaac wasn't convinced, so he called his son closer to him. Only when he smelled Esau's clothes that Jacob was wearing was he finally convinced. He then gave Jacob the blessing that really belonged to his older brother. He said something like this: "May you always have an abundance of grain and an abundance of wine. May nations bow low before you and people always serve you. May you be the lord over your brothers. May anyone that curses you be cursed, and anyone that blesses you be blessed."[2] Notice, in Isaac's blessing he declared great things concerning Jacob's future, and a study of history will show that those things came to pass.

On the other hand, shortly after Jacob left the room, Esau came in. He said, "Dad, sit up; I've got the meal I've prepared for you."

Now Isaac was confused. He said, "Who are you?"

"Dad, I'm Esau, your firstborn son." At that point, the Bible records that Isaac began to shake violently. He realized that he had been duped. He explained to Esau how his brother, Jacob, had come in and deceitfully tricked him out of his blessing.

Now, here's an amazing aspect of this awful story of treachery. Esau began to cry with a loud voice, saying, "Father, can't you still give me the blessing that belongs to the firstborn?"

Isaac's answer was insightful and powerful: "No, the words have already gone forth, and I cannot take them back. I said that Jacob will be blessed, and he will always be blessed."

Do you see the power of our words? Do you see the power of speaking blessings over your children? Isaac said, "Once the words go forth, I can't take them back." He gave Esau a lesser blessing, but it was not nearly as significant as the one he had given to Jacob.

We need to be extremely careful about what we allow to come out of our mouths. The next time you're tempted to talk down to somebody, to belittle your child or degrade him, remember, you can't ever get those words back. Once you speak them, they take on a life of their own.

Use your words to speak blessings over people. Quit criticizing your child and start declaring great things in store for her future.

We should never speak negative destructive words toward anybody, especially toward people over whom we have authority or influence. Just because you have your own business or supervise a large number of employees doesn't give you the right to talk down to them and make them feel badly about themselves. Quite the contrary! God is going to hold you accountable for what you say to those individuals under your authority, and He is going to judge you by a stricter standard. You should go out of your way to speak positive words that build up and encourage.

Similarly, it is important for a husband to understand that his words have tremendous power in his wife's life. He needs to bless her with his words. She's given her life to love and care for him, to partner with him, to create a family together, to nurture his children. If he is always finding fault in something she's doing, always putting her down, he will reap horrendous problems in his marriage and in his life. Moreover, many women today are depressed and feel emotionally abused because their husbands do not bless them with their words. One of the leading causes of emotional breakdowns among married women is the fact that women do not feel valued. One of the main reasons for that deficiency is because husbands are willfully or unwittingly withholding the words of approval women so desperately desire. If you want to see God do wonders in your marriage, start praising your spouse. Start appreciating and encouraging her.

"Oh, my wife knows I love her," one elderly fellow said. "I don't need to tell her. I told her back when we got married forty-two years ago."

No, she needs to hear it again and again. Every single day, a husband should tell his wife, "I love you. I appreciate you. You're the best thing that ever happened to me." A wife should do the same for her husband. Your relationship would improve immensely if you'd simply start speaking kind, positive words, blessing your spouse instead of cursing him or her.

Declare God's Goodness

You must start declaring God's goodness in your life. Start boldly declaring, "God's face is smiling toward me, and He longs to be good to me." That is not bragging. That is how God says we're going to be blessed—when we start declaring His goodness.

Allow me to make some declarations in your life:

- *I declare that you are blessed with God's supernatural wisdom, and you have clear direction for your life.*
- *I declare that you are blessed with creativity, with courage, with ability, and with abundance.*
- *I declare that you are blessed with a strong will and with self-control and self-discipline.*
- *I declare that you are blessed with a great family, with good friends, with good health, and with faith, favor, and fulfillment.*
- *I declare that you are blessed with success, with supernatural strength, with promotion, and with divine protection.*
- *I declare that you are blessed with an obedient heart and with a positive outlook on life.*
- *I declare that any curse that has ever been spoken over you, any negative evil word that has ever come against you, is broken right now.*
- *I declare that you are blessed in the city. You are blessed in the country. You are blessed when you go in. You are blessed when you come out.*
- *I declare that everything you put your hands to do is going to prosper and succeed.*
- *I declare that you are blessed!*

I encourage you to receive these words and meditate on them; let them sink down deeply into your heart and mind and become a reality in your life. Practice doing something similar with your family. Learn to speak blessings over your life, your friends, your future. Remember, a blessing is not a blessing until it is spoken. If you'll do your part and start boldly speaking blessings over your life and the lives of those around you, God will provide everything you need to live the life of abundance He wants you to have.

Learn to speak blessings over your life, your friends, your future.

PART 4

LET GO OF THE PAST

CHAPTER 17

Letting Go of
Emotional Wounds

We live in a society that loves to make excuses, and one of our favorite phrases is: "It's not my fault."

"Joel, I'm a negative person because I was raised in an unhealthy family environment," one man told me.

"My husband walked out on me. I've been rejected. That's why I'm always so depressed," said a woman in her early forties.

"I've lost my wife, and I just don't understand it. That's why I'm so angry," said another young man.

No, the truth is, if we are bitter and resentful, it's because we are allowing ourselves to remain that way. We've all had negative things happen to us. If you look hard enough, you can easily find reasons to have a chip on your shoulder. Anyone can make excuses and blame the past for his or her bad attitudes, poor choices, or hot temper.

You may have valid reasons for feeling the way you do. You may have gone through things that nobody deserves to experience in life. Perhaps you were physically, verbally, sexually, or emotionally abused. Maybe you've struggled to deal with a chronic illness or some other irreparable physical problem. Perhaps somebody took advantage of you in business and you lost your shirt, as well as your self-esteem. I don't mean to minimize those sad experiences, but if you want to live in victory, you cannot use past emotional wounds as an excuse for making poor choices today. You dare not use your past as an excuse for your current bad attitude, or as a rationalization for your unwillingness to forgive somebody. The fourth step toward living your best life now is *to let go of the past.*

It's time to allow emotional wounds to heal, to let go of your excuses and stop feeling sorry for yourself. It's time to get rid of your victim mentality.

Nobody—not even God—ever promised that life would be fair. Quit comparing your life to somebody else's, and quit dwelling on what could have been, should have been, or might have been. Quit asking questions such as, "Why this?" or "Why that?" or "Why me?"

Take what God has given you and make the most of it.

Instead, take what God has given you and make the most of it. You may have suffered much, endured great hardships, or been through a lot of negative things. You may have deep scars from emotional wounds, but don't let your past determine your future. You can't do anything about what's happened to you, but you can choose how you will face what's in front of you. Don't hold on to feelings of bitterness and resentment and let them poison your future. Let go of those hurts and pains. Forgive the people who did you wrong. Forgive yourself for the mistakes you have made.

You may even need to forgive God. Perhaps you've been blaming Him for taking one of your loved ones. Maybe you are angry at God because He didn't answer your prayers, or some situation didn't work out the way you had hoped. Regardless, you will never be truly happy as long as you harbor bitterness in your heart. You will wallow in self-pity, always feeling sorry for yourself, thinking that life hasn't dealt you a fair hand. You must let go of those negative attitudes and the accompanying anger. Change the channel and start focusing on the goodness of God.

CHANGE THE CHANNEL

We all know how to use the remote control to change the channels on the TV. If we see something we don't like, no big deal—we just flip channels. We need to learn how to mentally change channels when negative images of the past pop up in our minds unexpectedly. Unfortunately, when some people see those negative experiences on their minds' "screens," instead of quickly changing channels, they pull up a chair and get some popcorn, as though they're going to watch a good movie. They willingly allow themselves to relive all those hurts and pains. Then they wonder why they are depressed, upset, or discouraged.

Learn to change the channel. Don't let your mind or your emotions drag you down into despair. Instead, dwell on the good things God has done in your life.

You probably know some people who thrive on self-pity. They relish the attention that it brings them. They've lived that way for so long, self-pity has become part of their identity. He or she is known as the person that went through some great struggle, some horrible experience, the person who had something really awful happen to him or her. Certainly, when someone undergoes a traumatic experience, that person should be treated with compassion and care for as long as it takes to regain health and strength and get back on his feet. But the truth is, some people don't really want to get well. They like the attention too much.

Fifteen years ago, Phil and Judy's only son was killed in a freak accident at work. It was one of those senseless, unexplainable accidents for which there are no words of comfort. Family and friends hovered over the couple for several months, empathizing with them in their grief and attempting to nurture them back to a degree of normalcy.

Regardless of their comforters' sensitive efforts, Phil and Judy refused to let go of their grief. Whenever their son's name was mentioned, their eyes welled with tears and their woeful mourning began all over again. Slowly but surely, the comforters quit coming. People stopped calling. Family members avoided visiting.

Anytime an encourager bravely attempted to lift the couple's spirits, their efforts were met with sullen faces and a barrage of insults.

"You just don't know what it is like to lose your only son," Phil objected.

"No, but God does," somebody would tell them.

But Phil and Judy remained untouched. In their minds, nobody had ever felt pain the way they had. No consolation seemed adequate to their needs. They were forever to be known as the couple who tragically lost their son. Consequently, fifteen years after the fact, Phil and

Judy continue to languish in self-pity and self-induced isolation. Why? Because they don't want to get well.

If you've had something painful happen to you, don't let that experience be the focal point of your life. Stop talking about it; stop bringing it up to your friends. You must get beyond it. Unless you let go of the old, God will not bring the new. It is natural to feel sorrow and to grieve, but you shouldn't still be grieving five or ten years later. If you really want to be whole, if you really want to get well, you need to move on with your life.

Too often we keep reliving the painful memories of the past, negating God's desire to bring healing. Just as we are about to heal, we start talking about our painful experience again. We bring it up to our friends. We start reliving it, seeing it in our imagination. All of a sudden, we can feel those same emotions all over again, as though we were tearing open the old wound. It will never properly heal until we learn to leave it alone. Remember, your emotions follow your thoughts. When you dwell on painful experiences in your past, your emotions go right back there with you, and you feel the pain in the present. You can relive something in your mind and feel it today just as vividly as when it happened twenty years ago.

One day a few years after my father had passed away in 1999, I was over at my parents' home, and I was all alone in the house. I hadn't been there by myself in quite some time, and as I was walking through the den, for no apparent reason I started thinking about the night that my dad died. Daddy had a heart attack right there in that same room. In my imagination, I could see it all happening. I could see Daddy on the floor. I could see the paramedics working on him. I could see the look on my dad's face and I began to feel those same emotions of despair, sadness, and discouragement that I had known the night Daddy died.

For about fifteen or twenty seconds I stood there paralyzed, overwhelmed by my emotions. Finally, I caught myself, and thought, *What am I doing? Where is my mind going? Where are these emotions taking me?*

I had to make a decision that I was not going to allow myself to relive that night. I knew that it wasn't going to do me any good. It would only get me upset and discouraged. Rather than dwelling on the hurt from the past, I had to purposely start recalling all the good times that my dad and I had known in that den. I smiled as I remembered how we used to watch the TV show *Wheel of Fortune* together in that room. Daddy could always guess the puzzle long before the contestants. In my mind, I could see Daddy playing with our children in that den. He loved having children around, and they loved being with him.

I recalled how sometimes I'd walk in the den and Daddy would be in his favorite chair. He'd look up and say, "Joel, tell me all you know. It'll just take a second." Daddy thought he was real funny. And he was. He had a great sense of humor.

As I stood in that den, I had to willfully refuse to allow my mind to go back to painful memories of Daddy's death, and instead recall joyful moments from Daddy's life. But notice, it didn't happen naturally; it was a decision I had to make.

You must do something similar regarding the painful experiences from your past. Refuse to go back there emotionally; refuse to dredge up negative emotional memories. They will do you no good; in fact, strongly felt negative emotions can hold the potential to severely stifle your progress.

Think of it like this: Every person has two main files in his or her memory system. The first is a file filled with all the good things that have happened to us. It's full of our victories and accomplishments, all of the things that have brought us joy and happiness through the years.

The second file is just the opposite. It's filled with the hurts and pains of the past, all of the negative things that have happened to us. It's full of our defeats and failures, things that brought us sadness and sorrow. Throughout life, we can choose which file we will access. Some people repeatedly return to file number two and relive the painful things that have happened to them. They're always thinking about the times somebody did them wrong, the times they were hurt or suffered awful pain. They practically wear out file number two. They're so preoccupied with the negative things, they never get around to exploring file number one. They hardly think about the good things that have happened to them.

If you want to be free, if you want to overcome self-pity, throw away the key to file number two. Don't go back there anymore. Keep your mind focused on the good things God has done in your life.

DON'T GO THERE

An old joke says, "If you break your arm in three places, don't go to those places anymore." There may be more truth in that corny line than we realize. When the pains of the past beckon your attention, don't go back there. Instead, remind yourself, *No thanks, I'm going to think on things that are of good report, things that are going to build me up, not tear me down, things that encourage me and fill me with peace and happiness, not things that attempt to steal my hope and drain my spirit.*

Get Up and Get Moving

In the Bible, we read about a man in Jerusalem who had been crippled for thirty-eight years. He spent every day of his life lying on a mat by the pool of Bethesda, hoping for a miracle. This man had a deep-seated, lingering disorder.

I think many people today have lingering disorders. Their maladies may not be physical; they may be emotional, but they are deep-seated, lingering disorders nonetheless. They could stem from being unwilling to forgive, holding on to past resentments, blaming the past for their behavior, or other emotional wounds. These lingering disorders can affect your personality, your relationships, and your self-image. Just as the man lying by the pool, some people sit back year after year, waiting for a miracle to happen, waiting for some big event to come along to make everything better.

One day Jesus saw the man lying there in need. It was obvious that he was crippled, but Jesus asked the man what seemed a strange question: "Do you want to be made well?"[1]

"Do you want to be made well?"

I believe God is asking a similar question of us today: "Do you want to be well or do you want to continue lying around feeling sorry for yourself?"

Jesus asked a simple, straightforward question, but the man's response was interesting. He began listing all of his excuses. "I'm all alone. I don't have anyone to help me. Other people have let me down. Other people always seem to get ahead of me. I don't have a chance in life."

Is it any wonder that he remained in that condition for thirty-eight years?

I love the way Jesus answered him. He didn't even respond to his sad story. He didn't say, "Yes, friend, I agree with you. You've had a tough time. Let Me commiserate with you."

No, Jesus looked at him and said, in effect, "If you are serious about getting well, if you are serious about getting your life in order, if you really want to get out of this mess, here's what you must do: Get up off the ground, take up your bed, and be on your way." When the man did what Jesus told him to do, he was miraculously healed!

That's a message for us today. If you're serious about being well, if you really want to be made physically and emotionally whole, you must get up and get moving with your life. No more lying around feeling sorry for yourself. You must stop going back to file number two all the time. Stop making excuses; stop blaming people or circumstances that disappointed you. Instead, start forgiving the people that hurt you.

Today can be a turning point in your life, a time of new beginnings. Don't waste another minute trying to figure out why certain evil things have happened to you or your loved ones. Refuse to live with a victim mentality any longer.

You might be saying, "I just don't understand why this is happening to me. I don't understand why I got sick. Why did my loved one die? Why did my marriage break apart? Why was I raised in such an abusive environment?"

You may never know the answer. But don't use that as an excuse to wallow in self-pity. Leave it alone, get up, and move on with your life. Many of the "why" questions of life will remain a conundrum, but trust in God, and accept the fact that there will be some unanswered questions. Keep in mind, just because you don't know the answer doesn't mean that one does not exist. You simply haven't discovered it yet.

Usually, we can deal with a situation if we can locate a file in our thinking in which to put it. "He got into trouble because he was running with the wrong crowd . . ."

But what happens when things don't make sense? When a good person is stricken with a serious illness? Or a child is born with a birth injury? Or a husband or wife walks out of a marriage? What happens when life doesn't fit neatly into our categories?

Each of us should have what I call an "I Don't Understand It" file. When something comes up for which you have no reasonable answer, instead of dwelling on it and trying to figure it out, simply place it in your I Don't Understand It file.

In the meantime, you must muster enough faith to say, "God, I don't understand it, but I trust You. And I'm not going to spend all my time trying to figure out why certain things have happened. I'm going to trust You to make something good out of it. You're a good God, and I know You have my best interests at heart. You promised that all things will work together for my good."

That is faith, and that is the attitude God honors.

My mother had polio when she was growing up. She had to wear a heavy brace on her leg for many years, and even today, one leg remains shorter than the other. Mother could have easily said, "God, this isn't fair. Why did this happen to me?"

But instead, she took up her bed and got moving with her life. In 1981 when she was diagnosed with terminal cancer, she didn't collapse and say, "Poor me. I should have known it. I had polio; now I've got cancer. I always get the short end of the stick."

Mother didn't do that. She dug in her heels and fought the good fight of faith. She didn't go around complaining. She went around speaking words of faith and victory. She refused to see herself as the victim. She saw herself as the victor. And God brought her out of that difficulty. Your adversities can make you bitter or they can make you better. They can drag you down and make you a sour person, or they can inspire you to reach for new heights.

My dad could have said, "God, why did You let me be born into this impoverished family? We don't have a chance."

But he didn't use that as an excuse to stay in defeat or to feel sorry for himself. No, he got up and got moving with his life. When he began preaching at the age of seventeen he didn't have a church, so he preached on the streets, in the nursing homes, in prisons and jails, anywhere he could. He didn't have a car, so he walked or hitchhiked wherever he went. He could have easily withdrawn and said, "God, we've been through too much in life already. Please don't ask me to do any more. We're just poor, pitiful people."

But no, Daddy picked up his bed and got going, and you need to do the same thing. Your past does not have to determine your future. We can all sit back and make excuses to stay in mediocrity. That's easy. We can all sit back and make excuses to have a bad attitude, to have a poor self-image. Anyone can do that. But if we want to live in victory, we need to shake off self-pity and move on with our lives.

That's just what my sister Lisa had to do. She went through a very painful breakup in her marriage. It wasn't fair; she was mistreated and wronged. Yet for seven years, Lisa prayed and believed that her marriage could be restored. She did everything she knew how to do. But for some reason, it just didn't work out.

Lisa could easily have become bitter. She could have become depressed and said, "God, this is not fair. Why did this happen to me?"

But Lisa made a decision that she just wasn't going to sit around by the pool for thirty-eight years feeling sorry for herself. She wasn't going to stay in that black hole of depression. She decided it was time to get moving in her life. She didn't get bitter; she got better. She rose up out of those ashes. She said, "God, I don't understand it, but I'm going to trust You anyway. You know my heart. You know I've done everything I can do. I'm releasing it into Your hands."

Not long after she made that decision, God brought someone else into her life, and she and my brother-in-law, Kevin, have been happily married for many years.

Please understand, I'm not telling you to give up on your marriage. You must do what God is leading you to do. The point I want you to see is that sometimes we go through things we just don't understand. Through it all, we must learn to keep a good attitude and trust that God is still in control of our lives, even when events are not going the way we had planned or hoped.

In the Bible we find an interesting account of when King David's baby was dreadfully sick, near death.[2] David was extremely distraught; he prayed night and day, believing that God could heal his child. He wouldn't eat or drink; he didn't shave or shower. He didn't attend to any business. He wouldn't do anything but pray, crying out to God.

Despite David's passionate prayers, on the seventh day the child died. David's servants worried how they were going to tell the king that his baby was dead. They thought he would be so devastated, so distraught that he couldn't handle it. But when David finally figured out what had happened, he surprised them all. He got up off the floor. He washed his face and put on some fresh clothes. Then he asked his servants to bring him some food, and he sat down and ate a meal.

His servants were flabbergasted. They said, "David, when your child was alive, you fasted and prayed. But now that he's gone, you act as though nothing's wrong."

David answered, "Yes, I fasted and prayed when my son was sick, thinking that God might heal him. But now that he is gone, I cannot bring him back. He will not return to me, but I will go to be with him." Notice David's attitude. He didn't get bitter. He didn't question God. He could have snarled, "God, I thought You loved me. Why didn't You answer my prayers?"

David didn't do that. He dared to trust God in the midst of his disappointment. He washed his face and moved on with his life.

Friend, you and I have to learn to do the same thing. People may have mistreated you. Somebody may have walked out on you, or maybe you prayed fervently, yet God didn't answer your prayer the way you had anticipated. That's over and done. You cannot change the past; there's nothing you can do about it now. But you must make a decision. Are you going to sit around by the pool for thirty-eight years, or are you going to get up and get moving with your life? Are you going to keep going back to file number two, reliving all those painful memories, or are you going to stay in an attitude of faith? God is asking, "Do you really want to get well?"

If you do, you must walk out of any emotional bondage in which you have been living. Nobody can do it for you. You must rise up out of those ashes. You must forgive the people who have hurt you. You have to release all those hurts and pains. Leave the past behind. When you go through situations you don't understand, don't become bitter. Don't question God. Learn to do as David did: Just wash your face, keep a good attitude, and move on. Get ready for the new things God has in store for you.

If you will stay in an attitude of faith and victory, God has promised that He will turn those emotional wounds around. He'll use them to your advantage, and you will come out better than you would have had they not happened to you.

CHAPTER 18

Don't Let Bitterness Take Root

We all have unfair and unjust things happen to us; that's a part of life. When we are hurt, we can choose to hold on to that pain and become bitter, or we can choose to let it go and trust God to make it up to us.

I heard somewhere that 70 percent of people today are angry about something. Imagine that! Seven out of every ten people you encounter today will be angry. And that's not counting the people who pass you on the freeway!

People who harbor anger often don't realize it, but they are poisoning their own lives. When we don't forgive, we're not hurting the other person. We're not hurting the company that did us wrong. We're not hurting God. We're only hurting ourselves.

If you want to live your best life now, you must be quick to forgive. Learn to let go of the hurts and pains of the past. Don't let bitterness take root in your life. Maybe something happened to you when you were younger, somebody mistreated you, somebody took advantage of you. Perhaps somebody cheated you out of a promotion or lied about you. Maybe a good friend betrayed you, and you have a good reason to be angry and bitter.

For your emotional and spiritual health, you must let that go. It doesn't do any good to go around hating somebody. Nor does it make any sense to stay angry for what somebody's already done to you. You can't do anything about the past, but you can do something about the

future. You might as well forgive and start trusting God to make it up
to you.

The Scripture says, "Make sure that no root of bitterness shoots
forth and causes trouble and many become contaminated by it."[1] Notice, bitterness is described as a root. Think about that. You can't see
a root; it's deep down under the ground. But you can be sure of this: A
bitter root will produce bitter fruit. If we have bitterness on the inside,
it's going to affect every area of our lives.

Many people attempt to bury the hurt and pain deep in their hearts
or in their subconscious minds. They harbor unforgiveness and resentment, and then they wonder why they can't really live in victory, why
they can't get along with other people, why they can't be happy. They
don't realize it, but it's because their own hearts are poisoned. The
Bible says, "Out of the heart flow the issues of life."[2] In other words,
if we have bitterness on the inside, it's going to end up contaminating
everything that comes out of us. It will contaminate our personalities
and our attitudes, as well as how we treat other people.

A bitter root will produce bitter fruit.

A lot of people are trying to improve their lives by dealing with the
external fruit. They are attempting to rectify their bad habits, bad attitudes, bad tempers, or negative and sour personalities. They're dealing with the fruit of their lives, trying to change those things, and that
is noble. But the truth is, unless they get to the root, they will never be
able to change the fruit. Because as long as that bitter root is growing
on the inside, that problem will persist and keep popping up time and
again. You may be able to control your behavior for a while or keep a
good attitude for a short period of time, but have you ever wondered
why you can't really get free? Why you can't overcome that destructive
habit?

You have to go deeper. You must discover why you are so angry, why
you can't get along with other people, why you are always so negative.
If you'll look deeply and get to the root, then you'll be able to deal
with the problem, overcome it, and truly begin to change.

Poisons of the Past

I remember a young woman who came to my dad for spiritual help. She had gotten married and for several years could not have a normal relationship with her husband. For some reason, she just couldn't fully give herself to this man. She loved him, but she couldn't stand for him to be close to her and to be intimate with her. As you can imagine, this problem was destroying their relationship.

She tried to change, but she couldn't do it. She said, "God, what is wrong with me? Why do I act this way? Why can't I be a normal wife?"

One day she had a dream, and it reminded her of something that had happened when she was a young girl. In this dream, she saw herself out at the lake swimming, and several young boys came over and sexually assaulted her. She was so angry and so filled with hatred toward those boys, she began to scream, "I hate you! I hate you! I'll never let another man touch me as long as I live."

When she awakened, she realized that she still had all that anger and hatred in her heart toward those boys. It was buried deep down inside, and it was affecting her relationship with her husband many years later. She knew it wasn't going to be easy, but she recognized she had to deal with that unforgiveness, or she would never have a healthy relationship. She decided to release all that hurt and pain. She said, "God, You know it wasn't right. You know what they did to me. But I'm not going to hold on to it any longer; I'm not going to allow the pain from the past to poison my present and my future. God, I forgive those boys right now."

Interestingly, from that moment on, she was able to enjoy a healthy relationship with her husband. She couldn't change by dealing with the fruit, she had to get down to the root. And once the bitter root was gone, she was able to break free from her past.

Certainly, you do not need to go back and relive every negative experience, recalling all the painful memories of the past. Not at all. But you should examine your heart to make sure you haven't buried anger and unforgiveness on the inside. If you have areas in your life where you are constantly struggling, trying to change but finding yourself unable to do so, you need to ask God to show you what's keeping you from being free. Ask God to show you if you have any bitter roots that need to be dug up and extracted. If God brings something to light, be quick to deal with it. Be willing to change. Don't let the poisons of the past continue to contaminate your life.

Years ago there was a terrible outbreak of disease in a tiny village in a remote part of Africa. Both children and adults were getting sick and overcome with nausea. Several weeks passed, and the sickness became widespread, and people started dying. Word of the disease reached the main city in that area, and experts were dispatched to try to figure out what was causing the problem. They soon discovered that the water was contaminated. The village got its water supply from a mountain stream that was fed from a spring, so the experts decided to trek upstream and hopefully find the source of the pollution. They traveled for days and finally came to the mouth of the stream. But on the surface, they found nothing wrong. Puzzled, they decided to send some divers down to search as closely to the spring's opening as possible.

What the divers discovered shocked the experts. A large mother pig and her baby piglets were wedged right at the opening of the spring. Evidently they had fallen in, drowned, and somehow gotten stuck there. Now all that crystal clear, pure mountain springwater was being contaminated as it flowed past the decomposing remains of those dead pigs. In no time after the divers were able to extricate the dead pigs, the water began to flow clean and pure once again.

In our lives, something similar takes place. We've all had negative things happen to us. Maybe last week, last month, or ten years ago somebody hurt us. And too often, instead of letting it go and giving it to God, we've held on to it. We haven't forgiven, and just as those pigs soured that crystal-clear water, our own lives have become contaminated. The root of bitterness has taken hold.

Worse yet, after a while, we accept it. We make room in our hearts for that bitterness; we learn to live with it. "Well, I'm just an angry person. That's just my personality. I'm always like this. I'm always bitter. This is who I am."

No, with all due respect, that's not who you are. You need to get rid of the poison that is polluting your life. You were made to be a crystal-clear stream. God created you in His image. He wants you to be happy, healthy, and whole. God wants you to enjoy life to the full, not to live with bitterness and resentment, polluted and putrefied yourself and contaminating everyone else with whom you have influence.

Imagine yourself as a crystal-clear stream. It doesn't matter how polluted the stream may be right now, or how muddy or murky the waters may look in your life today. If you'll begin to forgive the people who have offended you, and release all those hurts and pains, that bitterness will leave and you'll begin to see that crystal-clear water once again. You'll begin to experience the joy, peace, and freedom God intended you to have.

Maybe that's why David said, "Search my heart, oh God, and point out anything in me that makes You sad."[3] We need to search our hearts and make sure we haven't let any roots of bitterness take hold.

It may not be a big thing that is polluting your stream. Maybe your spouse is not spending as much time with you as you'd like, and you can feel yourself starting to get resentful. You're short with your mate; sarcastic, cryptic, or unfriendly. You're intentionally becoming harder to get along with.

Watch out! That root of bitterness is contaminating your life. Keep your stream pure. Don't let your heart get polluted. The Bible talks about being quick to forgive, and the longer we wait, the harder it's going to be. The longer we hold on to resentment, the deeper that root of bitterness grows.

Sometimes, instead of forgiving quickly, letting go of the hurts and pains of the past, we quietly bury them deep down inside our hearts and minds. We don't want to talk about the issue. We don't want to think about it. We want to ignore it and hope that it will go away.

It won't. Just like those pigs trapped beneath the water, one day that contamination will show up in your life, and it will be a mess. It will cause you even more pain and sorrow, and if you refuse to deal with it, that bitterness could kill you.

A few decades ago, several American companies authorized by the U.S. government attempted to bury toxic waste products underground. They filled large metal containers with chemical waste and other life-threatening products, sealed the drums tightly, and buried them deep down below the topsoil. They thought that was the end of it. Within a short time, however, many of the containers began to leak and the toxic waste started seeping to the surface, causing all sorts of problems. In some locations, it killed off the vegetation and ruined the water supply. People had to move out of their homes. In one section near Niagara Falls, known as the Love Canal, an inordinate number of people began dying of cancer and other debilitating diseases. Many communities are still suffering the effects of toxic-waste burials to this day.

What went wrong? They tried to bury something that was too toxic. It couldn't be contained. They thought they could bury it, and be rid of it once and for all. But they didn't realize that the materials they were attempting to bury were so powerful. They were too toxic for the containers to hold. They never dreamed that one day these contaminants would resurface, and they would have to eliminate them all over again. But this time, the toxic materials would be dispersed, and much more difficult to deal with. Had they disposed of them properly in the first place, they wouldn't have had this terrible problem.

It's the same with us. When somebody hurts us, somebody does us wrong, instead of letting it go and trusting God to make it up to us, we bury it deep down on the inside. We attempt to cram unforgiveness, resentment, anger, and other destructive responses into our "leak-proof" containers. We seal those lids tightly. Then we put them aside and say, "Good. I'm not going to have to deal with that. I'm rid of it once and for all."

But unfortunately, just as that toxic waste tends to resurface, one day the things you have tamped into your subconscious or buried deeply in the recesses of your heart will rise to the surface and begin to contaminate your life. We can't live with poison inside us and not expect it to eventually do us harm.

Face it. You are not strong enough to contain the toxicity in your life. You need help from someone bigger and stronger than yourself. That's why you need to give that bitterness, resentment, and other contaminants to God. Forgiveness is the key to being free from toxic bitterness. Forgive the people who hurt you. Forgive the boss who did you wrong. Forgive the friend who betrayed you. Forgive the parent who mistreated you when you were younger. Get rid of all that poison. Don't let the root of bitterness grow deeper and continue to contaminate your life.

What does this toxic waste look like in our lives? For some people, it seeps out as anger. In other people it smells like depression. For others, it reeks of low self-esteem. It can show up in many different ways, sometimes doing damage before we even realize it has reappeared.

The famous boxer James "Lights Out" Toney was known for his aggressiveness in the ring. He fought like a man possessed. He wielded a powerful punch, and for many years, he was the middleweight champion of the world. One day after one of his victories, a reporter asked him, "James, what makes you so good? Why do you fight with such tremendous aggression and passion in the ring?"

The reporter expected the standard answer. Something like, "Well, you know, I'm just competitive. That's who I am. I love to box."

But that's not what Toney said. "Do you really want to know why I fight with such anger and aggression?" asked the boxer. "It's because my dad abandoned me when I was a child. He left me and my brothers and sisters alone, fatherless, to be raised by my mother all by herself. And now when I step into the ring I picture my dad's face on my opponent's. And I have so much hatred, so much anger toward him, I just explode."

Toney was driven by his anger. He had let that root of bitterness get a deep hold on him, and it was poisoning and contaminating his life. Yes, he was winning the applause of the crowd, the acclaim of the sports world, but he was miserable on the inside. You can have success on the outside, but if you're bitter on the inside, it's going to spoil and taint every victory. You must deal with the inside first. You must get to the root of the problem; then you can really be happy. Then you can experience true, untainted, unalloyed victory in your life.

You may be thinking, *Joel, I can't do it. It's too hard. I just can't forgive. They hurt me too badly.*

Wait a minute! You are not forgiving for *their* sake, you are forgiving for your sake. You are forgiving so that poison doesn't continue to contaminate your life. If somebody has done you a great wrong, don't allow them to continue to hurt you by hanging on to it. You're not hurting them at all. You're only hurting yourself.

I remember one time when I was a little boy, my dad and I were going to lunch with a man. He was driving, and we noticed he wasn't taking the shortest route to the restaurant. My dad politely and innocently said, "You know, there's a quicker way."

The man driving the car responded, "Oh, no. We don't go that way. Years ago somebody that lives on that street did our family wrong, and now we don't drive by their house anymore."

I didn't say anything, but even as a ten-year-old boy, I wanted to ask him, "Do you really think you're hurting that man? Do you really think that he's standing there by the window, looking outside, getting depressed because you're not coming by?"

Who are we kidding? When we hold on to poison from the past, we're only hurting ourselves. We're not hurting anybody else. We need to forgive so we can be free. Forgive so you can be made whole.

Forgive to Be Free

I recently watched a television program about Rudy Tomjanovich, the former coach of the Houston Rockets basketball team. The program recounted an event in 1973, when as a robust twenty-five-year-old, Rudy was playing for the Rockets. In the middle of a close game, a fight broke out at center court. Rudy rushed over there, running at full speed, to try to break it up. Just as he got there, a player whipped around and without even looking, swung as hard as he could. Unfortunately, the punch landed right in Rudy's face. It was called the punch heard around the world. It fractured Rudy's skull, broke his nose and cheekbones, and nearly killed him. Although Rudy was sidelined for months following the devastating blow, he eventually recovered.

One day after Rudy had recuperated, a reporter asked him, "Rudy, have you ever forgiven the player that did that to you?" Without hesitation, Rudy said immediately, "Absolutely. I've totally forgiven him."

The reporter shook his head as though he was perplexed. "Come on, Rudy, that guy nearly killed you. He caused you all that pain. He stole part of your career. Do you mean to tell me that you don't have any anger, any hatred or bitterness toward him?"

Rudy smiled. "I don't have any at all."

That reporter stared at him in disbelief. He finally asked, "Rudy, tell me, how'd you do it? How could you possibly forgive that man who hurt you so badly?"

Rudy replied, "I knew if I wanted to move on with my life, I had to let it go. I didn't do it for him. I did it for me. I did it so I could be free."

That's good advice. You need to forgive so you can be free. Forgive so you can be happy. Forgive so you can get out of that bondage. We have to remember, when we forgive we're not doing it just for the other person, we're doing it for our own good. When we hold on to unforgiveness and we live with grudges in our hearts, all we're doing is building walls of separation. We think we're protecting ourselves, but we're not. We are simply shutting other people out of our lives. We become isolated, alone, warped and imprisoned by our own bitterness. Those walls aren't merely keeping people out; those walls are keeping you penned in.

Do you realize that those walls will also prevent God's blessings from pouring into your life? Those walls can stop up the flow of God's favor. The walls of unforgiveness will keep your prayers from being answered. They'll keep your dreams from coming to pass. You must tear down the walls. You must forgive the people who hurt you so you can get out of prison. You'll never be free until you do. Let go of those wrongs they've done to you. Get that bitterness out of your life. That's the only way you're going to truly be free. You will be amazed at what can happen in your life when you release all that poison.

When I was growing up, we had a former Methodist minister in our church. His hands were so crippled with arthritis, he could hardly use them. They looked as though they had shriveled up and were deformed. He couldn't open a car door. He couldn't shake hands or anything like that. For as long as I'd known him, his hands had been that way. But one day, he went to my dad and showed him his hands—they were perfectly normal! He could move them like any of us, almost as though he had received a new set of hands.

My dad was surprised, but so happy for him. He said, "Man, what in the world happened to you?"

"Well, it's an interesting story," the former minister said. "Several months ago, you were talking about unforgiveness. You were speaking on how it keeps God's power from operating in our lives, and how it keeps our prayers from being answered. As I listened, I began to ask God to show me if I had any areas of unforgiveness and resentment in my life. And God began to deal with me. He brought to light several situations that had happened to me down through the years in which people had done me great wrong. I didn't even know it, but I still had anger and resentment in my heart toward those people. That's the odd part; I didn't realize I was carrying it around. But as soon as I saw it, I made a decision to forgive them and totally let it go. And then the most amazing thing began to happen. One by one, my fingers started straightening out. One week went by and this finger would get healed. The next week this finger got healed. The next week this finger. As I continued to search my heart and eliminate all that bitterness and resentment, God brought complete healing back to me, and now look at my hands. I'm perfectly normal!"

You, too, will be amazed at the great things that will start happening in your life when you rid yourself of bitterness and resentment. Who knows? Perhaps, like that Methodist minister, you may experience genuine physical and emotional healing as you search your heart and are willing to forgive. You may see God's favor in a fresh, new way. You may see your prayers answered more quickly as you let go of the past and get rid of all that poison you now harbor.

When my mother discovered that she was sick with cancer in 1981, one of the first things she did was to make sure she didn't have any unforgiveness in her heart. She sat down and wrote letters to her friends and family, asking us to forgive her if she had ever done any wrong toward us. She wanted to make sure that her heart was pure. She wanted to make sure that nothing she was doing or had done would interfere with God's healing power flowing into her.

You may be at a crossroads in your life. You may have issues to deal with; people you need to forgive. You can go one of two ways. You can ignore what you now know to be true and keep burying that bitterness in your life, pushing it deeper and allowing it to poison and contaminate you and those around you. Or, you can make a much better choice by getting it out in the open and asking God to help you to totally forgive and let it all go.

"But Joel," I hear you saying. "You don't know what they did to me."

No, I don't. But you must turn the issue over to God. He will make it up to you. God will make the wrongs right. He'll bring justice into your life. Don't be hardheaded and stubborn and miss out on God's best. Be willing to change.

I heard an old story about the captain of a ship that was sailing on a dark, pitch-black night. The captain suddenly noticed a bright light directly in front of him, and he knew that his ship was on a collision course with the light. He rushed to the radio and sent an urgent message, demanding that the vessel change its course ten degrees east.

A few seconds later, he received a message in return. The message said, "Cannot do it. Change your course ten degrees west."

The captain got angry. He sent another cryptic message, "I'm a navy captain. I demand you change your course."

He received a message back a few seconds later. It said, "I'm a seaman second class. Cannot do it. Change your course."

The captain was now furious. He sent one final message. It said, "I'm a battleship, and I'm not changing my course!"

He got a curt message in return. It said, "I'm a lighthouse. It's your choice, sir."

Many times, we are like that navy captain; we can be hardheaded and stubborn. We can think of all the reasons why we're not going to change: *They hurt me too badly. They did too much wrong to me. I'm not going to forgive.*

This book is your personal lighthouse, beaming truth into your life, saying you must change your course. Forgiveness is a choice, but it is not an option. Jesus put it this way: "If you don't forgive other people, then your Father in heaven is not going to forgive you."[4] When you hold on to unforgiveness, you are headed for trouble. You are on a destructive path. And God is saying to change your course.

Forgiveness is a choice, but it is not an option.

If you want to be happy, if you want to be free, get that junk out of your life. Quit holding on to it; let it go. Don't let the root of bitterness continue to poison your life. Search your heart. When God brings issues to light, be quick to deal with them. Keep your stream pure. Friend, if you'll do your part and keep the poison out of your life, you'll see God's favor and blessings in a new way.

Do you want God to bring justice in your life? How would you like for God to restore everything that has been stolen from you? Come on; I'll show you how that can happen.

CHAPTER 19

*Let God Bring Justice
into Your Life*

God has promised if we will put our trust in Him, He will pay us back for all the unfair things that have happened to us.[1] Maybe you were cheated in a business deal and you lost a lot of money. Maybe somebody lied about you, and that misinformation kept you from getting a promotion. Or maybe a good friend betrayed you.

Certainly, these kinds of losses leave indelible scars, causing you to want to hold on to your grief. It would be logical for you to seek revenge. Many people would even encourage you to do so. The slogan "Don't get mad, get even!" is a commonly accepted principle in America today.

But that is not God's plan for you. If you want to live your best life now, you must learn to trust God to bring about the justice in your life. The Bible says, "God is a just God and He will settle and solve the cases of His people."[2] That means you don't have to go around trying to pay everybody back for the wrong things they've done to you. You don't have to go around trying to get even with people. God is your vindicator. You need to start letting God fight your battles for you. Let God settle your cases. God has promised if you'll turn matters over to Him and let Him handle them His way, He'll make your wrongs right. He'll bring justice into your life.

Trust God to bring about the justice in your life.

Somebody in your life may not be treating you right. They may be saying things about you that aren't true, spreading vicious rumors, telling lies, trying to ruin your reputation. If you're like most people, you are probably tempted to get in there and set the record straight. And you're probably tempted to let them have it!

It takes faith to believe that God wants to vindicate you, but He really does. Don't make the mistake of sinking down to your offenders' level, getting into arguments and fighting. That will just make matters worse. Leave it up to God. Take the high road, respond in love, and watch what God will do. If you will do it God's way, He'll not only fight your battles for you, but in the end, you'll come out better off than you were before.

God Keeps Good Records

Sometimes God allows us to go through certain things to test us. If you have somebody in your life right now who is not treating you right, that situation may very well be a test of your faith. God is interested in seeing how you are going to respond. Will you become negative, bitter, or angry? Are you going to develop a vindictive attitude, always trying to pay people back? Or, are you going to turn it over to God, trusting Him to make the wrongs right? Are you going to pass that test so God can promote you?

Maybe your boss isn't treating you right. You're doing all the work, but it seems that you're not getting any of the credit. Everybody else gets promoted in the company except you. You may be tempted to mope around with a sour attitude, with a poor-old-me mentality.

Instead, you need to keep a good attitude and start trusting God to make it up to you. You must understand, you are not working merely for that person. You are not employed merely by that company. You are working for God! And God sees every wrong that's being done to you. God is keeping good records. He's closely watching your situation, and He said that He's going to pay you back. And friend, when God pays back, He always pays back in abundance.

When God wants you to be promoted, it doesn't matter whether your boss likes you or not; your future is not dependent on what your boss does or doesn't do. God is in control. The Bible says that promotion doesn't come from the north, south, east, or west. In other words, promotion doesn't come from your boss, your supervisor, or your company. No, true promotion comes from Almighty God. And when

God says it is time for you to advance up the ladder, all the forces of darkness cannot hold you down. You will be promoted.

Moreover, God will not allow somebody to continually mistreat you. If you will do your part, keep a good attitude, and turn your circumstances over to Him, sooner or later God will bring justice into your life. Sometimes when we don't see anything happening month after month, maybe even year after year, it's tempting to become manipulative, to attempt to make things happen on our own. When we do that, we risk interfering with God's plans and purposes, creating another mess for Him to clean up, and possibly even keeping God from doing what He really wants to do in that situation.

"But Joel, everybody is getting so far ahead of me," Darla lamented. "When is it going to be my turn? All my friends are getting married; everybody I graduated with is making big money and living comfortably; everybody is being promoted in my company *except me*."

You may have concerns similar to Darla's, but understand, God is a supernatural God. One touch of His favor can make up any lost ground, plus give you so much more. One touch of God's favor can bring the right person into your life or put you in charge of that entire organization.

One touch of God's favor can bring the right person into your life.

I met a man not long ago who worked as a mechanic at a large diesel-truck shop where they serviced 18-wheelers. He told me that for many years he was not treated properly at his place of employment. It was an extremely negative environment, and his coworkers often made fun of him because he wouldn't go out and party with them after work. Year after year, he put up with all sorts of injustice and ridicule. He was one of the best mechanics on staff, consistently one of their top producers, but for seven years, he never received a pay raise, he didn't get a bonus, he didn't get any sort of increase—because his supervisor didn't like him.

That mechanic could have grown bitter. He could have quit and found work elsewhere; he could have developed a chip on his shoulder and gotten mad at the world. But instead, he continued to do his best. He worked hard and kept his mouth shut, knowing that God was his vindicator. He wasn't working to please his supervisor; he was working to please God.

One day, out of the blue, the owner of the company called him. This owner wasn't involved in the day-to-day operations, so the mechanic had never before met him. But the owner told him that he was ready to retire, and he was looking for somebody to take over the business. "I'd like you to have it," the owner said to the mechanic.

"You know, sir, I'd love to have it," said the mechanic, "but I don't have enough money to buy your business."

"No, you don't understand," replied the owner. "You don't need the money. I have money. I'm looking for somebody to take over the business. I'm looking for someone I can trust to continue the work I have started. I want to *give* it to you."

Today, the mechanic owns that company free and clear!

During our conversation, I asked him, "What caused that owner to call you?"

He said, "Joel, to this day I don't know how he got my name. I don't know why he chose me. All I know is that almost overnight, I went from being the lowest man on the totem pole to the person in charge of the whole company!" He laughed and said, "You know, Joel, they don't make fun of me in the shop anymore . . ."

Friend, that is a good example of God bringing justice into that man's life. That's God paying him back for all those wrongs. God settled his case. God made his wrongs right. And God wants to do the same sort of thing for you.

You may say, "Joel, that sounds kind of far out to me."

Understand, we serve a God who wants to do more than you can ask or think. It doesn't matter how people are treating you. Keep doing the right thing; don't get offended; don't let them get you upset; don't try to pay them back, returning evil for evil.

Instead, keep extending forgiveness; keep responding in love. If you do that, then when it comes time for you to be promoted, God will make sure it happens. He'll make sure you get everything you deserve, and more!

Turn It Over to God

The key is, you must turn it over to God. Let Him do it His way. The Scripture says, "Never avenge yourselves, but leave the way open for [God's] wrath."[3] Notice, if you try to pay people back, you are closing the door for God to do it. You can either do it God's way, or you can do it your way. If you're going to let God handle it, you can't have the attitude of: *I'm going to show them what I'm made of.* That will prevent God from avenging you His way. If you want to keep that door open so God can bring true justice into your life, you have to totally turn it over to Him.

Somebody may be saying nasty things about you behind your back. Your attitude should be: *No big deal. God's got me covered. He's going to make it up to me.*

If somebody cheats you out of some money: *No big deal. God's promised me double. They don't owe me anything. God, I'll give it to them, because I know You can repay me with twice as much. I'm not going to worry about it; I release it right now.*

If somebody invites all your friends out to dinner but they exclude you, your attitude should be: *No big deal. God knows what I need. He will bring new friends into my life.*

What a liberating way to live! When you truly understand that you don't have to fix everything that happens to you, you don't have to get all upset and try to pay somebody back for what they did or didn't do. You don't have to get worried or try to manipulate the situation. When you know that God is fighting your battles, and He has promised to make your wrongs right, you can walk with a new confidence, with a spring in your step, a smile on your face, and a song in your heart. You are free!

When you have that kind of attitude, you are leaving the door wide open for God to pay you back. And remember, God always pays back abundantly.

A few years ago, Victoria and I had somebody in our lives who really did us wrong in a business deal. This person didn't keep his end of the bargain. He did some things that were questionable and ended up cheating us out of a lot of money.

Many times, Victoria and I were tempted to fight the battle in our own strength. We were tempted to want to pay him back and make his life miserable. After all, he made us suffer; why not make him suffer? It was difficult, but we had to force ourselves to do the right thing, which was to turn the matter over to God.

We said, "God, You see what's happening. You know we're being mistreated. You know that what this man is doing is wrong. But God, we're not going to try to get even. We're not going to try to avenge ourselves. We're going to leave that door open, counting on You to make it up to us."

This process continued for several years, and we didn't see any change. We had to keep reminding ourselves that God is a God of justice. *God is going to pay us back for doing the right thing. God is going to settle our case.*

One day, out of the clear blue, God supernaturally stepped in and turned that situation around. He not only moved that man out of our lives, but He paid us back in abundance for everything he had taken. Sadly, the man who tried to cheat us eventually lost his family, his business, his reputation—everything. And I certainly don't wish that on anybody, but that, too, is the justice of God. You cannot go around continually doing wrong, cheating people, and sowing bad seeds and not expect it to eventually catch up to you. We will reap exactly what we've sown.

Victoria and I were recently discussing how much God has paid us back. I don't say it arrogantly, but God has blessed us abundantly. He has prospered us through several real estate deals so we live in a lovely home and have all the material things we need. He's blessed us with wonderful children and a fantastic extended family. He's promoted us and given us positions of leadership. He's done more than we can ask or think. But had we not learned how to pass those kinds of tests, I really don't believe we'd be where we are today. If we had been stubborn and fought with the man who was doing us wrong, or if we had become bitter and angry, or held resentment in our hearts toward that man, God would not have promoted us.

If you will leave your situation up to God, in the end you'll come out much better off. You will be far ahead of where you would have been had you tried to solve matters in your own strength. God can truly bring justice into our lives.

Maybe you've been working through a situation and you've been doing the right thing for a long time. You've been taking the high road and forgiving somebody again and again. You keep overlooking their faults. You keep biting your tongue when they are rude to you. You have kept a good attitude even though they have mistreated you. Perhaps this has been going on month after month, maybe year after year, and now you're tempted to get discouraged. You're wondering, *Is God ever going to change this situation? Is God ever going to bring about justice? Does He even care about what I'm going through?*

Don't give up! Keep doing the right thing. God is building character in you, and you are passing that test. Remember, the greater the struggle, the greater the reward.

The Scripture says, "Don't get tired of doing what's right for in due season you shall reap if you don't faint."[4] Don't grow weary; God will bring justice into your life.

We must trust God to bring justice in His timing, not ours. Sometimes, it doesn't happen overnight. Sometimes you're going to have to love somebody who's unlovable for a long period of time. Sometimes you're going to have to do the right thing when the wrong thing is happening to you, and it may be a long time before you see any kind of change. It may require a strong will on your part, and a determination to trust despite the odds.

When David was just a young man, he was anointed by the prophet Samuel to be the next king of Israel. Not long after that, he defeated the giant Goliath, and he became an instant hero throughout the land. People loved him, and his popularity ratings soared off the charts. But King Saul, Israel's ruler at the time, became extremely jealous of David and started doing all sorts of unfair things to David.

Sometimes Saul would get sick, and David would play his harp for the king, soothing his mind and helping Saul to feel better. But one day as David was playing the harp for him, Saul suddenly picked up his spear and hurled it at David! The spear barely missed him. David ran out of the room, fearing for his life. When he realized that Saul was trying to kill him, he fled to the mountains to hide. He had to live on the run, going from cave to cave, month after month.

Think of it. David hadn't done anything wrong. He had treated Saul with respect and honor, yet Saul turned around and paid him back by attempting to kill him. Don't you know David could easily

Let God Bring Justice into Your Life   171

have been bitter? He could have easily said, "God, why is this guy try-ing to hurt me? I didn't do anything to him. God, I thought You chose me to be king. What's going on here?"

But David didn't do that. He kept a good attitude, refusing to hurt Saul, even when he had the opportunity. Although Saul wasn't treating him right, David still respected Saul's position of authority.

Somebody in your life who has authority over you—a boss, a su-pervisor, a parent, or somebody in a position of leadership—may be treating you unfairly. You know that what they are doing is wrong, and they probably know it, too. Consequently, you may be tempted to treat that person with disdain or disrespect. It's easy to rationalize or justify a wrong attitude toward that person. After all, *My boss is rude. He's ungodly. I don't have to treat him respectfully.* Or, *My parents argue and fight all the time. I'm not going to obey them.* Or, *My spouse doesn't go to church with me. How am I supposed to respect a person like that?*

The truth is, whether that person is behaving correctly or not, God expects us to honor his or her position of authority. Don't make ex-cuses and try to justify in your mind why you are free to speak or act disrespectfully toward that person. If you refuse to live under author-ity, God will never promote you to a position of greater authority.

It's easy to respect those in positions of authority as long as they are being kind to us or when we agree with that person. But the true test comes when you get a "Saul" in your life, when somebody treats you unfairly for no apparent reason.

Like David, many people today have been chosen by God to do something great. God wants to place them in positions of honor, po-sitions of leadership, but for some reason they don't ever pass the test. Instead of trusting God, they're always trying to manipulate circum-stances, to bring justice on their own. Instead of just letting offenses go, forgiving the offender and trusting God to make the wrongs right, they're always trying to pay back the "Sauls" in their lives. But there is a better way.

Back in the late 1950s, my dad had everything in the world going for him. He was a successful pastor of a thriving church in Houston, and the congregation had just built a big, beautiful new building. Daddy was on the state board for his denomination, and everyone regarded

John Osteen as a rising leader, on his way up in the hierarchy of the church. But in 1958, Daddy developed a desire to delve more deeply into the things of God. He wasn't satisfied to grow stagnant in his spiritual journey, and he didn't want the church to become complacent either.

As Daddy studied the Scriptures, he realized that God wanted to do more for His people than what most folks were accustomed to receiving. Daddy was excited about what he was learning from the Bible, and he began to share his insights with the church. He told the congregation that he saw more clearly that God was a good God, a heavenly Father, rather than a demanding, impossible-to-please judge. Daddy taught the people that God wanted them to be happy, healthy, and whole, and he began to pray for people who were sick or otherwise in need.

Much to my dad's surprise, many of the people in that congregation didn't appreciate his fresh discoveries. They were steeped in their traditions, and because Daddy's enthusiastic, fiery messages weren't exactly what they were used to hearing, it made some of them uncomfortable. Even though Daddy was teaching them right out of the Bible, they were upset that the supernatural God Daddy described didn't fit into their denominational guidelines.

The congregation took a vote to see whether they wanted Daddy to stay or to leave. When the ballots were all counted, Daddy had plenty of votes to stay, but during the next few months some of the people treated him so badly and were so disrespectful to him that he knew the best thing he could do for the church was to just move on. Naturally, he was disappointed and heartbroken. He had poured his heart and soul into that place, and now he would have to start all over again.

It wasn't fair; it wasn't right. The congregation didn't treat him as he deserved, and Daddy could have easily left there bitter. He could have harbored anger and resentment in his heart toward some of those people. But Daddy let those hard feelings go. His attitude was: *God, I know You're going to make this up to me. I know You will prosper me wherever I go, and You will bring about justice in my life.*

Daddy made the decision that he was going to go with God, and in 1959, he left the safety and security of that large, established church, and he went down the road to a small, run-down, abandoned feed store called East Houston Feed & Hardware. It was a beat-up, dirty building with holes in the floor. But Daddy and approximately ninety other people cleaned it up, and on Mother's Day, they started what they called "Lakewood Church."

The critics said, "It's never going to last, John. You don't have a chance. Nobody will come." They said, "It's going to blow over."

Sure enough, it did. It blew over the whole city! Today, it's blowing over the entire world! More than forty-five years later, Lakewood Church is still going strong, still seeing God's miracles, blessings, and favor, still touching people all over the world.

God knows how to bring justice into your life as well. If you will leave your concerns in God's hands, He will settle your cases. He will make your wrongs right. He's promised to take that evil and turn it around and use it to your advantage. It doesn't matter how badly somebody has hurt you, or how far their actions or words have set you back, God can turn that situation around and make it all up to you, plus much more!

God will make your wrongs right.

Leave it to God. Live a life of forgiveness. Don't go around trying to pay people back, trying to get revenge. God sees every wrong that's being done to you. God sees every person that's ever hurt you. He's keeping the record, and the Scripture says if you don't avenge yourself, God will pay you back. And friend, He'll not only pay you back, He'll pay you back in *abundance*.

CHAPTER 20

Defeating Disappointments

One of the most important keys to living your best life now, as well as moving forward into the great future God has for you, is *learning how to overcome the disappointments in life*. Because disappointments can pose such formidable obstacles to letting go of the past, you need to be sure you have dealt with this area before taking the next step to living at your full potential.

Let's be honest; all of us face disappointments from time to time. No matter how much faith you have or how good of a person you are, sooner or later, something (or somebody!) will shake your faith to its foundations. It may be something simple, such as not getting that promotion you really hoped for; not closing the big sale that you worked on so hard; not qualifying for a loan to buy that house that you really wanted. Or, it may be something more serious—a marriage relationship falling apart, the death of a loved one, or an incurable, debilitating illness. Whatever it is, that disappointment possesses the potential to derail you and wreck your faith. That's why it is vital that you recognize in advance that disappointments will come, and that you learn how to stay on track and deal with them when they do.

Often, defeating disappointments and letting go of the past are the flip sides of the same coin, especially when you are disappointed in yourself. When you do something wrong, don't hold on to it and beat yourself up about it. Admit it, seek forgiveness, and move on. Be quick to let go of your mistakes and failures, hurts, pains, and sins.

The disappointments that disturb us the most, however, are usually those caused by other people. Many individuals who have been hurt by others are missing out on their new beginnings because they keep re-opening old wounds. But no matter what we have gone through, no matter how unfair it was, or how disappointed we were, we must release it and let it go.

Somebody may have walked out on you. Somebody may have done you a great wrong. You may have prayed fervently for a loved one's life to be saved, yet your loved one died. Leave that with God and go on with your life. The Bible says, "The secret things belong to God."[1] Leave them there.

Disappointments almost always accompany setbacks. When you suffer loss, of course you will feel strong emotions. Nobody expects you to be an impenetrable rock or an inaccessible island in the sea. Not even God expects you to be so tough that you simply ignore the disappointments in life, shrugging them off as though you are impervious to pain. No, when we experience failure or loss, it's natural to feel remorse or sorrow. That's the way God made us. If you lose your job, most likely you are going to experience a strong sense of disappointment. If you go through a broken relationship, that's going to hurt. If you've ever lost a loved one, there's a time of grieving, a time of sorrow. That is normal and to be expected.

But if you are still grieving and feeling sorrow over a disappointment that took place a year or more ago, something is wrong! You are hindering your future. You must make a decision that you are going to move on. It won't happen automatically. You will have to rise up and say, "I don't care how hard this is, I don't care how disappointed I am, I'm not going to let this get the best of me. I'm moving on with my life."

The enemy loves to deceive us into wallowing in self-pity, fretting, feeling sorry for ourselves, or having a chip on our shoulders. "Why did this happen to me? God must not love me. He doesn't answer my prayers. Why did my marriage end in divorce? Why did my business not succeed? Why did I lose my loved one? Why didn't things work out in my life?"

You can't unscramble eggs.

Such questions may be valid, and may even be helpful to consider for a season, but after that, quit wasting your time trying to figure out something that you can't change. You can't unscramble eggs. What's done is done. Let the past be the past and go on. So you've suffered some setbacks; you didn't get what you were praying about; things didn't go your way. Friend, you are not alone. Many fine, upstanding individuals have experienced something similar.

Don't Become Trapped in the Past

My dad married at a very early age—probably not one of the best decisions Daddy ever made—and, although he went into the relationship with the best of intentions, unfortunately, things didn't work out. The marriage failed. Daddy was heartbroken and devastated. He thought sure that his ministry was over, that God's blessings had lifted from his life. He didn't think he would ever preach again, much less have a family. Dealing with his divorce was the darkest hour of my dad's life. He could easily have given up and sunk into a black hole of depression. I'm sure he was tempted to feel condemned and guilty. No doubt, he was tempted to internalize the blame and not accept God's forgiveness. He could have allowed that disappointment to thwart him from fulfilling his destiny.

But years later, Daddy told me how he had to shake himself out of his doldrums. He had to quit mourning over what he had lost and start receiving God's mercy and love.

The Bible says, "The mercies of God are fresh and new every single day." God knows we're going to make mistakes. God knows we are not perfect, so He provides fresh, new mercy and grace every day. God doesn't condone our sins; He doesn't wink at our wrongdoing. But God doesn't automatically condemn us either. The Bible says, "The Lord . . . is patient toward you, not wishing for any to perish but for all to come to repentance."[2]

If you're going to avoid getting trapped in your past, you must learn to forgive yourself. You must be willing to accept God's mercy. You can't be so critical of yourself that you won't receive what God has to offer.

Maybe you made some bad choices, and now you are trying to correct the things you've done wrong. That's noble, and to the extent that you can make restitution for any hurt you have inflicted on others, you should attempt to do so. But you must understand, you can't always repair every broken piece of your life or somebody else's life; you can't fix every mistake or clean up every mess that you have made. You may be trying to pay a debt that you cannot possibly pay. Perhaps it is time that you simply receive God's mercy and forgiveness so you can move on with your life.

Please don't misunderstand. I'm not suggesting that you take the easy way out, ignoring or abdicating responsibility for your actions. Quite the contrary. As much as you are able, you should seek forgiveness from and make restitution to those whom you have hurt. But frequently, little can be done to correct the past. When you know the situation is over and done, the best thing to do is just move on.

My dad made a decision that he was not going to allow his past to poison his future. He accepted God's forgiveness and mercy, and little by little, God began to do a fresh work in Daddy's life, restoring his spiritual strength as well as his ministry. Daddy began to preach once again, and to do what God wanted him to do. He began to fulfill God's destiny for his life.

Yet Daddy never dreamed he would ever get married again and have a family. Then one day, my dad met an attractive young woman with an unusual name—Dodie—who was working as a nursing student at one of the local hospitals where Daddy visited some of his ailing church members.

Daddy fell head over heels for the woman, and he started looking for any possible reason he could find to go to that hospital so he could see her. I mean, he would visit your great-aunt's third cousin's next-door neighbor if you asked him to! He was almost *hoping* members of his congregation would get sick so he could go to the hospital.

The young nursing student didn't recognize what was going on. But Daddy was at the hospital so much, she once told one of her friends, "That minister has the sickest congregation I've ever seen!" She didn't realize he was there to see her.

You've probably already guessed that Daddy married Dodie Pilgrim, and God blessed them with four average children and one exceptional child, whom they named Joel!

God not only restored my dad's ministry, He increased it. Daddy traveled all over the world for more than fifty years, ministering to millions of people. He founded Lakewood Church in Houston in the late 1950s and pastored the congregation for more than forty years.

God gave my dad a new family, too. Today, all five of his children are active in the ministry, carrying on the work that God started in Daddy many years ago. But I don't believe any of that would have happened had Daddy focused on his disappointments, refusing to let go of the past.

God wants to do more than you can ask or think as well. He wants to restore good things to you in abundance. If you will focus on the right things, God will take your most horrendous battlefield and turn it into your greatest blessing field.

I'm not saying to take the easy way and just bail out of a marriage or some other difficult situation. Daddy went through hell on earth. If you knew the circumstances surrounding the divorce he experienced, you would understand that he didn't take the easy road. But neither did he allow himself to be trapped in the past. Let go of your past disappointments, failures, and sins. God wants to do a new thing. He wants to restore to you in abundance everything the enemy has stolen from you. Quit dwelling on those disappointments, mourning over something you've lost, and start believing God for a fantastic future!

I'm often asked to pray for individuals who are believing for a relationship to be restored. Some are praying for their marriage to be restored; others are asking God to heal a business situation or a rift between coworkers. I encourage people to persevere, to continue praying, and believing for good things to happen. But we must also understand that God will not change another person's will. He has given every human being free will to choose which way he or she will go, whether to do right or wrong. Sometimes, no matter how hard we pray or how long we stand in faith, things don't turn out as we hope.

God will not change another person's will.

You may be heartbroken over a failed relationship or a bankrupt business, but I challenge you to not stay heartbroken. Don't carry around all that hurt and pain year after year. Don't let rejection fester inside you, poisoning your future. Let it go. God has something new in store for you.

When God allows one door to close, He will open another door for you, revealing something bigger and better. The Bible says that God will take the evil that the enemy brings into our lives, and if we'll keep the right attitude, He'll turn it around and use it for our good.[3] God wants to take your scars and turn them into stars. He wants to take those disappointments and turn them into reappointments. But understand, whether you will experience all those good things in your future depends to a large extent on your willingness to let go of the past.

You can't put a question mark where God has put a period.

You can't put a question mark where God has put a period. Avoid the tendency to dwell on what you could have done, which college you should have attended, which career you should have pursued, or that person you wish you would have married. Quit living in a negative frame of mind, stewing about something that is over and done. Focus on what you *can* change, rather than what you cannot. Shake yourself out of that "should have, could have, would have" mentality and move on. Don't let the regrets of yesterday destroy the hopes and dreams of tomorrow.

Surely, we all can look back and see things in our lives that we wish we would have done differently. But the Bible says, "Make the most of each day."[4] Yesterday is gone; tomorrow may not come. You must live for today. Start right where you are. You can't do anything about what's gone, but you can do a great deal about what remains.

You may have made some poor choices that have caused you awful heartache and pain. Perhaps you feel that you have blown it, that your life is in shambles and beyond repair. You may feel disqualified from God's best, convinced that you must settle for second best the rest of your life because of the poor decisions you made. But friend, God desires your restoration even more than you do! If you'll let go of the past and start living each day with faith and expectancy, God will restore everything that the enemy has stolen from you.

Backup Plans

Let's be frank; sometimes, because of wrong choices, disobedience, or sin, we miss out on God's "Plan A." The good news is, God has a "Plan B," a "Plan C," and whatever it takes to get us to His final destination for our lives.

Worse yet, maybe you weren't the person who made the bad choices, but somebody else's foolish decisions caused you to experience wrenching heartache and pain. Regardless, you must stop dwelling on it. Let the past be the past. Forgive the person who caused you the trouble and start afresh right where you are today. If you continue to dwell on those past disappointments, you will block God's blessings in your life today. It's simply not worth it.

The prophet Samuel suffered a horrible disappointment in his relationship with the first king of Israel, a man named Saul. As a young man, Saul was humble and shy. Then, at God's direction, Samuel picked him out of the crowd and declared him to be the king of Israel. Samuel did his best to help Saul be a king who was pleasing unto God.

Unfortunately, Saul refused to live in obedience to God, and God eventually rejected him as the king. Imagine how Samuel must have felt. Maybe you've invested a lot of time, effort, money, emotion, and energy in a relationship; you did your best to make it work out. But for some reason, things got off course, and now you feel as though you have been robbed.

That's how Samuel must have felt. Devastated. Heartbroken. Disappointed. But as Samuel was nursing his wounded heart, God asked him an important question: "Samuel, how long are you going to mourn over Saul?" God is asking us similar questions today: "How long are you going to mourn over that failed relationship? How long are you going to mourn over your broken dreams?" That's the problem with excessive mourning. When we focus on our disappointments, we stop God from bringing fresh new blessings into our lives.

God went on to tell Samuel, "Fill up your horn with oil and be on your way. I'm sending you to the house of Jesse for I have chosen one of his sons to be the new king."[5] In other words, God said, "Samuel, if you will quit mourning and get going, I'll show you a new, better beginning."

Remember, God always has another plan. Yes, Saul was God's first choice, but when Saul wouldn't walk in obedience, God didn't say, "Well, Samuel, I'm so sorry. Saul blew it and that ruins everything." No, God always can come up with another plan. If you will stop feeling sorry for yourself and, instead, do what the Bible says, your future can be brighter than ever.

Notice what God told Samuel to do: *Fill your horn with oil.* Have a fresh new attitude. Put a smile on your face. Get the spring back in your step and be on your way.

Samuel could have said, "God, I just can't do this. I'm too heartbroken. I gave so much of myself in that relationship and now it's gone, wasted."

But if Samuel would not have trusted God at that point, he might have missed King David, one of the greatest kings in the Bible. Similarly, if we wallow in our disappointments, we risk missing out on the new things God wants to do in our lives. It's time to get up and get going. God has another plan for you. And it is better than you can imagine!

My sister Lisa and her husband, Kevin, tried for years to have a baby, but Lisa could not conceive. She and Kevin longed to have a child, so Lisa tried all sorts of medical procedures, enduring a long, drawn-out process that included several operations, all to no avail. Finally her doctor said, "Lisa, let's try one more surgery. Hopefully this time it will help you to get pregnant." So she went through that, and she and Kevin tried for another year or so, but she still couldn't conceive.

At the end of that process, Lisa was exhausted, emotionally and physically drained. She went back to the doctor one more time to see if there was any possibility of her becoming pregnant, and the doctor offered no hope. "Lisa, I hate to tell you this," he said, "but we've done everything we can possibly do. You're just not going to be able to have a child."

Lisa was heartbroken. She thought, *God, we've endured all this time and effort. We tried so hard. We prayed and believed. We spent all this money. God, it's all such a waste. It seems so unfair.*

Sometimes we don't understand why certain things don't work out. I can't tell you why one person is healed and another person is not, when they are both praying and believing and standing in faith. But we must get to that point where we trust God, even when we don't understand Him. Some things we shouldn't even try to figure out; we should let them alone and go on. God is in control. The Bible says, "God's ways are higher and better than our ways."[6] God knows what He is doing. He knows what is best for us. And God always has another plan. If you'll quit dwelling on your disappointments, God will show you what the plan is.

That's exactly what Kevin and Lisa did. They finally came to the point where they said, "God, we're putting this totally in Your hands. We've done everything we know to do. Yes, we're disappointed, but we're not going to be trapped in the past. We're going to move on with our lives, knowing You are in control. You are a good God, and You have good things in store for us."

A few months later, they received a telephone call from a dear friend of ours, Nancy Alcorn. Nancy is the founder and president of Mercy Ministries of America, a ministry that takes care of young women at risk, including those dealing with premarital pregnancies. When a young woman gives birth to a baby and wishes to give up the child for adoption, Mercy Ministries helps place that child with a loving Christian husband and wife.[7]

"Lisa, I don't even know why I'm calling you," Nancy said. "I normally would not do this, but we have a teenager who is about to give birth to twin girls, and we were just wondering if you and Kevin might be interested in adopting them? It may not work out, though. I know you and Kevin have all the other qualifications, but one of the birth mother's stipulations is that her baby be placed in a family with twins in their background."

Little did Nancy know that Kevin, Lisa's husband, has a twin sister, and it was always his dream that he would one day raise twins. God answered the specific prayer of a young lady giving up her baby for adoption, while fulfilling a dream of Kevin's and Lisa's at the same time! A few months later, Lisa and Kevin were able to adopt, at childbirth, two beautiful baby girls. God had another plan!

But if Lisa had not been willing to let go of her own plan, if she had not been willing to get over her disappointments, I don't believe God's new plan would have opened up for her and Kevin.

Maybe you have put a lot of time, effort, and resources into your plan. You've prayed about it; you have believed. Maybe you have spent a lot of money. But now you can clearly see that the door is closing, and you are disappointed. You say, "God, how can I ever let go of this? It's going to be such a waste. I put so much into it, and all I can see is failure."

Right there is where you must dare to trust God, knowing that He has another plan, a better plan. He wants to do something new in your life. And you must let go of the old so you will be ready and able to receive the new plan God has for you. God will do more than you can even ask or think.

Recently, Kevin and Lisa adopted another child, a baby boy. Lisa quipped, "How about that! God has given me three beautiful children, and I have not had to spend a single month being pregnant!"

We all encounter circumstances that can cause us to grow negative, bitter, or disappointed with ourselves or God. But I love what the apostle Paul said: "Forgetting what lies behind and straining forward to what lies ahead, I press on toward the goal."[8] In other words, Paul was saying, "I'm not going to dwell on yesterday's disappointments or my past failures. I'm not going to think about what I would have done or should have done. I'm leaving all that behind, and I'm looking ahead for the good things God has in store for me." That's the kind of attitude we should have as well.

Every morning when you get up, refuse to dwell on what you did wrong the day before. Refuse to dwell on yesterday's disappointments. Get up each day knowing that God is a loving and forgiving God, and He has great things in store for you.

Paul said, "I'm straining forward. I press toward the mark." Those words imply a strong effort. It's not always easy to get over some of those bumps in the road, those disillusionments and disappointments. It's going to take a strong will. Sometimes, it may take courage; sometimes nothing but faith in God and sheer determination will see you through. But you can say, "I refuse to be trapped in the past. I'm not going to let the past destroy my future. I'm pressing on. I'm straining forward, knowing that God has great things in store for me."

When you make mistakes—and we all do—humble yourself and receive God's forgiveness and mercy. Be willing to forgive yourself. Don't live in regret. Regret will only interfere with your faith. Faith must always be a present-tense reality, not a distant memory. God will turn those disappointments around. He will take your scars and turn them into stars for His glory.

PART 5

FIND STRENGTH
THROUGH ADVERSITY

CHAPTER 21

Getting Up on the Inside

Many people give up far too easily when things don't go their way or they face some kind of adversity. Instead of persevering, they get all bent out of shape. Before long they're down and discouraged. That's understandable. Especially when we've struggled with a problem or a weakness for a long time, it's not unusual to come to a place where we acquiesce. We simply accept it and say, "Well, I've always had this sickness. I guess I'll never get well." "My marriage has been dry and dull for years; why should I expect anything to change now?" "I've banged my head on my company's glass ceiling one too many times. Apparently, this is as high as I can go."

But if you want to live your best life now, you have to be more determined than that. The fifth step to living at your full potential is finding strength through adversity. Our attitude should be: *I may have been knocked down a few times in life, but I am not going to stay down; I am determined I'm going to live in victory. I'm determined I'm going to have a good marriage. I'm determined I'm going to work my way out of these problems.*

We all face challenges in life. We all have things that come against us. We may get knocked down on the outside, but the key to living in victory is to learn how to get up on the inside.

I heard a story about a little boy who was in church with his mother, and he had so much energy, he just could not sit still. In fact, he kept standing up on the seat. His mother said, "Son, sit down."

He'd sit down for a few seconds, then he'd get right back up.

She'd gently reprimand him again, "Son, I said to sit down!"

This happened several times, and then the little boy stood up and simply would not sit down. His mother took her hand, put it on his head, and pushed him down onto the seat. The boy sat there smiling. Finally, he looked at his mother and said, "Mom, I may be sitting down on the outside, but I'm standing up on the inside!"

Sometimes that's what we have to do in life. Our circumstances may force us to sit down for a while, but we must not stay down. Even when we are sitting down on the outside, we must see ourselves as standing on the inside!

Even when we are sitting down on the outside, we must see ourselves as standing on the inside!

You may have received a bad report from the doctor. Maybe you lost your largest client at work. Perhaps you just found out that your child is in trouble. You may be facing some other serious setback, and you feel as though life has caved in on top of you, knocking you off your feet and pushing you down.

But the good news is, you don't have to stay down. Even if you can't get up on the outside, get up on the inside! In other words, have that victor's attitude and mentality. Stay in an attitude of faith. Don't allow yourself to lapse into negative thinking, complaining, or blaming God. Set your face like a flint and say, "God, I may not understand this, but I know You are still in control. And You said all things would work together for my good. You said You would take this evil and turn it around and use it to my advantage. So Father, I thank You that You are going to bring me through this!" No matter what you face in life, if you know how to get up on the inside, adversities cannot keep you down.

Keep on Standing Firm

The Scripture says, "When you've done everything you know how to do, just keep on standing firm."[1] You may be in a situation today where you have done your best. You've prayed. You've believed. You've placed your faith firmly on the truth of God's Word. But it just doesn't look like anything is happening. Now you're tempted to say, "What's the use? It's never going to change."

Don't give up! Keep standing. Keep praying; keep believing; keep hoping in faith. "Don't cast away your confidence," one translation of the Bible says, "for payday is coming."[2] I like that! *Payday is coming!* Friend, God will reward you if you will keep standing up on the inside. You may be in the hospital, or lying flat on your back at home. But even if you cannot stand up physically, nothing can keep you from standing up on the inside. That sickness may have you down physically, but you don't have to be down spiritually or emotionally. You can keep on getting up in your heart, mind, and will.

Maybe you work around people who are always putting you down, mistreating you, trying to make you feel badly about yourself. Let that trash talk go in one ear and out the other. They may try to knock you down on the outside, but they can't knock you down on the inside. Don't let those people steal your joy. Don't let that problem or adversity cause you to become discouraged or depressed. Just keep standing up on the inside.

I talked to a man the other day who had recently lost his job. He had been making a good salary working in a prestigious position, but then suddenly he was let go. When he first told me what had happened, I was certain that he was going to be upset and distraught. But I was wrong. When he came to see me, he was as happy as could be. He had a big smile on his face, and said, "Joel, I just lost my job, but I can't wait to see what God has in store for me next!"

He had been knocked down by circumstances outside his control, but he was still standing up on the inside. He had a victor's mentality. His attitude was: *This thing is not going to defeat me. This thing is not going to steal my joy. I know I'm the victor and not the victim. I know when one door closes, God will open up a bigger and a better door.*

Your attitude should be similar. You can say, "Even if the enemy hits me with his best shot, his best will never be good enough. He may knock me down, but he cannot knock me out. When it's all said and done, when the smoke clears and the dust settles, I'm still going to be standing strong." The Bible says no man can take your joy. That means no person can make you live with a negative attitude. No circumstance, no adversity can force you to live in despair. As Eleanor Roosevelt, wife of wheelchair-bound President Franklin D. Roosevelt, often said, "No one can make you feel inferior without your consent."

No matter what you are going through or how difficult it may seem, you can stay standing up on the inside. It will take courage; it will definitely take determination, but you can do it if you decide to do so. You must act on your will, not simply your emotions.

Before he became king of Israel, David and his men were out patrolling one day, doing what God had told them to do. But while they were away, some bandits attacked their city. The marauders burned down all the homes, stole their possessions, and kidnapped the women and children. When David and his men returned, they were devastated. They wept until they could not weep any more. But as David sat out there among the ruins, watching the smoke and ashes fill the air, he made a decision that changed his destiny. He was knocked down on the outside, but he decided he was going to get up on the inside. And that victor's spirit began to rise within him. Instead of just sitting around mourning over what he had lost, the Bible says that David "encouraged and strengthened himself in the Lord his God."[3] In other words, he got up on the inside. He said to his men, "Get your armor back on. We're going to attack the enemy." And they did just that. As David and his men persevered, God supernaturally helped them to recover everything that had been stolen. But I don't believe any of that would have happened if David had not first gotten up on the inside.

You may be sitting around waiting for God to change your circumstances. *Then* you're going to be happy, *then* you're going to have a good attitude, *then* you're going to give God praise. But God is waiting on you to get up on the inside. When you do your part, He'll begin to change things and work supernaturally in your life.

Are you going through a dark time in your life? Perhaps somebody deceived you, took advantage of you, or mistreated you, and now you are tempted to sit around mourning over what you have lost, thinking about how unfair it was, and how your life will never be the same. You need to change your attitude. You have to get up on the inside. Develop that victor's mentality and watch what God will do.

In the New Testament, we read about Paul and Silas, two of Christianity's earliest missionaries. One day they were teaching about God and trying to help people. But some of the religious leaders didn't approve of what Paul and Silas were doing, so they went to the local authorities and falsely accused Paul and Silas of being troublemakers. The authorities had them arrested, beaten, and thrown into prison.

Did Paul and Silas murmur and complain? Did they start blaming God? No, in the midst of that adversity, the Bible says, they were "singing hymns of praise to God."[4] In other words, they were standing up on the inside. When you give God praise and stay in an attitude of faith in the midst of your adversities, God's miracle-working power will show up. The Bible records that at midnight while they were singing praises to God, suddenly there was a great earthquake. The prison doors flew open and the chains fell off Paul and Silas.[5]

Friend, your circumstances are subject to change suddenly, too, especially when you start standing up on the inside. When you face adversity, don't be a crybaby. Don't be a complainer. Don't wallow in self-pity. Instead, have the attitude of a victor.

You may be weary and tired, worn down, and ready to give up. You may be saying, "I'm never going to break this addiction. I've had it for so long. I wouldn't even know how to function without it." Or, "My income is so low, and my debts are so high; I don't see how my financial situation will ever get better." Or, "I've been praying for years, but it doesn't look as though my children want to serve God." "I've had about as much as I can take."

Don't allow yourself to wave the white flag of surrender. You must get out of that defeated mentality and start thinking and believing positively. Your attitude should be: *I'm coming out of this thing! I may have been sick for a long time, but I know this sickness didn't come to stay. It came to pass. I may have struggled with this addiction for years, but I know my day of deliverance is coming. My children may not be doing right, but as for me and my house, we will serve the Lord.*

With God's help, you can get back up on the inside. You must show the enemy that you're more determined than he is. Shout aloud if you must, "I'm going to stand in faith even if I have to stand my whole lifetime! I'm not going to give up and settle for mediocrity. I'm going to keep believing for the best. I'm going to keep standing up on the inside no matter how long it takes."

God wants you to be a winner, not a whiner.

God wants you to be a winner, not a whiner. There is no reason for you to be perpetually living "under the circumstances," always down, always discouraged. No matter how many times you get knocked down, keep getting back up. God sees your resolve. He sees your determination. And when you do everything you can do, that's when God will step in and do what you can't do.

Learn to Be Happy

The Old Testament hero David is one of my favorite characters in the Bible, but David wasn't perfect. He made mistakes, he became discouraged, but he prayed, "God, renew a right, persevering, and steadfast spirit within me."[6] You may need to pray something similar. "God, please help me to get rid of this negative attitude. Help me to get rid of this self-pity. Help me to not give up. God, renew a right spirit in me."

Friend, life is too short to trudge through it depressed and defeated. No matter what has come against you or what is causing you to slip and fall, no matter who or what is trying to push you down, you need to keep getting up on the inside. If you want to give your enemy a nervous breakdown, learn to keep a good attitude even when the bottom falls out! Learn to be happy even when things don't go your way.

When many people face adversity, they allow their doubts to cloud their determination, thus weakening their faith. They don't persevere; they don't keep a good attitude. Ironically, because their spirits are not right, they remain in bad situations longer than necessary. Medical science tells us that people with a determined, feisty spirit usually get well quicker than people who are prone to be negative and discouraged. That's because God made us to be determined. We were not created to live in depression and defeat. A negative spirit dries up your energy; it weakens your immune system. Many people are living with physical ailments or emotional bondage because they are not standing up on the inside.

The Bible tells us that many of the saints of old died in faith. But you can die in faith only if you live a faith-filled life. When it's my time to go, I want to spend my last day here on this earth full of joy, full of faith, and full of victory. I've made up my mind that I'm going to live my best life now, and when my days are done, I'm going to die standing up on the inside.

You need to make a decision to do the same thing. Get rid of the mind-set that's saying you can't do it; you can't be happy; you have too much to overcome. Those are all lies from the enemy. You can be happy if you want to be. You can stand strong if you have a determined spirit. You can do whatever you need to do. When you face adversity, remind yourself, "I am full of God's can-do power. I can overcome. I can live in victory. I can stand up on the inside." Learn to tap into the can-do power that God has placed inside you, rather than rolling over in the face of adversity.

Don't Back Down

Growing up, my family had a dog named Scooter. He was a great big German shepherd, and he was the king of the neighborhood. Scooter was strong and fast, always chasing squirrels here and there, always on the go. Everybody knew not to mess with Scooter.

One day my dad was out riding his bicycle, and Scooter was bounding along beside him. Daddy looked over at Scooter and smiled. He was so proud of that dog. He could see Scooter's muscles rippling as he ran; he looked as though he could fight a tiger. But about that time, a tiny Chihuahua came yelping out of one of the homes, about thirty or forty yards in front of them. That spunky Chihuahua raced toward Scooter, barking up a storm.

Daddy thought at the time, *You poor little dog. You are messing with the wrong dog. Scooter could put one paw on you, and you'd be a goner!* But that little dog kept coming with full force, barking at the top of his lungs. Daddy was concerned that Scooter was just going to tear him up.

But much to my dad's surprise, the closer that little dog got to Scooter, the more Scooter began to hang his head like a coward. When that little dog finally got face-to-face with Scooter, Scooter just lay down on the ground, rolled over, and put all four legs up in the air! Apparently, Scooter was not nearly as big on the inside as he was on the outside.

Have you ever done something similar? Although we know that we have all God's resources at our disposal, when adversity comes barking, too often we just back down, roll over, and let the one with the loudest voice and the most annoying personality take control. We have the most powerful force in the universe inside us. We are filled with God's can-do power. We are made to be more than conquerors. But too often, just like Scooter, when trouble comes we back down and don't use what God has given us. We just give up and say, "I can't do this. It's too tough for me."

It's time to stand up on the inside, to tap into God's power. Stand strong and fight the good fight of faith. Remember, if you get knocked down, don't stay down. Get back up. Don't be like Scooter and roll over in the face of adversity; learn to do as David and encourage yourself in the Lord your God.

God has destined you to live in victory, but you have to do your part. Make a firm decision that no matter what comes against you in life, you are going to keep standing up on the inside.

CHAPTER 22

Trusting God's Timing

Human nature tends to want everything right now. We're always in a hurry. Most of us get impatient when we miss a turn on a revolving door! When we pray for our dreams to come to pass, we want them to be fulfilled immediately. But we have to understand, God has an appointed time to answer our prayers and to bring our dreams to pass. And the truth is, no matter how badly we want it sooner, no matter how much we pray and plead with God, it's not going to change His appointed time. It's still going to happen on God's timetable.

Because we sometimes don't understand God's timing, we live upset and frustrated, wondering when God is going to do something. "God, when are You going to change my husband? When are You going to bring me a mate? God, when is my business going to take off? When are my dreams going to come to pass?"

When you understand God's timing, however, you won't live all stressed out. You can relax knowing that God is in control, and at the perfect time He is going to make it happen. The Scripture says, "The vision is for an appointed time. Though it tarry, wait earnestly for it, for it will come to pass."[1] Notice, it's called an "appointed time." It may be next week, next year, or ten years from now. But whenever it is, you can rest assured that it will be in God's perfect timing.

I would love to tell you that if you prayed hard enough, and if you had enough faith, your prayers would always be answered within twenty-four hours. But that's simply not true. God is not like an ATM machine, where you punch in the right codes and receive what you requested (assuming you've even made a deposit!). No, we all have to wait patiently. That's a part of learning to trust God. The key is, *how* are we going to wait? What will be our physical, emotional, and spiritual demeanor? Are we going to wait with a good attitude and expectancy, knowing that God has great things in store? Or are we going to be upset, frustrated, and muttering complaints? "God, You never answer my prayers. When is my situation ever going to change?"

Consider this: If you know you have to wait anyway, why not make a decision to enjoy your life while you're waiting? Why not be happy while God is in the process of changing things? After all, there's nothing we can really do to make it happen any faster. We might as well relax and enjoy our lives, knowing that at the appointed time God is going to bring His plan to pass.

See, you don't have to struggle. You don't have to go around always wondering why God is, or is not, doing something. No, when you are trusting God, you can be at peace knowing that at the right time, God will keep His promise. It's going to happen, and the good news is, it's not going to be one second late. Imagine how much pressure that can take off you!

If you are unmarried and are believing for a mate, you don't have to worry. You don't have to beg God incessantly. You don't have to pray every fifteen minutes reminding God to send your mate. No, you can relax, knowing that at exactly the right time, God is going to bring the perfect person into your life, and he or she will not be one second late.

By the same token, if you are believing for your family members to develop a relationship with God, you don't have to quote Scripture to them at every family function as though you were firing a spiritual machine gun. You don't have to shove the Bible down their throats. You don't have to be upset because they won't come to church with you as much as you would like. You can relax and live your life in front of your loved ones, speaking naturally about your relationship with God and knowing that at the appointed time, God is going to speak to your family members.

Maybe you have some areas in your own life in which you need to improve, areas in which you need to change, and you've been extremely hard on yourself because you're not growing as fast as you would like. Lighten up and allow God to change you in His own timing. We all want to change overnight, but the Bible tells us that God changes us little by little. You can quit struggling, stop worrying about it, and simply do your best to love God and live for Him, love others, and let God change you in His own way and in His own timing.

Do you see how liberating it can be when you understand the concept of God's timing? When you are truly living by faith, you can relax in what the Bible calls the "rest" of God. That's a place where you're not worried, you're not struggling, you're not trying to figure everything out, wondering why something is or isn't happening. The rest of God is a place of total trust. When you're in God's rest, you know that at the perfect time, God is going to perform everything He promised; He will bring it into being.

Why isn't God working in my life? you may be wondering. *I've been praying, believing, and waiting, but it seems God is not doing anything about my marriage. That difficult situation at work hasn't changed. None of my dreams is coming to pass.*

Understand, God is at work in your life whether you can see anything happening externally or not. In fact, one could almost make a case that God often works the most when we see it and feel it the least. You may not see any progress. Your situation may look the same as it did three months or even three years ago, but you must trust that deep inside your life, God is at work.

**God often works the most when we see it
and feel it the least.**

Beyond that, behind the scenes, He's putting all the pieces together. He's getting everything lined up, and one day, at the appointed time, you will see the culmination of everything that God has been doing. Suddenly, your situation will change for the better.

In Due Season

David had a big dream for his life. He had a desire to make a difference, but as a young man he spent many years as a shepherd, caring for his father's sheep. I'm sure there were plenty of times when he was tempted to think that God had forgotten him. He must have thought, *God, what am I doing out here? There's no future in this place. I want to do something big for You. When are You going to change this situation?* But David understood God's timing. He knew that if he would be faithful in obscurity, God would promote him at the right time. He knew God would bring his dreams to pass in due season. He said, "God, I'm trusting You. My times are in Your hands."[2] He was saying, in effect, "God, I know You are in control. Although I don't see anything happening, You are working behind the scenes, and at the right time, You're going to change this situation."

You know the story. God brought David out of those fields, he defeated Goliath, and eventually he was made king of Israel.

Perhaps you have a big dream in your heart—a dream to have a better marriage, a dream to own your own business, a dream to help hurting people—but like David, you don't really see any human way your dream could happen.

I have good news for you! God isn't limited to natural, human ways of doing things. If you will trust God and keep a good attitude, staying faithful right where you are and not getting in a hurry and trying to force things to happen, God will promote you at the right time, in your due season. He will bring your dreams to pass.

If you're not seeing God move in your life right now, one of two possibilities must be considered. Either your requests are not God's best and will probably not be answered the way you'd like, or it must not be the right time. If God were to answer that prayer the way you are hoping, it could interfere with His ideal plan for you.

God Sees the Big Picture

Today, our television program is aired on networks across the United States and in numerous countries around the world. That has been a dream come true for me. I loved broadcasting my dad's ministry all over the world. But toward the end of my dad's life, he didn't want to do too much of that anymore. He just wanted to relax and serve the church.

At one point I had arranged for a large number of radio stations to carry our weekly broadcast. I said, "Daddy, if you'll come down to the studio for maybe an hour a week, we can make all these radio programs."

To my dismay, Daddy responded, "Joel, I don't want to do that. I'm seventy-five years old, and I'm not looking for anything else to do."

I was so disappointed. I thought, *God, I'm young, and I have all these dreams to touch the world; I have lots of energy; I don't want to do less. I want to do more!*

But something deep within me kept saying, *Be patient. It's not the right time.*

I made a decision that I would keep a good attitude and honor my dad. I didn't get in a hurry. I didn't get frustrated and start struggling and trying to make things happen in my own strength or in my own timing. No, I simply remained faithful and kept doing the best I could.

At the time, it didn't seem that God was doing anything with Daddy's dream or mine to broadcast messages of hope all over the world. But a few years later, when my dad went to be with the Lord, it all became clear to me. I never dreamed that I would be the pastor. I never dreamed that I would be the guy in front of the camera one day. But now I realize that God put those dreams in my heart for my own life, for my own ministry, not just Daddy's. Had I not been patient and stayed in God's perfect timing, I don't believe I'd be where I am today.

We don't always understand God's methods. His ways don't always make sense to us, but we have to realize that God sees the big picture. Consider this possibility: You may be ready for what God has for you, but somebody else who is going to be involved is not ready yet. God has to do a work in another person or another situation before your prayer can be answered according to God's will for your life. All the pieces have to come together for it to be God's perfect time.

But never fear; God is getting everything lined up in your life. You may not feel it; you may not see it. Your situation may look just as it did for the past ten years, but then one day, in a split second of time, God will bring it all together. When it is God's timing, all the forces of darkness can't stop Him. When it's that appointed time, no man can keep it from happening. When it's your due season, God will bring it to pass.

Suddenly, things will change. Suddenly, that business will take off. Suddenly, your husband will desire a relationship with God. Suddenly, that wayward child will come home. Suddenly, God will bring your hopes and dreams to pass.

Shelby was an attractive woman in her mid-thirties who genuinely desired to be married. She had prayed and prayed but had never even had a serious relationship with a man. In fact, she told me that she hadn't been out on a date within the last two or three years. She was tempted to be discouraged, assuming that nothing was happening, and that she might spend the remainder of her life as a single woman.

But one day she was driving home from work when she had a flat tire and had to pull her car over to the side of the freeway. A few seconds later, another car pulled over behind her, and out stepped a handsome young man. He not only changed Shelby's tire, he invited her out to dinner. About a year later they got married, and today they are wonderfully happy and in love.

Now, think about the odds of such an occurrence. That certainly was not an accident or a coincidence. That was God at work in the lives of two young adults. Think about the timing involved in their meeting. Her tire had to go bad at just the right time. There had to be just the right amount of traffic on the freeway. Had there been too many cars, he would have been late; too few cars, he would have been early. That young man had to catch just the right elevator leaving the office. He had to get stopped by just the right amount of traffic lights. All the timing had to go down to the split second in order for his car to be shortly behind Shelby's when her tire went flat.

Don't ever think that God is not at work in your life. He's making things happen even when you don't realize it. Just stay in an attitude of faith and learn to trust His timing.

When I was in my early twenties, I had an experience similar to Shelby's. I had never really dated much during high school or college. I was a sports nut, and I was busy playing baseball four or five nights a week. I really didn't have any time for a social life. But I eventually tired of hanging out with all those old ugly guys, and I decided I was going to find somebody a little better looking.

I prayed that God would lead me to the right person. I said, "Father, I know You have somebody already picked out for me, so I'm trusting You to bring us together at the right time."

Two or three years went by and nothing much happened, but I didn't get in a hurry or try to force things. I didn't get upset and say, "God, why aren't You doing anything?" No, I just did my best to stay in the rest of God. I said, "Father, I know You are in control and even though I don't see anything happening, I know You are working behind the scenes on my behalf."

One day I noticed that my watch had stopped. My friend Johnny and I were going up to the gym to work out, so I decided to stop at a jewelry store along the way to get a new watch battery. I went into the store and met the most beautiful girl I had ever seen! I thought, *God, You have just answered my prayers!*

We struck up a conversation, and I discovered that she was a good Christian girl. I thought, *That's great, because if you weren't a Christian, you were about to become one!*

She not only sold me a battery for my watch, she sold me a whole new watch! And she's been spending my money ever since.

But think of all the factors that had to fall into place for me to meet Victoria. My watch battery had to stop. I had to have a reason to go to a jewelry store, not simply a Wal-Mart or a convenience store. Then I had to stop at the particular store where Victoria was working. Keep in mind, there are hundreds of fine jewelry stores in Houston. Then she had to be working that specific shift. She could have been off that day. Somebody else could have waited on me. But all these pieces came together perfectly, because God was in control.

To live your best life now, you must learn to trust God's timing. You may not think He's working, but you can be sure that right now, behind the scenes, God is arranging all the pieces to come together to work out His plan for your life.

You may be experiencing some difficult times, and perhaps your circumstances have seemed static and immobile for quite a while. You may not be able to fathom how your situation can ever move forward. But you need to know that God had the answer to your prayer even before you had the need. God has been arranging things in your favor long before you ever encountered the problem.

A pastor of a large church in America unfortunately got off track and made some very poor decisions, resulting in his resignation. His family fell apart, and he left the ministry. It was a very sad situation. By all outward appearances, he had a bleak future. Several years went by, and the pastor was trying to get his life back together. He still had a heart to serve people, so he decided to travel to South America to assist some missionaries there. While he was in Brazil, he visited a little church. When he met the pastor, something very strange happened. The Brazilian pastor looked shocked and then began to weep. The pastor clasped the American's hands and began to pray in Portuguese.

As the pastor prayed for him, the American felt an unusual presence enveloping him, almost like a warm glow purging him of his hurt and pain. He said, "For the first time in several years, I felt that I was able to let go of the past. I felt totally free and totally restored."

When the prayer ended, the American asked his interpreter, "Who is this man? And why was he praying for me like that?"

Through the interpreter, the Brazilian pastor said, "Twenty years ago, I was praying and suddenly your face came into my mind. And God said to me, 'One day you will help bring healing and restoration to this man.' Today is that day, and you are that man."

Now here's the truly amazing aspect of this story: Twenty years prior to that event, the American was not even a Christian, much less a pastor. He wasn't even serving God. But God knows the end of the story before the first word is written. Twenty years earlier, He had placed a vision in one man's heart that involved another person, then for two decades, God designed events in both of their lives to bring them together on that platform in that little church in Brazil, so one man could see the fulfillment of his dream, and another man could be reassured of God's love and forgiveness.

In the same way, God already has the answer to your prayers before you have the need. He has already been arranging things in your favor. And who knows, maybe five or ten years ago, God spoke to somebody about the situation you're going through right now, and He is shaping events to bring your paths together. You can't fake that sort of thing. You'd be foolish to try to manipulate such events. No, God is in control. You may not think anything is happening, but remember, God often works the most when we see it and feel it the least. Learn to trust His timing. Don't get in a hurry; don't grow impatient; don't try to force doors to open. Don't try to make things happen in your own strength. Let God do it His way.

Let God do it His way.

I remember a number of times when my dad tried to start construction on a new sanctuary for Lakewood Church. The congregation had grown too large for our facility, so several times over a five-year period, Daddy had architects draw up some preliminary plans for a new building. But just as he was about to break ground, Daddy would sense a caution from God. He didn't feel right about pressing ahead. He didn't have a peace in his heart about the matter, so he'd put it all on hold.

At that time, my dad was in his early sixties, and a number of younger ministers across the country were building large sanctuaries. Daddy felt pressured to build before it was too late. He'd get all fired up about starting the new project. Two or three times, he announced to the congregation, "This fall, we're going to break ground for our new sanctuary!"

Fall rolled around, and Daddy would get up in front of the church and say, "I've changed my mind. It's not the right time. I don't feel a peace about it." See, Daddy was smart enough to know that he needed to stay in God's perfect timing. And the congregation possessed enough confidence in him to patiently abide by Daddy's convictions.

The sad truth is, if you push hard enough, and if you're so stubborn that you must have things your way, God will sometimes allow you to undertake a project without His blessing or at the wrong time. The problem with that, of course, is when you start something in your own strength and in your own timing, you're going to have to finish it and maintain it in your own strength. When you let God start something, He'll finish it for you. He'll provide everything you need.

When we try to force open doors and make things happen in our own strength, the end result is a constant strain on us and a drain on our resources. Life becomes a constant struggle. Nearly all joy, peace, and victory dwindle from your existence. That is not a place of contentment and satisfaction.

If you are in an area like that today, you need to do your best to get out of it. I'm not suggesting that you break up your marriage relationship or renege on business contracts. That would only exacerbate the problem. But if you are doing things that are not bearing any fruit, and they are giving you a perpetual headache, there's a good chance that God didn't initiate that endeavor or relationship. Or perhaps it is part of God's plan for your life, but you are out of His timing, and you are proceeding under your own power according to your own timetable.

Be careful! If God isn't in what you are doing, you need to make a change. Here is where many people miss God's favor: They know God has spoken to them; He has placed a dream within their hearts. But they then set about trying to fulfill God's plan on their own. We must be aware that if we get out of God's timing, it's the same as getting out of God's will. We need to be patient and let God bring His plan together at the appointed time.

That is not to say that we should sit back passively and expect God to do everything. No, we have to aggressively pursue our dreams. But if a door is not opening, don't try to make things happen in your own strength.

My dad was a big enough person to get up and tell the congregation, "I missed it. I thought this was the time we were supposed to begin building, but it is not. It's just not the right time."

Amazingly, when God finally did lead Daddy to start construction, it was during what seemed to be the worst possible time. It was two weeks before Christmas, and Daddy had just gotten out of the hospital following open-heart surgery. Added to that, the economy in Houston was at an all-time low. The city was in one of the worst recessions that we had ever seen. More than twelve thousand businesses had gone bankrupt during the previous year. By all logical business standards, beginning a new building—one paid for by donations—looked as though it was going to be a major mistake. Cynics and friends alike told my dad, "You'd better not start right now. You're never going to raise the money. That building's going to sit there unfinished."

Daddy thanked them for their opinions, but when it's God's timing, it doesn't matter what the surrounding circumstances look like. It doesn't matter what people are telling you. If God says it's time, then He will bring it to pass.

Daddy initiated the building program, and in less than one year's time, the congregation gave enough money that the building was built debt-free! Had Daddy tried to do that in his own strength, in his own timing, even if the economy would have been red hot, it still would have been a constant struggle.

Understand, when you get out of God's timing, you are stepping out of His favor. When you step out of His favor, you are operating on your own in the dark. I'm not saying that when we do something for God, we're not going to have adversity. But fighting the good fight of faith outside God's timing can leave you constantly struggling, never having anything go your way, never having any joy. On the other hand, when you're in God's timing, you can be in the midst of the biggest challenge of your life, and you'll still be filled with joy. God will give you all the grace you need. If you will learn to trust His timing, He's promised that at the right time, He will bring your dreams to pass and answer your prayers. The answer will come, and it will be right on time.

CHAPTER 23

The Purpose of Trials

No matter how successful we are, we all face challenges, struggles, and times when things don't go our way. When calamities occur, some people immediately think they have done something wrong, that God must surely be punishing them. They don't understand that God has a divine purpose for every challenge that comes into our lives. He doesn't send the problems, but sometimes He allows us to go through them.

Why is that? The Bible says temptations, trials, and difficulties must come, because if we are to strengthen our spiritual muscles and grow stronger, we must have adversities to overcome and attacks to resist. Moreover, it's in the tough times of life that we find out what we're really made of. The pressure exposes things that we need to deal with—things such as wrong attitudes, wrong motives, areas where we're compromising. As odd as this may seem, the trials can be beneficial.

It's in the tough times of life that we find out what we're really made of.

The Scripture says, "Don't be amazed at the fiery ordeal that's taking place to test your quality as though something strange was happening."[1] Notice, the trial is intended to test your quality, to test your character, to test your faith. In other words, "Don't think it's a big deal when you go through these tough times." All through life, you will face various tests, and even though you may not enjoy them, God will use those trials to refine you, to cleanse and purify you. He's trying to shape you into the person He wants you to be. If you will learn to cooperate with God and be quick to change and correct the areas that He brings to light, then you'll pass that test and you will be promoted to a new level.

Tests of Faith

I've discovered in the struggles of life that God is more interested in changing me than He is in changing my circumstances. I'm not saying that God won't change the circumstances. Certainly, He can and often does. But most of the time, I'm tested in the areas where I am the weakest.

You've probably found something similar to be true. If you have a problem with jealousy, it seems as though everybody you meet has more or better material possessions than you do. You notice that your best friend wears a brand-new outfit every time you turn around. The person you work next to, who makes half as much money as you do, comes driving up in a brand-new car. Your long-lost relative calls to tell you that she just won the lottery!

Are you going to pass the test? Are you going to keep a good attitude and rejoice with those who rejoice and be sincerely happy for them? Or are you going to get all negative and bitter and say, "God, I work harder than they do. Nothing good ever happens to me. I go to church every Sunday. Why can't I get a new car?"

That's a test of your faith. That's God bringing to light impurities in your character. That's God trying to refine you. If you'll learn to work with God, and let go of that jealousy, you'll be amazed at the blessings and favor and victory that will come into your life.

I'm a very focused and goal-oriented person. When I have a project to do, I like to get it done right then and there. I've been that way my whole life. In elementary school, when the teacher would give us a homework assignment on a Monday that wasn't due until Friday, I'd go home on Monday night and do the whole thing! I didn't want anything hanging over my head.

When I go to a restaurant, I order before they even give me a menu. I'm trying to tell you in a roundabout way that sometimes I'm impatient. I don't like to wait; I don't like to be inconvenienced. But I've discovered that the more impatient I am, the more I find myself in situations where I have to wait around. If I'm in a hurry to get out of the grocery store, inevitably I'll get in the line with a brand-new cashier who is plodding through his or her first day on the job, and the person in front of me will have twenty-three items that don't have a price tag on them!

At home, I've noticed that the more impatient I am, the longer it takes Victoria to get dressed for an occasion. Ironically, when I'm not in a hurry or being impatient, Victoria will beat me getting dressed. She'll be out in the car waiting with the kids. But every time I'm impatient, one thing after another will delay us. Little Alexandra will have taken Victoria's makeup. The iron won't work right. My wife can't find our daughter's shoes. Interesting, isn't it? Victoria doesn't realize it, but God is using her to refine me while she's getting dressed!

God deliberately uses situations such as these so I can recognize the problem in myself and learn to deal with it. He's working something out of me so I can rise to a new level and be the person He really wants me to be.

In a similar way, God will use people in your life. Your own husband or wife, your in-laws, or your own children may be the unwitting mirrors that God uses to reveal areas where you need to change.

"Joel, I can't stand my boss. He irritates me to no end. I don't know why I have to work with him day in and day out. When is God ever going to change that man?"

Have you considered that God may want to change *you*? God may have purposely arranged for you to be in close proximity to that person who grates against you. He may be trying to teach you how to love your enemies. Or, He may be trying to toughen you up a little and teach you to have some endurance, to not run from everything that is hard, uncomfortable, or inconvenient.

A husband moans, "God, why did You put me with this woman? She can't do anything right. She can't even cook. She burns the toast. She can't make a meat loaf. God, when are You going to change her?"

She's probably going to continue to cook just like that until you learn how to get over it, have a better attitude, and start appreciating the fact that at least she's trying to do something for you. You could be eating a TV dinner!

A parent complains, "God, these kids are driving me bananas. If You would just make them behave, then I'll be happy."

God is not going to change anyone you are dealing with until He first changes you.

God is not going to change anyone you are dealing with until He first changes you. But if you'll quit complaining about everybody around you and, instead, start taking a good look inside and working with God to change you, God will change those other people. Examine your own heart and see if there are attitudes and motives that you need to change.

One day I was driving to church, and I was running a bit late for an important meeting. I knew that if could avoid any traffic jams, I'd get there just in time. But I caught every single stoplight going out of the neighborhood. I even got stopped by a light that I had never before seen turn red, not in my entire lifetime!

I started praying as I drove, but the more I prayed, the longer it took me to get through the traffic lights. I finally steered onto the highway and took off toward the church as fast as I could drive, praying the whole time that God would give me the discernment to know which hill the policemen were waiting behind. I had just enough time to make it to my meeting.

But as I kept going, much to my chagrin, the traffic started moving slower and slower. I thought, *Oh, no! What is going on?* Eventually, the traffic came to a complete stop. I thought, *God, I've got to get to this meeting. You've got to help me.* In a couple of minutes, the lane next to me started moving. I tried everything I possibly could to get into that lane, but it was just one of those days. Nobody was willing to let me squeeze in. I had my blinker on, I was smiling and waving, I was holding up money, I was blowing kisses, I was doing everything, yet nobody would let me in!

Finally, a sweet little old lady was kind enough to let me pull into the lane in front of her. I thought, *All right! At last, I can get going!* But just as I tramped down on the gas pedal, the flow of traffic in that lane came to a complete stop, and I had to slam on the brakes. Meanwhile, my previous lane started moving! I was so frustrated that I didn't even want to think about trying to get back in that other lane.

I didn't realize that God was testing me in the area of my patience. I sat stewing in that traffic for about ten minutes, and when it started inching forward, I noticed the problem. A car had stalled and had been pulled off to the right side of the road by a wrecker.

As I drew nearer to the flashing lights, compassion for a stranded motorist was the farthest thing from my mind. Instead, I was thinking, *I wish you'd keep that old piece of junk off the road; here you are holding everybody up, and you're making me miss my meeting!* My attitude was terribly sour. About that time, my heart sank. I looked over at the disabled vehicle and I saw what looked to be a Lakewood Church bumper sticker on it. Sure enough, when I drove by, I slowed down and looked over, and saw a man smiling and waving at me. I smiled back and waved at him like I was his best friend. I thought, *If he only knew the truth!*

That's when it dawned on me that perhaps God was trying to teach me something. Maybe God was using the traffic jam to bring to light impurities in my character. This was God showing me areas in which I needed to improve.

God often allows you, too, to go through situations to draw out those impurities in your character. You can rebuke until your "rebuker" wears out. You can pray, you can resist, you can bind, you can loose, you can sing and shout, you can do it all, but it's not going to do you any good! God is more interested in changing you than He is in changing the circumstances. And the sooner you learn to cooperate with God, the sooner you'll get out of that mess. The quicker you learn your lesson and start dealing with those bad attitudes and start ruling over your emotions, the quicker you'll go to the next level in your spiritual journey. We must recognize the refining purpose of trials. We can't run from everything that's hard in our lives.

Perhaps you are in a trial, and you're doing what I did. You're praying for God to deliver you out of that negative situation. That is a legitimate prayer, but maybe you're missing the point of why you were allowed to go through that trying time.

Recognize that God wants to do a work in you. He's molding you and refining you. But you're so busy trying to evade the difficulty, the work is not being done. You're so focused on all the circumstances and all the people around you that you haven't taken time to look deep inside and deal with the issues God is bringing to light.

Perhaps you get worried and full of fear when important things don't go your way. Have you ever thought that God may be allowing those events to teach you to trust Him and to see if you will stay peaceful and calm in the midst of the storm? Have you considered that God may be allowing some of that to teach you how to rule over your emotions? He may be trying to toughen you up, to help you develop some backbone and stability in your life.

We often pray, "God, if You will change my circumstances, then I'll change." No, it works the other way around. We have to be willing to change our attitudes and deal with the issues God brings up; then God will change those circumstances.

God loves you far too much to allow you to go through life in mediocrity. He will often permit pressure to be applied to your life, to test you, and only as you pass those tests will you advance. He will put people and circumstances in your path that grate on you like sandpaper, but He will use them to rub off your rough edges. You may not always like it; you may want to run from it, you may even resist it, but God is going to keep bringing up the issue, again and again, until you pass the test.

Work in Progress

Remember, the Bible says, "We are [God's] workmanship."[2] That means we are a work in progress, not a finished product. One way or the other, God is going to get His way. Either you can learn the hard way, as I did in that traffic, and say, "Okay, God, I'll do it Your way. I understand. I'll be calm; I'll be patient." Or, you can do it the easier way: When struggles come your way, look deep inside and be quick to change. Be willing to deal with any issues that God brings up. Work with God in the refining process rather than fighting against Him.

Scripture says that God is the potter and we are the clay.[3] Clay works best when it is pliable, malleable, and moldable. But if you are hard, crusty, and set in your ways, God will have to pound away on that old, hard clay to get out the lumps.

Certainly, none of us enjoy going through struggles, but you have to understand that your struggle may be an opportunity for advancement and promotion. The very thing that you are fighting against so tenaciously may be the springboard that catapults you to a new level of excellence. Your challenges may become your greatest assets.

Many years ago, fishing for codfish up in the Northeast had become a lucrative commercial business. The fishing industry recognized that a great market for codfish existed all over America, but they had a major problem in the distribution. At first, they simply froze the fish, as they did all their other products, and shipped it out all across the country. But for some reason, after the codfish was frozen, it lost its taste. So the owners decided to ship the fish in huge tanks filled with fresh seawater. They thought for sure that would solve the problem and keep the fish fresh. But to their dismay, this process only made matters worse. Because the fish were inactive in the tank, they became soft and mushy, and once again they lost their taste.

One day, somebody decided to put some catfish in the tank with the codfish. Catfish are a natural enemy of codfish, so as the tank traveled across the country, the codfish had to stay alert and active and be on the lookout for the catfish. Amazingly, when the tank arrived at its destination, the codfish were as fresh and tasty as they were in the Northeast.

Like that catfish, perhaps your adversity was dropped in your path for a purpose. Perhaps it was put there to challenge you, to strengthen you, to sharpen you, to keep you fresh, to keep you alive and active and growing. Granted, at times, it feels as though you have a great white shark in the tank rather than a catfish, but the adversity you are facing could very well be something that God is using to push you and challenge you to be your best. The trial is a test of your faith, character, and endurance. Don't give up. Don't quit. Don't whine and complain, saying, "God, why is all this happening to me?"

The trial is a test of your faith, character, and endurance.

Instead, stand strong and fight the good fight of faith. God is giving you an opportunity for promotion. It is the struggle that gives us the strength. Without opposition or resistance, there is no potential for progress. Without the resistance of air, an eagle can't soar. Without the resistance of water, a ship can't float. Without the resistance of gravity, you and I can't even walk.

Yet our human tendency is to want everything easily. "God, can't You teach me patience without having to go through the traffic jam?

God, can't You teach me how to love and trust You without ever having a problem?"

Unfortunately, there are no shortcuts; there's no easy way to mature physically, emotionally, or spiritually. You must remain determined and work with God. The Bible says, "Work out your own salvation."[4] Salvation is more than a onetime prayer. It is constantly working with God, dealing with the issues He brings up and keeping a good attitude, fighting through until you win the victory.

Some bumblebees were taken along on a space mission for a study on the effects of weightlessness. Similar to humans in space, the bees floated around with such great ease, they didn't even have to use their wings. It looked as though they were thriving in the weightless environment without work, struggle, or adversity. But after three days, all the bees died. The experiment was summed up with these words: "They enjoyed the ride, but they didn't survive." Bees were never meant to go through life without using their wings, not having any resistance. In the same way, you and I were never made to float through life on flowery beds of ease.

God never promised that we wouldn't have challenges. In fact, He said just the opposite. His Word says, "Be truly glad! . . . These trials are only to test your faith, to see whether or not it is strong and pure . . . So if your faith remains strong after being tried in the test tube of fiery trials, it will bring you much praise and glory and honor on the day of his return."[5]

When you go through difficult times, make sure you pass the test. Don't be stubborn and hardheaded. Recognize that God is refining you, knocking off some of your rough edges. Stand strong and fight the good fight of faith. God has called each of us to be champions; you are destined to win. If you will work with God and keep a good attitude, then no matter what comes against you, the Bible says that all things—not just the good things in life, but all things—will work together for your good.[6]

CHAPTER 24

Trusting God When Life Doesn't Make Sense

In 1958, when my dad's future looked so bright in the denomination in which he was serving, my sister Lisa was born with a birth injury similar to cerebral palsy. The doctors told my parents that she would never be normal, never walk, and would probably need twenty-four-hour care. Mother and Daddy were devastated.

It was one of the darkest hours in our family's history. Mother and Daddy could easily have become bitter. They could have easily said, "God, this is not fair. Why did this happen to us? Here we are doing our best to serve You, and You allow something like this to occur."

But no, Daddy knew that adversity could be a stepping-stone to something greater. He knew God would not allow a trial without having a purpose for that trial. Instead of being negative and running away from God, Daddy ran to God. He began to search the Scriptures as never before, and he discovered the God of the Bible in a fresh way—as a loving God, a healing God, a restoring God, and, yes, as a God of miracles. Daddy went back to his church and preached with a new fire and enthusiasm. Beyond that, he and Mother began believing that Lisa could be healed.

Daddy studied the Bible and began preaching messages about hope, healing, and living in victory. He honestly thought the congregation would be thrilled with the message that God wanted good things for His people—after all, who could argue with that?

But, as I mentioned earlier, some people became upset and Daddy eventually resigned from that church. In that dark hour, Lakewood Church was born. God used the adversity to enlarge my dad's vision, ushering him into a whole new era of ministry. What the enemy meant for evil, God turned around and used it to His advantage. And in the midst of the struggle, God healed Lisa's body. To this day, my sister is healthy and well. But I don't believe any of that would have happened if my dad had not handled his adversities correctly.

Many people immediately respond negatively to adversities and trouble, rather than believing that God can bring good out of the situation. I'm not saying God sends the trouble, but I am saying God will use any adversity you face to take you to a higher level if you'll just do your part and keep standing strong.

Two Kinds of Faith

In my life, I've discovered two kinds of faith—a *delivering* faith and a *sustaining* faith. Delivering faith is when God instantly turns your situation around. When that happens, it's great. But I believe it takes a greater faith and a deeper walk with God to have that sustaining faith. That's when circumstances don't change immediately, but you say, "God, I don't care what comes against me, I don't care how long it takes, this thing is not going to defeat me. It's not going to get me down. I know You're on my side. And as long as You are for me, that's all that matters." Sustaining faith is what gets you through those dark nights of the soul when you don't know where to go or what to do, and it seems that you can't last another day . . . but because of your faith in God, you do.

When you have that kind of attitude, the adversary doesn't have a chance with you. Besides, it's not usually adversities that cause our problems; it's how we respond to our adversities. You can have a little bitty problem and it can defeat you. On the other hand, I've seen people dealing with huge problems—tragic deaths in the family, incurable diseases, divorce, bankruptcy, and all sorts of other calamities—yet they are happy and at peace. They are living in an attitude of faith. They are believing for things to change. They are determined to live in victory!

When you face adversity, you need to remind yourself that whatever is trying to defeat you could very well be what God will use to promote you. For example, when Daddy went to be with the Lord back in January 1999, God placed a strong desire in my heart to pastor Lakewood

Church. All of the critics said we would never make it, and with good reason. I had never preached before! *Ever!*

A Willing Heart

I had spent seventeen years behind the scenes at Lakewood managing our television production. Over the course of those years, Daddy tried many times to get me out in public to speak, but I never had the desire to do it. I was comfortable and content working behind the scenes. But about a week before my dad went to be with the Lord, he and Mother were over at Kevin and Lisa's home eating dinner. During the meal, Daddy said to them, "I'm going to call Joel and ask him if he'll speak for me this Sunday."

My mother laughed and said, "John, you're just wasting your time. Joel is not going to get out there and speak in front of anybody."

(Thanks for that vote of confidence, Mom!)

Nevertheless, Daddy telephoned me at my house. And just as Mother said, I responded, "Daddy, I'm not a preacher. I don't even know how to preach. You're the preacher." I laughed and told him, as I had many times before, "You get up there and preach, and I promise you this; I'll make you look good."

We laughed, and I hung up the phone and sat down to eat dinner.

While Victoria and I were eating, Daddy's words kept flitting through my mind, and with no other provocation, I began to have an overwhelming desire to preach. I didn't really understand it at the time, but I knew I had to do something. Keep in mind, I had never even prepared a sermon, let alone considered standing up in front of thousands of people to speak. Nevertheless, I called Daddy right back and said, "Daddy, I've changed my mind. I think I'll do it."

Of course, Daddy nearly passed out!

I studied all week and prepared a message, and the next Sunday I spoke at Lakewood Church for the first time. The message was well received by the congregation. None of us, however, could have imagined that would be the last Sunday of Daddy's life. He passed away Friday night—five days later.

We had church that Sunday and, of course, the congregation was grieving the loss of my father, their pastor and friend, yet there was an air of confidence in the building. On Monday morning, three days after Daddy's death, I was at home contemplating all the events that had taken place and spending a little time in prayer. We were to have a special memorial service in Daddy's honor later that week.

All of a sudden, I felt that overwhelming desire to speak once again. I called my mother and said, "Mother, who's going to speak this Sunday?"

She said, "Ah, well, Joel, I don't know. We're just going to have to pray and believe that God will send the right one."

"Well, I'm just sort of thinking about . . . maybe that I would like to do it."

That's all Mother needed to hear. My mother has an interesting habit. When she is on the telephone and finishes her part of the conversation, she's through. She just hangs up. She doesn't give you any time to respond. So when I said, "I'm thinking about speaking," she jumped right in and said, "Oh, Joel, that would be great. I can't wait to tell the people. We'll see you later."

Click. The line went dead.

"Now wait a minute!" I said. "I said I was thinking about speaking. I didn't say I was going to do it."

Too late; Mother was already long gone.

Well, that's just my mother, I thought. *I can always back out on her. It's not going to hurt her feelings. She'll forgive me.*

Two days later, at the memorial service for my dad, and in front of eight thousand people, Mother turned around and said, "I'm so happy to announce to you that my son Joel will be speaking this Sunday."

And I thought, *Dear God, now I'm stuck!*

Later that night, I was watching all the news reports about my dad. The Houston media gave Daddy glowing tributes as they reported his passing away. I was about to turn the television off and go to bed when I heard a newscaster say one final thing about Daddy's memorial service. "And by the way," the news anchor announced, "Osteen's son Joel will be ministering this Sunday."

I said, "All right, God. I got the message. I'll do it."

So I wasn't surprised when after Daddy went to be with the Lord, almost every subsequent media report discussed how Lakewood Church had little chance of surviving. They talked about how we would never make it. The naysayers were quick to point out that no large church with a strong, dynamic leader such as my dad had ever survived after the death of that leader. One article specifically opined, "The worst thing that could happen is for one of the sons to take over."

I quipped to Victoria, "Now, I could understand that if they knew my brother, Paul, but they don't even know me!"

As much as I tried to make light of the reports, the words still stung. There I was, trying to get my nerve up to speak, trying to build my confidence, and the media were already predicting our church's demise!

I knew I had to make a choice: Would I believe God or would I believe the negative reports? I decided not to dwell on public opinion or popularity polls. I refused to let those negative reports poison my heart and mind. I declined to listen to anyone who seemed intent on talking me out of fulfilling my destiny. More important, I knew God had raised up Lakewood Church to be a beacon of hope for more than forty years, and He wasn't going to let it go down the drain just because Daddy had graduated to heaven.

Interestingly, the naysayers predicted that we'd be doing well if we merely maintained the status quo. But God had other plans. Lakewood continued to grow, and in 2003, *Forbes* magazine named Lakewood Church "the largest church in America," with twenty-five thousand people attending each weekend. And we're still growing!

If you will handle adversity in the right way, God has promised that He will turn your challenges into stepping-stones for promotion. God wants to do new and unusual things in our lives. He's looking for people who will trust Him with their whole hearts. He's looking for people who won't limit Him with their small-minded thinking.

God has promised that He will turn your challenges into stepping-stones for promotion.

You may say, "Joel, I'm just an ordinary person. How could God ever use me? What could I ever do?"

Friend, God uses ordinary people like you and me to do extraordinary things. God is not looking for great power. He's not looking for great education. God is simply looking for a willing heart. God is not looking for ability; He's looking for availability. Just give God what you have. If you'll give God the little that you do have, He'll take that and multiply it and increase it. And He'll make more out of your life than you've ever dreamed possible. God's plan for your life is so much bigger and so much greater than you can imagine.

I'm convinced that one day we will look back at what we considered to be the worst thing that could happen to us, and we'll realize that God used even that time of adversity to refine us, mold us, shape us, and prepare us for good things to come. Interesting, isn't it? Adversity often pushes us into our divine destiny.

Adversity often pushes us into our divine destiny.

And sometimes we need a push! Had God not pushed me out of my comfort zone, I would probably still be behind the scenes today. God wants us to constantly be growing, and sometimes He'll use a little adversity or some tension to get us moving forward. He will allow pressure to push you, to stretch you, to get you out of your comfort zone. He knows just how much you can take, and in your times of distress, keep in mind, God is enlarging you. The struggle is giving you strength. Furthermore, God knows the gifts and talents that He has placed within each one of us. He knows what you are capable of, and He's going to do everything necessary to get you into your divine destiny. You'll be amazed at what you can accomplish when God puts a little pressure on and you get out of that safe zone and step over into the *faith* zone.

PART 6

LIVE TO GIVE!

CHAPTER 25

The Joy of Giving

One of the greatest challenges we face in our quest to enjoy our best lives now is the temptation to live selfishly. Because we believe that God wants the best for us, that He wants us to prosper, that we have the favor of God, and that He has much more in store, it is easy to slip into the subtle trap of selfishness. Not only will you avoid that pitfall, but you will have more joy than you dreamed possible when you *live to give*, which is the sixth step to living at your full potential.

Society teaches us to look out for number one. "What's in it for me? I'll help you, but what will I get in return?" We readily acknowledge this as the "me" generation, and that same narcissism sometimes spills over into our relationship with God, our families, and one another.

Many people nowadays are blatantly and unashamedly living for themselves. They're not interested in other people. They don't have time to help others in need. They focus only on what they want, what they need, what they feel will most benefit themselves. Ironically, this selfish attitude condemns them to living shallow, unrewarding lives. No matter how much they acquire for themselves, they are never satisfied.

Friend, if you want to experience a new level of God's joy, if you want Him to pour out His blessings and favor in your life, then you're going to have to get your mind off yourself. You must learn to be a giver and not a taker. Quit trying to figure out what everybody can do for you, and start trying to figure out what you can do for somebody else. We were not made to function as self-involved people, thinking only of ourselves. No, God created us to be givers. And you will never be truly fulfilled as a human being until you learn the simple secret of how to give your life away.

You must learn to be a giver and not a taker.

When I'm tempted to be upset or worried, or when I lose my joy, the first thing I ask myself is, "What am I focused on? Where is the emphasis? What am I thinking about?" Nine times out of ten I'm thinking about *my* problems. I'm thinking about some concern or frustration in my life. I'm thinking about what I must do tomorrow. When I get all caught up in *me*, it's a formula for depression and discouragement. We must learn to get our focus off ourselves. The late singer Keith Green said it well: "It's so hard to see when my eyes are on me."

We Were Created to Give

You may not realize it, but it is extremely selfish to go around always dwelling on your problems, always thinking about what you want or need, and hardly noticing the many needs of others all around you. One of the best things you can do if you're having a problem is to help solve somebody else's problem. If you want your dreams to come to pass, help someone else fulfill his or her dreams. Start sowing some seeds so God can bring you a harvest. When we meet other people's needs, God always meets our needs.

I met a man not too long ago who was extremely disgruntled with life, disappointed with God and himself. He had been highly successful at one time, but through a series of poor choices, he lost his business, his family, his home, and his entire life savings. Now, he was basically living out of his car.

He was deeply depressed, so I attempted to cheer him up and encourage him. After I finished praying for him, I gave him some practical advice. "Listen, sir, you've got to get your mind off your problems," I told him. "Get your mind off the mistakes you've made and all the things you've lost." I told him, "If you really want to be happy, if you really want to be restored, you've got to change your focus and go out and help somebody else in need. You've got to sow some seeds.

"Do you know that no matter how big your problem is today, somebody else has a bigger problem, a tougher road, a more heartrending story than yours? You can help make a difference in somebody's life. You can help ease somebody's burden. You can cheer somebody up, and give somebody a fresh new hope."

The man promised that he would take my advice. He connected with some men at Lakewood who help people overcome addictions. Instead of moping in his car, thinking about what a failure he was, he began spending his time helping to care for those drug addicts. He became a friend to many of the addicts, listening to their struggles, encouraging them, praying for them, and challenging them to believe for a better life. He became a giver.

He showed up at church a few weeks later, and I'll never forget seeing him walk through the front lobby. He was beaming with joy. He had a smile from ear to ear. I said, "Hey, man, you look great. What's going on?"

He said, "Joel, I've spent the last two weeks taking care of cocaine addicts, and I've never had so much joy in all my life." He wiped a tear from his eye as he said, "I've never been so fulfilled." He said, "I spent my whole life living for myself, building my career, doing what I wanted to do, whatever I thought would bring me happiness. But now I see what really matters."

We were created to give, not to simply please ourselves. If you miss that truth, you will miss the abundant, overflowing, joy-filled life that God has in store for you.

Interestingly, my new friend went on to tell me how that week somebody had come by and offered him a job. He was moving out of his car and into an apartment. On and on, he related the great things that had begun happening to him in just a matter of weeks since he became a giver rather than a taker. And it all started when he got his mind off himself and began to help other people.

When you reach out to other people in need, God will make sure that your own needs are supplied. If you're lonely today, don't sit around feeling sorry for yourself. Go help someone else who is lonely. If you're down and discouraged, don't focus on your own need. Get your mind off yourself and go help meet someone else's need. Go visit the nursing home or a children's hospital. Call a friend and encourage that person. You need to sow some seed so God can bring you a harvest.

If you are believing for your child to find God, go help somebody else's child to develop a relationship with God. If you're struggling financially, go out and help somebody who has less than you have.

You may say, "Joel, I don't have anything to give." Sure you do! You can give a smile. You can give a hug. You can mow somebody's lawn. You can bake somebody a cake. You can visit someone in the hospital or in a senior citizens' center. You can write somebody an encouraging letter. Somebody needs what you have to share. Somebody needs your smile. Somebody needs your love. Somebody needs your friendship. Somebody needs your encouragement. God didn't make us to function as "Lone Rangers." He created us to be free, but He did not intend for us to be independent of each other. We really do need one another.

A Rescuing Hug

I heard an amazing story about a set of twins who were just a few days old. One of them had been born with a serious heart condition and wasn't expected to live. A few days went by and one baby's health continued to deteriorate; she was close to death. A hospital nurse asked if she could go against hospital policy and put the babies in the same incubator together, rather than in individual incubators. It was a big ordeal, but finally the doctor consented to allow the twins to be placed side by side in the same incubator, just as they had been in their mother's womb.

Somehow, the healthy baby managed to reach over and put her arm around her little sick sister. Before long, and for no apparent reason, her heart began to stabilize and heal. Her blood pressure came up to normal. Her temperature soon followed suit. Little by little she got better, and today they are both perfectly healthy children. A newspaper caught wind of the story and photographed the twins while still in the incubator, embraced in a hug. They ran the photo with the caption "The Rescuing Hug."

Friend, somebody needs your hug today. Somebody needs your love. Somebody needs to feel your touch. You may not realize it, but there is healing in your hands. There is healing in your voice. God wants to use you to bring hope, healing, love, and victory to people wherever you go. If you'll dare to take your mind off your troubles, get your mind off your own needs and, instead, seek to be a blessing to other people, God will do more for you than you could even ask or think.

Focus on Being a Blessing

Don't live a self-centered life. You have so much to give, so much to offer. When you center your life around yourself, not only do you miss out on God's best, but you rob other people of the joy and blessings that God wants to give them through you. The Scripture says, "We should encourage one another daily."[1] It's easy to criticize and condemn, to point out everyone's flaws and failures. But God wants us to build people up, to be a blessing, speaking words of faith and victory into their lives.

"Joel, I don't have the time," I hear you saying. "I'm so busy."

How long does it take to give somebody a compliment? How long does it take to tell your wife, "I love you. You're great. I'm glad you're mine." How long does it take to tell your employee, "You are doing a fine job. I appreciate your hard work."

It's not enough to think kind compliments; we need to express them. As the old saying puts it: "Love is not love until you give it away." We should get up each morning with an attitude that says: *I'm going to make somebody else happy today. I'm going to help meet somebody else's need.* Don't go through life as a taker; become a giver.

"But, Joel, I have so many problems and so many needs of my own . . ."

Yes, but if you get your mind off your problems and begin to help others, you won't have to worry about your needs. God will take care of them for you. Something supernatural happens when we get our eyes off ourselves and turn them to the needs of those around us.

The Old Testament teaches, "When you feed the hungry, when you clothe the naked, when you encourage the oppressed, then your life is going to break forth like the dawn. Then your healing is going to quickly come."[2] In other words, when you reach out to hurting people, that's when God is going to make sure your needs are supplied. When you focus on being a blessing, God makes sure that you are always blessed in abundance.

I'll never forget what my mother did when she was diagnosed with terminal cancer back in 1981. After she got out of that hospital, she could easily have come home and just sunk into a deep pit of depression. But Mother didn't do that. She didn't stay focused on herself. She didn't constantly dwell on that sickness. In her time of greatest need, in the darkest hour of her life, what did she do? She went to church and prayed for other people who were sick or in need. She sowed those seeds of healing. And just as the Scripture says, as she began to help other people in need, her light broke forth like the dawn, and her own healing came.

I'm convinced that many people would receive the miracle they have been praying about if they would simply turn their attention away from themselves, away from their own needs and problems, and start to focus on being a blessing to other people. All too often we spend most of our time trying to be blessed. "God, what can You do for me? God, here's my prayer list. Can I have it by next Tuesday?"

We should concentrate more on being a blessing than trying to be blessed. We need to look for opportunities to share God's love, His gifts, and His goodness with others. The truth is, the more you help others, the more God will make sure that you are helped.

Let's get practical. If you have things lying around your house or in storage that you are never going to use again, why not give those things away to someone who could use them? Those extra things aren't doing you any good stacked in your attic, basement, or garage. If it's not meeting a need, turn it into a seed!

If it's not meeting a need, turn it into a seed!

A few years back I bought an expensive top-of-the-line, state-of-the-art push lawn mower. I was so proud of that lawn mower. Then, about that time, my dad went to be with the Lord, and a lot of things changed in my life. I became a pastor and my schedule became much busier. So busy, in fact, that I didn't have time to mow my own lawn anymore. I had to hire someone to do it.

I stored my state-of-the-art lawn mower in my garage with all my other lawn equipment. Every time I pulled my car into the garage, I could see it and enjoy it.

One day as I pulled into the garage I heard a voice deep inside saying, *Joel, you ought to give away all that lawn equipment.*

My first reaction was, *Hey! Wait a minute. I paid a lot of money for that lawn mower. I've hardly even used it. It's brand new. Besides I may need it again one day. What if I get fired?*

Our minds can conjure up all kinds of excuses when God begins unclasping our sticky fingers. Human nature wants to hold on to everything. So, being the deeply spiritual man that I am, I totally ignored that voice.

Week after week went by, and every time I pulled into my garage, I felt convicted. There was my brand-new lawn mower—hardly used— and it was not doing anybody a bit of good. There was my leaf blower, my weed-eater, and my edger. There was all that other wonderful lawn-care stuff.

I knew I was never going to use it again. I knew that twenty years from now it would probably still be sitting there. But I just couldn't bear the thought of giving away something so new, something I loved so much. After all, I had hardly even used it!

I pulled into the garage another day, and I heard the voice again: *Joel, you either give that lawn mower away, or you're going to start mowing your own lawn again.*

I gave it away less than thirty minutes later!

You probably have some items like that lying around your house as well. Clothes you haven't worn in years, cooking utensils still packed in boxes from your last move, books, your children's crib and baby clothing, and all sorts of other things that you haven't used in ages! Most clutter experts say, "If you haven't used an item within the past year, give it away!" If it's not meeting a need, turn it into a seed. Remember, we will reap what we sow. When you do good for other people, that's when God is going to make sure that His abundant blessings overtake you.

If you want to live your best life now, you must develop a lifestyle of giving: living to give instead of living to get. Have an attitude that says, *Who can I bless today?* rather than *How can I get blessed today?*

To catch monkeys years ago, hunters would take a large barrel and fill it with bananas and other treats appealing to monkeys. Then they'd cut a hole in the side, just large enough that the monkey could barely get his hand and his arm through it. The monkey would reach in the barrel and grab one of those treats. But when he clenched his fist, it would be too big to back out of the hole. That monkey would be so stubborn and so intent on holding on to what he had in his hand, even when his captors converged on him, he wouldn't turn it loose. He was easy prey for the men with the nets.

Sadly, monkeys are not alone when it comes to selfishness. Many people live like that, too. They live with their hands clenched. They are so focused on holding on to what they have, they don't realize that it is robbing them of the freedom and the abundant blessings that God has in store for them. They are selfish with their money, with their resources, and with their time.

How about you? Are you so focused on getting what you want, what you need, that you don't obey that still, small voice when God tells you to bless others? Open your hands; don't hold on so tightly. God will not fill a closed fist with good things. Be a giver, rather than a taker. You won't have to look far before you find someone you can help. There's a whole world out there that's crying out for help. You have an opportunity to live unselfishly, displaying the character of God. God is a giver, and you are never more like God than when you give.

God promised the Old Testament patriarch Abraham, "I will bless you [with abundant increase of favors] and make your name famous and distinguished, and you will be a blessing."[3] We often read such promises, and say, "All right, God! Come on; pour out Your blessings on me!" But notice, there's a catch. We must do something; better yet, we must *be* something. God is implying that we will not be blessed simply so we can live lavishly or self-indulgently. We will be blessed *to be* a blessing. Indeed, unless we are willing to be a blessing, God will not pour out His favor and goodness in our lives. We will receive from God in the same measure we give to others.

"But Joel, you just don't understand. I don't have anything to give. I don't have a lawn mower lying around like you did."

Perhaps not. But it all depends on your attitude. You must be faithful in the little you have right now before God will bless you with more. A lot of people say, "God, when are You going to bless me?" But if we'd listen more carefully, maybe we'd hear God saying, "When are you going to start *being* a blessing?"

Whatever you give will be given back to you.

Giving is a spiritual principle. Whatever you give will be given back to you. If you give a smile, you will receive smiles from others. If you are generous to people in their time of need, God will make sure that other people are generous to you in your time of need. Interesting, isn't it? What you make happen for others, God will make happen for you.

Live to Give

I saw an interesting report about a young man in Saudi Arabia. He was extremely wealthy and lived in an ornate palace almost too grand to describe. He had scores of automobiles and airplanes. He owned several cruise ships just for his personal use. The man was rich beyond anything my mind could fathom.

But what intrigued me about him was the interesting way in which he used part of his wealth. Every couple of months or so, he would bring in hundreds of poor people from his country. He met with them individually and discussed their needs. Then, in most cases, he would give the people whatever they needed. If they needed a car, he would buy them a car. If they needed a home, he would buy them a home. If they needed money for an operation, he provided that as well. Whatever the need, he would meet it. He gave away hundreds of thousands of dollars and literally millions more in property and materials. Is it any wonder why his business continues to flourish?

I doubt that the Saudi man practices the Christian faith, but the principles of giving are spiritual principles. They work regardless of nationality, skin color, or even religion. If you give unselfishly, it is going to be given back to you. If you meet other people's needs, God will make sure your own needs are supplied in abundance.

The Bible says, "When you help the poor you are lending to the Lord."[4] That Saudi man has developed a lifestyle of giving, especially to the poor, and not surprisingly, that which he sows comes back to him exponentially. He has lent to God by helping the poor, and God will not be in debt to any person.

You may be thinking, *Well, if I had all that money, I would do the same thing.*

No, that's where you miss it. You have to start right where you are. You must be faithful with what you have, then God will trust you with more. You may not have a lot of extra money to give, but you can buy somebody's dinner every once in a while. You can give somebody a kind word. You can go out of your way to pray for somebody in need.

Now is the time to develop an attitude of giving. Friend, the closest thing to the heart of our God is helping hurting people. God loves when we sing and when we pray. He loves when we come together to celebrate His goodness. But nothing pleases God any more than when we take care of one of His children. Jesus said, "If you even give as much as a cup of water to somebody in need, I see it and I'm going to reward you." He said, "Inasmuch as you did it to one of the least of these My brethren, you did it to Me."[5]

Somebody needs what you have to give. It may not be your money; it may be your time. It may be your listening ear. It may be your arms to encourage. It may be your smile to uplift. Who knows? Maybe just like that little baby, putting your arm around somebody and letting him or her know that you care can help begin to heal that person's heart. Maybe you can give a rescuing hug.

John Bunyan, author of the classic book *The Pilgrim's Progress,* said, "You have not lived today until you have done something for someone who cannot pay you back." Make a decision that you will live to give. Be on the lookout each day for somebody you can bless. Don't live for yourself; learn to give yourself away, and your life will make a difference.

CHAPTER 26

Showing God's Kindness and Mercy

How we treat other people can have a great impact on the degree of blessings and favor of God we are experiencing in our lives. Are you good to people? Are you kind and considerate? Do you speak and act with love in your heart and regard other people as valuable and special? Friend, you can't treat people poorly and expect to be blessed. You can't be rude and inconsiderate and expect to live in victory.

Are you good to people?

The Bible says, "See that none of you repays another evil for evil, but always aim to show kindness and seek to do good to one another and to everybody."[1] Notice the words *aim* and *seek* in this verse. God is saying we must be proactive. We should be on the lookout to share His mercy, kindness, and goodness with people. We must aim for kindness and seek to do good. Moreover, we need to be kind to people even when they don't deserve it. We need to walk in love and be courteous even when somebody is unkind to us.

When that coworker walks by you and doesn't give you the time of day, God expects you to go the extra mile and be friendly to him anyway. If you are on the phone and somebody speaks harshly or is discourteous to you, it's easy to think, *I'll just tell her off and then hang up. She doesn't know me. She's never going to see me.* But God expects us to be bigger and better than that.

When that checker at the grocery store jumps down your throat for no reason, your initial response may be to act rudely in return. That's the easy way; anybody can do that. But God wants us to live by higher standards. The Bible says, "We are to love our enemies. We are to do good to them that spitefully use us." Daddy often said, "Everybody deserves to have a bad day once in a while." We've got to give people room to have a bad day.

If somebody flies off the handle at you, instead of retaliating and giving them a piece of your mind, why not show them some of God's grace and mercy? Aim for kindness and give them a word of encouragement. After all, you don't know what they may be going through. That person's child may be in the hospital. His or her mate may have just walked out; they may be living in hell on earth. If you return their venom with more vitriol, you could escalate the conflict, or your response could be the final straw that causes them to give up and sink into utter despair. Neither scenario is pleasing to God.

When you are placed in awkward situations where somebody doesn't treat you right, you have a golden opportunity to help heal a wounded heart. Keep in mind, hurting people often hurt other people as a result of their own pain. If somebody is rude and inconsiderate, you can almost be certain that they have some unresolved issues inside. They have some major problems, anger, resentment, or some heartache they are trying to cope with or overcome. The last thing they need is for you to make matters worse by responding angrily.

Evil is never overcome by more evil. If you mistreat people who are mistreating you, you will make matters worse. When you express anger to somebody who has been angry with you, it's like adding fuel to a fire. No, we overcome evil with good. When somebody hurts you, the only way you can overcome it is by showing them mercy, forgiving them, and doing what is right.

Keep taking the high road and be kind and courteous. Keep walking in love and have a good attitude. God sees what you're doing. He sees you going the extra mile to do what's right, and He will make sure your good actions and attitude will overcome that evil. If you'll keep doing the right thing, you will come out far ahead of where you would have been had you fought fire with fire.

The Bible says, "God is our vindicator." He will not let you lose out. You may think you're getting the short end of the stick, but when it's all said and done, God will make sure that you don't lose anything truly valuable. Moreover, He'll make sure you get your just reward. Your responsibility is to remain calm and peaceable even when those around you are not.

Overcome Evil with Good

I called a restaurant one night to order a pizza. I often ordered pizzas from this particular establishment, and each time I placed an order, the clerk asked for my phone number. I got in the habit of giving them my phone number right up front so we could save a bit of time.

On this night, a woman answered the phone. I politely said, "Hello, my phone number is 713 . . ."

"Sir, I am not ready for your phone number," the woman snarled into the phone. "And when I get ready for your phone number, I will ask you for your phone number!"

I could hardly believe that someone working with the public could be so cantankerous and rude. My initial instinct was to respond, "Listen, lady! I'll give you my phone number whenever I feel like it. I'll call you at midnight with my phone number if I want to!" My mind instantly considered ordering about twenty or thirty pizzas and sending them to the wrong addresses. In my imagination, I could see that lady running all over town attempting to deliver pizzas to people who hadn't ordered them!

Fortunately, I was able to maintain my composure. I kept telling myself, *You are the pastor of a church. Behave!*

I don't always do what's right, but in this case, I made a decision that I was going to overcome evil with good. I recognized that the woman was just having a bad day; something was bothering her that had nothing to do with me or my phone number. I decided I was going to be a part of the solution rather than part of the problem. I took her on as a personal mission project, determined that I would do whatever I could to cheer her up.

I began by complimenting her work. (I had to really use my imagination!) I said, "You make the best pizzas in the world. I've been ordering from you folks for years, and your food is wonderful. Your delivery is great; you are always on time; you're running a first-class operation." On and on I went, trying to encourage her. I said, "I appreciate your being so efficient and answering the phone so quickly.

And I'll tell you, when I talk to your boss, I'm going to recommend that he give you a raise." By the time I got through, she not only took my phone number, she threw in some hot wings and sodas and coupons for more pizza!

That's overcoming evil with good. I didn't know what she was dealing with at work or what she was going through at home. Who knows what was going on in her personal life? But it wasn't hard to figure out that she was having a bad day. She needed somebody to encourage her, to cheer her up, to let her know that she mattered, and to tell her she was good at her job. That pizza order was a small matter, but it was a giant opportunity for me to share God's kindness with a woman who needed it.

The Bible says, "Love overlooks a person's faults."[2] That's not always easy, but love believes the best in every person. Anybody can return evil for evil, but God wants His people to help heal wounded hearts.

Anybody can return evil for evil, but God wants His people to help heal wounded hearts.

If somebody is not treating you right today, go out of your way to be kinder than usual to that person. If your husband is not serving God, don't go around beating him over the head with your Bible, preaching at him, nagging him, coercing him to come to church with you. No, just start being extra kind to him. Start loving him in a fresh way. The Bible says, "It is the goodness of God that leads people to repentance." If you will be extra good and inordinately kind, before long God's goodness expressed through you will overcome that evil. Friend, love never fails.

If anybody had a right to return evil instead of love, it was Joseph, the famed young man with the coat of many colors. His brothers hated him so much they threw him into a deep pit and were going to kill him, but "out of the kindness of their hearts" they decided instead to sell him into slavery. Years went by, and Joseph experienced all sorts of troubles and heartaches. But Joseph kept a good attitude, and God continued to bless him. After thirteen years of being in prison for a crime he didn't even commit, God supernaturally promoted him to the second highest position in Egypt.

Joseph was in charge of the food supply when a famine struck the land, and his brothers traveled to Egypt, hoping to buy provisions for their families. At first they didn't recognize Joseph. Joseph finally said, "Don't you know who I am? I am Joseph, your brother. I'm the one you threw into the pit. I'm the one you tried to kill, the brother you sold into slavery."

Can you imagine what was going through his brothers' minds? Imagine the fear that must have gripped their hearts! This was Joseph's opportunity to pay back his brothers for the years of pain and suffering they had caused him. Now their lives were in his hands.

Joseph could have ordered them killed or imprisoned for life. But Joseph said, "Don't be afraid. I'm not going to harm you. I'm going to do good to you. I'm going to give you all the food you need."

Is it any wonder why Joseph was so blessed? No wonder God's hand of favor was on him in such a strong way. Joseph knew how to extend mercy. Joseph knew how to treat people right.

The Bible says, "Love doesn't hold a grudge. Love doesn't harbor unforgiveness."[3] You may have people in your life who have done you great wrong, and you have a right to be angry and bitter. You may feel as though your whole life has been stolen away by somebody who has mistreated you or deceived you. But if you will choose to let go of your grudge and forgive them, you can overcome that evil with good. You can get to the point where you can look at the people who have hurt you and return good for evil. If you do that, God will pour out His favor in your life in a fresh way. He will honor you; He will reward you, and He'll make those wrongs right.

When you can bless your worst enemies and do good to those who have used or abused you, that's when God will take that evil and turn it around for good. No matter what you've gone through, no matter who hurt you or whose fault it was, let it go. Don't try to get even. Don't hold a grudge. Don't try to pay them back. God says show mercy. Aim for kindness. Seek to do good.

You may be thinking, *But Joel, that's just not fair!*

No, it's not. But life is not fair. We have to remember that God is the one keeping the score. He is in control. And when you bless your enemies, you will never lose. God will always make it up to you.

Go the Extra Mile

God told Abraham to pack up his family and head toward a better land. Abraham moved all his flocks, his herds, his family, and even his extended family members. They traveled for months and finally made it to their new land. After living there for a while, they discovered that the portion of land where they settled wasn't able to support them with enough food and water for all the people and their flocks and herds.

Abraham said to his nephew Lot, "We need to split up." He said, "You choose whichever part of the land you would like to have, and I'll take whatever is left." Notice how kind Abraham was to his nephew. Lot looked around and saw a beautiful valley with luscious green pastures and rolling hills and ponds. He said, "Abraham, that's what I want. That's where my part of the family will settle."

Abraham said, "Fine; go and be blessed." Abraham could have said, "Lot, you're not going to have that land. That's the best land. I've done all the work. I've led this journey. God spoke to me, not to you. I should get the first choice." Abraham didn't do that. He was bigger than that. He knew God would make it up to him.

But I'm sure after Abraham realized what was left over for him, he was disappointed nonetheless. His portion was arid, barren, desolate wasteland. Think of it; Abraham had traveled a long distance. He'd gone to great effort in search of a better land, in search of a better life. Now, because of his generosity and kind heart, he was relegated to living on the scruffy part of the land. I'm sure he thought, *God, why do people always take advantage of my goodness? God, why do I always get the short end of the stick? That boy Lot wouldn't have had anything if I hadn't given it to him.*

Maybe you feel that you're the one who's doing all the giving in some situation. Perhaps you are the parent of an ungrateful child. Maybe your former spouse is taking advantage of you in a divorce settlement. Possibly your company is talking about "downsizing" after you have given them the best years of your life. Perhaps you are the one who's always going the extra mile. You're the peacemaker in the family. Because people know you are kind, generous, and friendly, they tend to take advantage of you or not appreciate you.

But God sees your integrity. Nothing that you do goes unnoticed by

God. He's keeping the records, and He will reward you in due time. That's what He did for Abraham.

In essence, God told Abraham, "Because you preferred your brothers, because you treated your relative kindly, because you went the extra mile to do what is right, I'm not going to give you a small portion of land; I'm going to give you an abundant blessing. I'm going to give you thousands and thousands of acres; miles and miles of land. All that you can see is going to be yours."

Don't grow weary in well doing. God is a just God, and He sees not just what you are doing but why you are doing it. God judges our motives as well as our actions. And because of your unselfishness, because you prefer others, because you're aiming for kindness, one day God will say to you as He did to Abraham, "As far as you can see, I'm going to give it to you."

Sometimes when we're good to people and we go the extra mile, we have a tendency to think, *I'm letting people walk all over me. I'm letting them take advantage of me. They're taking what rightfully belongs to me.*

That's when you have to say, "Nobody is taking anything from me. I am freely giving it to them. I'm blessing them on purpose, knowing that God is going to make it up to me."

Think of the biblical story of Ruth. Her mother-in-law, Naomi, was an older woman who had just lost her husband. Ruth and another daughter-in-law named Orpha lived with Naomi because their husbands had also died. When Naomi lost her husband, she told those young women, "I'm going to move back to my homeland. Why don't you do the same thing and just get on with your lives?" Orpha took Ruth's advice and went her own way. But Ruth wouldn't do that.

She said, "Naomi, I'm not going to leave you all alone. You need somebody to take care of you. I'm going to watch after you. I'm going to stay close to you."

When Naomi and Ruth moved to Naomi's homeland, they had no provision there. They had no money and nothing to eat. So each day Ruth went into the wheat fields and followed behind the reapers who were harvesting the crop. She picked up any leftover wheat and grain that fell on the ground. She was finding just a little here, a bit there.

Then at night, Ruth and Naomi would make a meal from the gleanings of wheat. It wasn't much, but the women were able to survive.

God saw Ruth out there working hard in the fields trying to take care of Naomi. God knew that Ruth could have taken care of herself, selfishly living her own life. God knew she had nothing to gain by being concerned about the older woman. And because of her acts of kindness and her good-heartedness, God instructed a man by the name of Boaz, the owner of all those fields, to help her. He said, "Boaz, tell your workers to leave handfuls of wheat and handfuls of grain behind for Ruth." Now, when Ruth went out to the fields, she gathered up more than she could handle. She was blessed in abundance.

God sees your acts of kindness and mercy as well. When you are kind to people, when you go around doing good to people, God arranges for others to leave behind "handfuls" of good things for you. You will find a handful of blessings over here, a handful of blessings over there, supernatural favors over here, an unexpected promotion over there. Everywhere you go, you will discover the supernatural blessings of God lying in your path, left there for you by God.

CHAPTER 27

Keep Your Heart of Compassion Open

When my dad and I were traveling overseas to a Third World country, our plane stopped to refuel on a small island out in the middle of nowhere. We had an hour layover, so we all got off the plane to stretch. The airport was nothing more than a makeshift building with a thatched roof and a few benches and a snack bar. I went over to get something to eat, and when I came back, I saw my dad talking to a bedraggled-looking guy who looked to be about my age.

I had noticed the fellow when I got off the plane. Actually, it was difficult not to notice him. He was lying on the floor outside the building, and it seemed obvious that he had been there for quite some time.

He and Daddy talked that whole hour while the plane was being serviced. When it came time for us to leave, I watched my dad pull out his wallet and give the young man some money. When we got back on the plane, I asked, "Daddy, what was that all about? What was that young man doing here? What's his story?"

He said, "Joel, he was headed back home to the States, but he ran out of money. He's been here for a couple of weeks, all alone, stranded. So I gave him enough money to get home."

Daddy's eyes welled with tears as he said, "When I got off the plane and saw him lying there on the ground, I had so much compassion for him. I just wanted to pick him up and hug him. I wanted to love and comfort him, and tell him that he was going to make it." He said, "All I could think about, Joel, was, *What if that was one of my sons? What if that was you? What if that was Paul? What if that was one of my daughters? How I would want somebody to help one of my children!*"

Daddy was sowing seeds of compassion and love. He was making a difference in the world. There's no telling what kind of impact he made on that young man's life. Who knows? Maybe that fellow had never before experienced the love of God and the goodness of God. But he'll never forget that moment. He'll never forget the time some stranger, just passing through on a plane, willingly gave him help in a hopeless situation. Perhaps, at his lowest moment, he'll remember that somebody cared for him, somebody was concerned, so surely there must be a God who loves him.

Seeds of God's goodness and compassion were planted in that young man's heart, and he'll never be the same. But notice, it all started out of a heart filled with compassion, when Daddy took time to listen to the young man's story.

The Ability to Empathize

One definition of *compassion* is simply "feeling what other people feel, being concerned, showing that you care." In other words, when you see somebody in need, you feel their pain. You take time to comfort them. When somebody is discouraged, you feel that discouragement. You take it to heart and you do your best to cheer them up. If you see somebody struggling financially, you don't just pat them on the back and give them a quick Scripture verse. No, you take time for them, and you do what you can to help. You have a genuine concern. You show them that you really care.

Everywhere you go these days people are hurting. People are discouraged; many have broken dreams. They've made mistakes, and now their lives are in a mess. They need to feel God's compassion and His unconditional love. They don't need somebody to judge and criticize them, or to tell them what they're doing wrong. (In most cases, they already know that!) They need somebody to bring hope, somebody to bring healing, somebody to show God's mercy. Really, they're looking for a friend, somebody who will be there to encourage them, who will take the time to listen to their story and genuinely care.

**This world is desperate to experience the love
and compassion of our God.**

This world is desperate to experience the love and compassion of our God. More than any other human attribute, I believe our world is crying out for people with compassion, people who love unconditionally, people who will take some time to help their fellow sojourners on this planet.

We're all so busy. We have our own priorities and important plans and agendas. Often, our attitude is: *I don't want to be inconvenienced. Don't bother me with your problems. I've got enough problems of my own.* But the Scripture says, "If anyone sees his brother in need yet closes his heart of compassion, how can the love of God be in him?"[1] Interesting, isn't it? God's Word implies that we each have a heart of compassion, but the question is whether it is opened or closed.

Furthermore, the Bible says, "We are to continually walk in love being guided by love and following love."[2] When God puts love and compassion in your heart toward someone, He's offering you an opportunity to make a difference in that person's life. You must learn to follow that love. Don't ignore it. Act on it. Somebody needs what you have.

Certainly, when God created us, He put His supernatural love in all of our hearts. He's placed in you the potential to have a kind, caring, gentle, loving spirit. You have the ability to empathize, to feel what other people are feeling. Because you were created in the image of God, you have the moral capacity to experience God's compassion in your heart. But too often, because of our own selfishness, we choose to close our hearts to compassion.

How can you tell if your heart is open or closed? Easy. Are you concerned about other people, or are you concerned about only yourself? Do you take time to make a difference, to encourage others, to lift their spirits, to make people feel better about themselves? Do you follow the flow of love that God puts in your heart toward somebody in need? Or are you too busy with your own plans?

If you want to live your best life now, you must make sure that you keep your heart of compassion open. We need to be on the lookout for people we can bless. We need to be willing to be interrupted and inconvenienced every once in a while if it means we can help to meet somebody else's need.

We need to be on the lookout for people we can bless.

If you study the life of Jesus, you will discover that He always took time for people. He was never too busy with His own agenda, with His own plans. He wasn't so caught up in Himself that He was unwilling to stop and help a person in need. He could have easily said, "Listen, I'm busy. I have a schedule to keep. I'm on My way to the next city, and I've already been delayed." But no, Jesus had compassion on people. He was concerned about what they were going through, and He willingly took the time to help. He freely gave of His life. I believe He demands nothing less from those who claim to be His followers today.

Many people are unhappy and are not experiencing life to its fullest because they've closed their hearts to compassion. They are motivated by only what they want and what they think they need. They rarely do anything for anybody else unless they have an ulterior goal in mind. They are self-involved and self-centered.

But if you want to experience God's abundant life, you must get your focus off yourself and start taking time to help other people. You must exhibit and express God's love and goodness wherever you go. You must be a person of compassion.

"But Joel, I've got so many problems," I hear you saying. "If I spend all my time helping other people, how am I ever going to get my problems solved and my needs met? When am I ever going to get my life straightened out?"

Take my word for this: If you will focus on meeting other people's needs, God will always make sure your needs are supplied. God will take care of your problems for you.

Take the Time to Listen

Interestingly, Jesus was very patient with people. He took the time to listen to their stories. He wasn't in a big hurry. He didn't try to see how quickly He could get rid of a person so He could move on to somebody more important or do what He wanted to do. Instead, He patiently took the time to listen to each person's struggles. And He did what was necessary to meet their needs.

Sometimes if we would just take the time to listen to people, we could help initiate a healing process in their lives. So many people today have hurt and pain bottled up inside them. They have nobody they can talk to; they don't really trust anybody anymore. If you can open your heart of compassion and be that person's friend—without judging or condemning—and simply have an ear to listen, you may help lift that heavy burden. You don't have to know all the answers. You just need to care.

More than our advice, more than our instruction, people need our listening ears. Many people simply need somebody they can talk to, somebody with whom they can be honest. They just need a friend they can count on. You will be amazed at what a positive impact you can have in the world if you will just learn to be a good listener.

The other day a man came up to me and began telling me about his problem—in great detail. The person went on and on. About four or five times, I tried my best to jump in, to interrupt his monologue long enough to give him my expert advice, but I couldn't get an opening. I thought, *I have a wonderful piece of advice. I've got a great Scripture for you. I know exactly what you need to do.* I tried and tried, but I just could not get a word in edgewise. I kept listening and listening, looking all the while for my opportunity, but it never came. Finally, the fellow finished telling me all about his struggle, and just as I was about to give him my great wisdom, he let out a big sigh, and said, "Boy, I feel so much better. God just spoke to me and told me what to do." Then he turned around and walked away! I was so disappointed I almost ran after him.

Then I realized that he didn't need my profound wisdom; he didn't need my solution to his problem. He didn't need my advice; he just needed my ears to listen.

We need to learn to be better listeners. God can speak to people and tell them what to do while they're speaking to you about their struggle. Don't always be so quick to give your opinion. Be sensitive to what the real need is in the person you hope to help. Too frequently, what we really want to do is just shut them down, give them a quick word of encouragement, a semi-appropriate Scripture verse, and a fifteen-second prayer; then we can go on and do what we want to do. But God wants us to take time for people, to hear with our hearts, to show them we're concerned, to show them we really care.

Reaching Out

I used to feel compassion for people all the time, but I didn't know what it was. I thought I was just feeling sorry for them. But one day I realized that was God speaking to me, wanting me to pour out His love and show His mercy to people in need. Throughout life, God will lead us to people in need. If you are sensitive to it, you will discern His supernatural love welling up inside you, directing you toward a person or situation that God wants to help through you. But you must recognize what is happening and then follow that love. A lot of times we make God's leading too complicated. We all want God to speak to us, to lead us, to tell us where to go and to whom we should extend kindness, love, mercy, or some physical aid. We think we'll feel goose bumps or hear thunder in the heavens. But friend, when you feel love, you are feeling God. That's God talking to you. When you feel compassion toward someone, that's God's way of telling you to be a blessing to that person. Go encourage them. See how you can make his or her life better.

You may be in a crowded restaurant when, suddenly, you feel a tremendous concern and compassion for somebody sitting across the room. You sense a heavy burden for them, and you have a desire to help them. You may not even know that person, but you want his or her life to be better. That may well be God talking to you, prompting you to be a blessing to that person. Why not buy their dinner? Slip them a note and tell them that you're praying for them. Stop by their table to extend a word of encouragement. Do something to express the love that God is prompting within you.

Certainly, you must be discerning. Make sure that it is God prompting you and not some other motive. But more often than not, when you reach out with concern and compassion, your overture will not be squelched or rejected.

"Come on, Joel, those people in that restaurant are doing fine. They're over there laughing and having a good time. They look as though they don't have a problem in the world. They don't need my money. They're going to think I'm crazy if I pay for their dinner or tell them I'm praying for them."

Perhaps, but probably not. God would not give you such a strong level of compassion for them if they didn't need what you have to give.

They may be smiling on the outside, but you don't know what they're going through on the inside. Only God can see a person's heart. And God knows when people are hurting. He knows the people who are lonely. He knows the people who are about to make a wrong decision. And if you'll dare to step out in faith and reach out to them in love, letting them know you're concerned, you could be the one who helps turn a life around or keeps a person's life on the right course. You never know what one word of encouragement might do. You don't know the impact just one simple act of kindness might have.

A few years back, I woke up one morning and I had a real strong concern and compassion for an old friend of mine. I hadn't seen him in years, and hadn't talked to him for at least fifteen years, but he was one of my best friends growing up. We played a lot of sports and spent a lot of time together. All day long, I kept thinking about him, for no apparent reason. I was just hoping that he was doing okay.

It finally dawned on me that maybe God was speaking to me, and I needed to take action. I decided to give my old buddy a call to say hello and see how he was doing. I had no idea how to get in touch with him. But I finally tracked him down and called him.

My friend answered the phone, and I said, "Hey, man, this is Joel Osteen. I've been thinking about you all day long. How have you been doing?"

The phone went completely silent. Not a word. I thought, *This is very odd.* I didn't know what was going on, but I stayed on the line. After about fifteen or twenty seconds, I noticed that my buddy was all broken up on the other end of the line. I could tell that he was weeping. This fellow was one of the toughest athletes around as we were growing up. I had never seen him shed a tear. But he was now. When he finally composed himself, he said, "Joel, my wife just recently left me. And I've been so depressed and discouraged." He said, "I'm not a religious person, but I prayed, 'God, if You're still out there, if You really love me, if You're concerned at all, just give me some kind of sign.' And then the phone rang, and it was you."

God knows what He's doing. He knows who's hurting. He knows who's at the end of their rope. If you will follow that flow of love and compassion wherever it leads, you may be the answer to a desperate, lonely person's prayer. You may not fully realize the impact one brief phone call can have. You may not realize the significance of what it means to a hurting, lonely person to hear the words "I've been thinking about you. I've been concerned about you. I love you. I believe in you. I want to be praying for you. I'm going to stand with you." You may have forgotten how powerful and life-changing those simple words of hope can be. Let love lead you through life. Don't ever ignore that feeling of compassion inside you. Learn to follow the flow of God's divine love. He will direct your paths and show you where and how to express it.

Sometimes, you may have to risk appearing silly or superspiritual, or downright foolish, but it would be better to err on the side of being too compassionate than to miss a person for whom you may be the last hope. About fifteen years ago, during a service at Lakewood Church, my mother was at the podium sharing a Scripture and welcoming visitors as usual. Suddenly, Mother put her head down, and for no apparent reason, she began to weep. Sitting in the audience, my family and I wondered what was going on. Mother stood there silently for thirty or forty-five more seconds. Finally, she lifted her head and said, "Don't do it. Don't do it. Somebody here is about to do something you shouldn't do. Please, don't do it!"

It was a moving time in our service. The entire congregation spent a few minutes praying. About that time, we noticed a beautiful young lady walking from the very back of the auditorium. She was crying as she approached the front of the building. After talking with her, we discovered that she had been extremely depressed because she was pregnant and not married. Her mind was filled with torment to the degree that she felt her life just wasn't worth living. She had already written her suicide note and left it at home. But something told her to go to church one more time. She had not intended to change her mind, but Mother's words, "Don't do it. Don't do it," supernaturally pierced her heart. All at once, she realized God loved her. God was concerned about her. God had a future for her. That one moment saved her life and totally turned her life around.

How we need to learn to follow the flow of God's compassion! Had Mother thought, *Oh, that's silly. People will think I'm being overly dramatic or foolish*, a young woman and her baby may not be alive today.

God may be prompting you about somebody to whom you need to reach out. If somebody's name keeps coming up in your mind, and you feel compassion toward them, do something about it. Don't put it off; make a phone call; stop by to visit that person, or make contact in another appropriate manner.

"I'll pray for them privately," you may say. "Isn't that good enough?" It might be, if that is what God is directing you to do. But often, God wants you to do more than pray for them. He wants you to contact that person to whom He wants to express love and compassion. Perhaps He wants you to go see them face-to-face, to look them in the eye and tell them that God loves them and you love them. He may instruct you to put your arms around that "untouchable" person and let them feel your concern. If he or she is too far away, God may direct you to pick up the phone and let them hear your voice expressing His love for that person. Don't rule out a road trip, but if God leads you to travel to a distant location to express His love and compassion, He will provide specific, unequivocal directions.

You may be feeling a special love toward your parents. Perhaps you've been saying, "As soon as I get time, I'm going to visit them. As soon as I get through this busy season at work, as soon as my kids get a break from school, then I'm going to go." Don't put it off. We have to understand, when God's compassion rises up in us and we feel a special love toward someone, it is there for a specific reason. God didn't stimulate compassion within you for that person just because He was bored and didn't have anything else to do. No, God put that concern in your heart and mind on purpose. Now you need to respond to it. Recognize that although your understanding may be limited, God can see the future. He can see the big picture for our lives. We must learn to quickly follow that flow of compassion.

An Irreplaceable Moment

Early one morning a few years ago, I got a phone call from my dad. At that time, Daddy had been on kidney dialysis for about two months. He said, "Joel, I didn't sleep too much last night, and I really need to get up to the clinic to take dialysis. Can you come and take me?"

I said, "Sure, Daddy. I'll be right there." I looked at my watch and was surprised that it was around four o'clock in the morning. I quickly dressed and drove toward Mother and Daddy's home. As I was driving, I felt tremendous love and concern for my dad. Not a normal affection; it was a supernatural love. I began to think about how good Daddy had been to me, how proud I was to have him as my father, and how well he had always treated our family. I just had this extreme desire to express my love to my dad. He knew I loved him, but this was something different.

So early that morning, on the way to the clinic, I made sure my dad knew how much I loved him. I told him, "Daddy, I'm going to do everything I can to make your life better, to make your life more comfortable, to make you more proud of me."

Normally, when I took Daddy to dialysis, after he got all hooked up and the procedure was under way, there wasn't much else to do, so I would leave and then return to pick him up later. The dialysis procedure usually took four or five hours, so I would go to work, run errands, or simply go back home till Daddy was done. But this day, something down inside told me to stay with Daddy. I just pulled up a chair and decided I would visit with him and just be there for him.

I hadn't planned on taking Daddy to dialysis, so I had a lot of things scheduled for that day. But I just knew God wanted me to be there with my dad. Daddy eventually fell asleep, so I ran out and got us some breakfast and brought it back to the clinic. Daddy and I had a good time eating breakfast together and visiting. Finally, he finished the dialysis and I took him home.

As I was about to walk out the door of my parents' kitchen, Daddy called me back and gave me a great big hug. It wasn't his usual sort of hug. He hung on to me. He said, "Joel, you're the best son a father could ever hope to have." It was a real special moment between us. I felt that we really connected somehow. I felt that I had accomplished my goal of letting my dad know how much I loved him.

I left that morning feeling so good, knowing that Daddy knew I loved him, knowing that he was proud of me, and knowing that I had followed that flow of compassion toward him.

And that was the last time I ever saw my dad alive.

That was the last time I ever got to hug him, the last time I ever got to tell him I loved him. Later that same day, Daddy had a heart attack and unexpectedly went to be with the Lord.

Despite my grief and tears, I later thought, *God, how good You are to me. Here that whole time I thought I was following the flow of love for my dad's sake, just for his benefit. But now I realize You put that love in my heart just as much for my own sake.* How rewarded I feel today, knowing that on the last day of my dad's life, I was able to express my love to him. How fulfilled I feel, knowing that I have no regrets. There's nothing more I would have said, nothing I would have done differently. I'm at perfect peace.

But what if I would have been too busy that day? What if I had not followed that flow of compassion God put in my heart? What if I had not been sensitive to that love and followed after it and expressed my feelings to my dad? I would have missed out on something precious, an irreplaceable moment in history—Daddy's and my own.

Most of the time, when we reach out to other people, when we follow that flow of love, we think we're doing it for their sakes, for their benefit. But I can tell you firsthand, sometimes God puts that compassion in our hearts as much for our own benefit as for others'.

Keep your heart of compassion open.

Keep your heart of compassion open. Learn to be quick to follow that flow of love God puts in your heart. Be sensitive and obedient to do what God wants you to do. You won't be sorry—not now, or a million years from now!

CHAPTER 28

The Seed Must Lead

One of the main hindrances to living your best life now is selfishness. As long as you are focused on what you want, what you need, you will never experience God's best. But if you really want to thrive, you must learn to be a giver.

The Scripture says, "Whatsoever a man sows, that he will also reap."[1] All through the Bible, we find the principle of sowing and reaping. Just as a farmer must plant some seed if he hopes to reap the harvest, we, too, must plant some good seed in the fields of our families, careers, businesses, and personal relationships.

What if the farmer decided that he didn't really feel like planting, that he was tired, so he "felt led" to sit around and hope the harvest would come in? He'd be waiting around his whole life! No, he must get the seed in the ground. That's the principle God established. In the same way, if we want to reap good things, we, too, must sow some good seeds. Notice, we reap what we sow. If you want to reap happiness, you have to sow some "happiness" seeds by making other people happy. If you want to reap financial blessings, you must sow financial seeds in the lives of others. If you want to reap friendships, you should sow a seed and be a friend. The seed always has to lead.

The reason many people are not growing is because they are not sowing. They are living self-centered lives. Unless they change their focus and start reaching out to others, they will probably remain in that condition.

Some people say, "Joel, I've got a lot of problems. I don't care about sowing seeds. I want to know how I can get out of my mess." This *is* how you can get out of your mess. If you want God to solve your problems, help solve somebody else's problem. Get some seed in the ground!

FAMINE IN THE LAND

In biblical times, a great famine struck the land of Canaan. People didn't have any food or water, and they were in desperate need. So Isaac did something that people without insight may have thought rather odd: "In the middle of that famine, Isaac sowed a seed in the land. And in the same year he received one hundred times what he planted and the Lord rewarded him greatly."[2] In his time of need, Isaac didn't wait around, expecting someone else to come to his rescue. No, he acted in faith. He rose up in the midst of that famine and sowed a seed. God supernaturally multiplied that seed, and it brought him out of his need.

Maybe you are in some sort of famine today. It could be a financial famine; or maybe you're simply famished for friends. It's possible you need a physical healing. Perhaps you need peace in your home. Whatever the need, one of the best things you can do is to get your mind off yourself and help meet somebody else's need. If you're down and discouraged today, don't sit around feeling sorry for yourself. Go find somebody to cheer up. Sow some seeds of happiness. That's the way to receive a harvest. The seed always has to lead.

When you meet other people's needs, God has promised that He will make sure your needs are supplied. If you want to see healing and restoration come to your life, go out and help somebody else get well. The Bible says, "In times of difficulty, trust in the Lord and do good."[3] It's not enough to say, "God, I trust You. I know You are going to meet all my needs." That's tantamount to the farmer not planting any seeds and expecting a fabulous harvest. Scripture says there are two things we must do in times of trouble. First, we must trust in the Lord: and second, we must go out and do something good. Go out and sow some seeds. If you need a financial miracle, go buy somebody a cup of coffee tomorrow morning, or give a little extra in the offering at church. If you don't have any money, do some physical work for somebody;

mow somebody's lawn, pull some weeds, wash their windows. Make someone a pie. Do *something* to get some seed in the ground.

If you are lonely or lacking in friends, don't sit at home month after month, all alone, feeling sorry for yourself. Go to the nursing home and find someone else who is lonely whom you can befriend. Go to the hospital and find somebody you can cheer up. If you'll start sowing those seeds of friendship, God will bring somebody great into your life. When you make other people happy, God will make sure that your life is filled with joy.

We need to be more seed-oriented than need-oriented. In your time of need, don't sit around thinking about what you lack. Think about what kind of seed you can sow to get yourself out of that need.

Plant Some Seed

When I was a young boy, Lakewood Church launched its first building program. We didn't have much money, but there was a little Spanish church down the street in a building program, too. One Sunday morning my dad got up and announced to the congregation that we were going to take up a special offering, not for our new building, but for that little Spanish church. Several thousand dollars came in that morning, and we sent the check straight down the road. Truth is, we needed the money more than they did, but Daddy understood this principle. He knew he had to get some seed in the ground. He knew one of the best things he could do in that time of famine was to plant some seed. It wasn't long before we had all the money we needed to get to work on our building project. We built that building, plus several others, and down through the years, we've lived by that principle: In the time of need, sow a seed.

In the time of need, sow a seed.

An intriguing Scripture verse says, "It is possible to give away and become richer! It is also possible to hold on too tightly and lose everything. Yes, the liberal man shall be rich! By watering others, he waters himself."[4] Daddy understood that if he generously took care of others, God would take care of his own needs. The same goes for you. If you will focus on giving generously to others, God will make sure your own life is refreshed, even if you must go through a dry, dreary wilderness.

A few years back, Dan lost his beautiful wife of many years. He was heartbroken. But he decided instead of staying focused on his pain, hurt, and loss, he wanted to help somebody else. He was retired from the phone company, so he wasn't sure how his skills could benefit anyone else. He said, "All I really know how to do is comfort other people who have lost a loved one." His attitude was: *I've been there. I know what you are going through.*

Dan started showing up at funerals where my dad was conducting the service. He often had no personal connection with the grieving family; sometimes he didn't even know the person who had passed away, but he went to the funerals simply to encourage other people, to show them love and compassion. Over time, my dad noticed that Dan had a gift for comforting mourners. One day Daddy invited Dan to be a part of the church staff, and today, Daniel Kelley heads Lakewood's "Comfort Ministry."

Daniel didn't stay focused on his problems. He didn't develop the selfish attitude of: *Who's going to help me make my life better?* He was proactive and on the offensive. As he began to meet other people's needs, God began to turn his own situation around. Not only did God bring him through that difficult period, but recently, God brought a beautiful woman into his life. Now he and Shirley are happily married, and together they continue to sow seeds of God's goodness.

God will do something similar for you. If you'll dare to sow a seed in your time of need, God will do more than you can ask or think. I rely on this principle in my own life. When I'm tempted to feel discouraged, I turn my attention away from myself and go help somebody else. I like to go to the hospitals and visit people when I'm starting to feel low. If I don't have time to do that, I keep a stack of prayer requests right next to my desk.

Recently, I had one of those days where everything that could go wrong, did. I had some major disappointments. I came home drained and discouraged. I sat down in my favorite chair and started watching TV, just thinking about all my troubles. The more I thought, the worse I felt. Finally I decided to sow a seed in my time of need. I went to my office and found one of those prayer requests. I called a young man who had been in the hospital for several months. I couldn't recall meeting him before, but as I began to encourage him, I could feel my joy coming back. I could feel my spirit being lifted. By the time I hung up the phone, I was a new person. I felt like I could leap over a wall.

Friend, in your times of difficulty, don't sit around feeling sorry for yourself. Go sow a seed. Moreover, you don't need to wait until you have a problem before you start sowing. We should constantly be on the lookout for ways that we can be a blessing, not just when our backs are against the wall. We should get up each day looking for ways to help others. If you will do that, the Bible says God's blessings will chase you down and overtake you.

Granted, the temptation to be selfish is strong. Many good people get sucked into the trap of living with the attitude: *What's in it for me? How can you help me? How can you make my life better? How can you solve my problems?*

Our attitude should be just the opposite: *Whom can I bless today? Where is a need that I can meet? Whom can I encourage? Whom can I cheer up?*

I've made up my mind. I'm going to be a giver in life. I'm going to do something good. I am looking for opportunities to sow some seeds. Why? I've simply learned that planting seeds works! And I want to make sure that I keep my harvest coming in, in a big way.

Do Something Out of the Ordinary

Somebody once wrote to me, "Joel, I sure like that tie you wore last week on television." So I just boxed it up and mailed it to him. I thought, *That is too good an opportunity to pass up.* (Now, don't write me and tell me you like my suit, or the car I drive. That's cheating. You know my secret!)

You may say, "Joel, I could never do something like that, giving something to somebody simply because they paid me a compliment."

Fine, but do what you can do. You can give somebody a ride. You can call somebody and encourage them. You can go to the grocery store for an elderly person. You can do something. Start today!

Learn to stretch your faith. Do something out of the ordinary. If you want an extraordinary harvest, sow an extraordinary seed. Instead of sitting at home watching TV every night, why not spend some of that time doing something good for somebody else? Instead of going out to eat at an expensive restaurant, why not save that money and sow it as a seed? If you normally give 10 percent of your income, stretch your faith a bit and give 11 percent. Get a little more seed in the ground and watch what God will do. The Scripture says, "For with the same measure that you use, it will be measured back to you."[5] In other words, if you give with a teaspoon, it's going to be given back to you with a teaspoon. If you give with a shovel, it's going to be given back with a shovel. And if you give with a dump truck, you're going to get dump truck loads of blessings in your life!

The Bible clearly says, "He who sows sparingly will also reap sparingly, and he who sows bountifully will also reap bountifully."[6] If you're not satisfied with where you are in life, increase the amount of seed you are sowing. The size of your harvest depends on the amount of your seed. Certainly, some people live on limited incomes. It takes everything they have to make it each month. In my heart, I want to tell them, "Just hold on to what you have. You need that money." But I know that God's principles are true. And I know it is imperative that the people with the greatest need continue to sow.

Victoria and I were at a hotel eating breakfast one morning and a young man was waiting on us. When he brought our check, I opened it and found a note that said, "Thank you." He had paid for our breakfast.

My first thought was, *Oh, my! That's so nice of him, but he's just a young man. He's probably not making more than minimum wage. He needs this money a lot more than we do.*

Beyond that, our breakfast was included with the price of our hotel room! All we had to do was sign the check, and it would be free anyway.

What a dilemma! Victoria and I quietly discussed what we should do. She said "Joel, don't you think we should tell him, so maybe he could get his money back?"

"Well, we could, but I don't think we should," I said. "Even though we want to do that, we can't rob him of his blessing. He's planted a seed by doing something good for us. We don't want to pull his seed out of the ground and give it back. That would be doing him a disservice."

Although we knew he needed that money, we also knew that when he planted that seed in the ground, God was going to multiply it back to him. We knew God would give him a greater harvest. So we accepted his generous gift and whispered a prayer that God would bless him abundantly.

Understand, sowing seed is not a replacement for tithing. In fact, it is usually when you give over and above the first 10 percent of your income that this principle kicks into high gear. The Bible says, "The tithe is the Lord's. And it is holy." That means the first tenth of your income doesn't belong to you. It belongs to God and should be given to your local church. When you hold on to it, you're really robbing from God. So if you are not sowing at all, the tithe is a good place to start!

You may be thinking, *Joel, I just can't afford to tithe.* No, the truth is, you can't afford to *not* tithe. First, it would be foolish to try to rob God; and second, you need to get some seed in the ground. If you will dare to take a step of faith and start honoring God in your finances, He'll start increasing your supply in supernatural ways. God will take that 90 percent you have left over, and He'll cause it to go further than the 100 percent with which you started. The Scripture says that when we tithe, God not only opens up the windows of heaven, but He will rebuke the devourer for your sake.[7] That means He'll keep the enemy off your money, off your crop, off your children, and away from your home. He'll make sure you get promoted. He'll cause you to get the best deals in life. Sometimes, He'll keep you from sickness, accidents, and harm that might cause other unnecessary expenses. All kinds of blessings come your way when you honor God in the area of your finances.

You can't rob God and expect Him to bless you at the same time.

On the other hand, you can't rob God and expect Him to bless you at the same time. You must realize, God doesn't need your money or your time or your talent. When God asks us to give, it's not because He's trying to get something from us. No, it's because He's trying to get us to put some seed in the ground so we can reap a harvest. God abides by the laws He has established, and if you don't sow, you will not reap. It's as simple as that. But if you are faithful and do what God tells you to do, God will honor the law of reaping and sowing. You may not have a lot to give, but God will bless you if you start where you are.

Don't wait until you have more; start now. That's the way you will receive more from God. You sow some seed, and then God will bless you with more. Then you can sow a little more seed, and on and on. That's how you increase. But if you are not being faithful with what you have right now, how can God trust you with more?

The Scripture is not ambiguous about this matter. It says, "In everything you do, put God first, and he will direct you and crown your efforts with success."[8] If you want to prosper in your finances, put God first. If you want to prosper in your business, put God first. When you honor God, God will always honor you. And it's interesting, the only place in the Bible where God tells us to *prove* Him—which means to test Him, or check Him out—is in the area of our finances. If you will be faithful and show God that you're trustworthy with what you have right now, there's no limit to what God will do in your life.

CHAPTER 29

Sowing and Growing

The Dead Sea is one of the most fascinating bodies of water on Earth. The water is so dense, due to the high mineral content, even a nonswimmer can stay afloat. A human being can actually sit down in the water and read a newspaper without sinking. Bus tours of the area stop long enough for skeptical or adventurous tourists to take a dip. Problem is, when you come out of the water, nobody wants to sit next to you! The water reeks with a wretched smell.

Fed by Israel's Jordan River, the Dead Sea has no outlet. All the fresh water flowing into it becomes stagnant. While it is interesting to look at and fascinating to study, the water is undrinkable, polluted, and putrid.

That is a good picture of a person who lives selfishly, who is a taker but not a giver. God did not create us to be a reservoir that only collects. He created us to be a river that's constantly flowing. When we live selfishly, always receiving, always taking but never giving, we become stagnant and polluted. Putting it bluntly, our lives will start to stink. We'll go around with a sour attitude; we'll be no fun to be around, always irritable and hard to get along with. And it's all because nothing is flowing out of us. Yes, God wants to pour good things into your life, but if you want to live your best life now, you must learn to allow those good things to flow through you to others. As you do, your supply will be replenished and your life will maintain its freshness.

Stop hoarding what God has given you and start sharing it with others. Share your time, your energy, your friendships, your love, and your resources. If God has given you joy, share it with somebody else. Make someone else happy; cheer up another person; be a friend to somebody. If God has given you talent and the ability to make money, don't simply accumulate more for yourself; share those resources with others. Don't allow yourself to become stagnant. You must keep your river flowing. That's the way to truly prosper in life and be happy.

If God has given you joy, share it with somebody else.

"Joel, I have a lot of difficult issues in my life right now. When I get out of all these problems, then I'll go out and help somebody else."

You have it backward. Go help someone first, then God will begin to turn your situation around. Remember the fundamental principle: You must sow the seed first, then you will reap a harvest. If you want to get well, sow a seed by helping somebody else get well. If you want to be happy, help somebody else enjoy a little happiness. If you're having financial difficulty, give some money to someone in need, help the poor, or sow a little extra in the church offering. You must plant some seed if you are hoping for a harvest!

When you go through difficult times, because of the stress it's easy to focus only on your needs, on what's wrong in your life. But if you want the best stress relief of all, get your mind off yourself and go help somebody else. Something supernatural happens when we turn our attention away from our own needs to the needs of others. God's supernatural power seems to be activated by unselfish gestures. When you have a problem, don't concentrate on your need, think about what kind of seed you can sow to get you out of that problem.

Sow a Seed in Your Time of Need

Some first-century Christians were struggling to survive in the Greek town of Corinth. The Bible says, "The people were in deep poverty and deep trouble."[1] What did they do in their time of need? Did they complain and pout? Did they say, "God, why do we have so much trouble coming against us?" Not at all. The Scripture records, "In the midst of their great trouble, they stayed full of joy and they gave generously to others."[2] Notice they sowed a seed in their time of need. They knew if they would help to meet other people's needs, God would meet theirs.

In your times of difficulty, do just what they did. Number one, stay full of joy. Number two, go out and sow a seed. Help someone else, and you will be helped.

If you lost your job, don't sit around feeling sorry for yourself, go volunteer someplace. Sow a seed while you're waiting for that next door of opportunity to open. If you are believing for a better car, instead of complaining about the one you have, sow a seed by giving somebody a ride. If you are believing for your business to be blessed, help somebody else's business to grow. Do something to get some seed in the ground.

I read about a woman who wanted to start a new business—a mobile pet grooming shop. She thought, *I can't really afford to advertise, but I need to groom some dogs if I'm going to get this business going. What kind of seed can I sow to bring in some clients?* She decided to go down to her local SPCA dog shelter and groom the dogs for free so they would be more likely to be adopted. She did that month after month, and her business began to grow. Today, she has more clients than she can handle. Her business is so blessed, her customers have to book appointments three to four months in advance!

If you will sow an extraordinary seed, you will reap an extraordinary harvest. I'm sure when that woman first showed up at the SPCA wanting to groom the abandoned animals, people must have thought her a bit odd, or that she was an obsessed pet lover, but she didn't care. She knew she had to get some seed in the ground, so she was aggressive. She put some action behind her prayers. She didn't merely pray, "God, please prosper my new business." She rose up in faith and sowed a seed in her time of need, and God supernaturally increased her.

You may say, "Joel, I sure wish God would do that for me."

He can, but the question is: What seed are you putting in the ground? Are you giving God anything to work with? If not, start planning and start planting!

The Bible says, "Give generously, for your gifts will return to you later. Divide your gifts among many, for in the days ahead you yourself may need much help."[3] Notice, God is giving us a principle here that will cause us to have our needs supplied during those tough times that occasionally come. Give generously right now, because in the future you may need some help.

Picture it this way: When you give, you are storing up God's goodness and His favor so in your time of need, you'll have a great harvest out of which God can "draw" to meet your need. You may not have any pressing needs today. That's great! But don't let that stop you from giving. You need to prepare for the future. When you do have a need, God will be right there to help you out. Giving is similar to taking a preventive medicine. You are storing up God's goodness.

One fellow said to me, "Joel, I've given and given, but I don't ever seem to reap a harvest. I'm always on the giving end, never on the receiving end."

"Even if you don't see anything happening right now, don't get discouraged," I told him. "Don't quit giving. You've got to understand that you are storing up God's goodness, and God has promised that your generous gifts will come back to you. One day when you need them the most, they will be there to help you out."

I mentioned earlier about my dad's encounter with a young man who had been stranded at an airport in a foreign land. Daddy helped that young man by giving him some money to make his way back home. Daddy understood this principle of storing up God's goodness, and he knew if he would help somebody's child in their time of need, God would make sure that somebody would be there to help him and his children in a time of need.

A few years later we were in India, traveling by car. It was late at night, and we had been traveling for a couple of hours on our way back to the hotel when our car broke down. We were stranded out in the middle of nowhere. Although it was one or two o'clock in the morning, a crowd quickly gathered. Before we knew it, we had about fifty or sixty people surrounding us and staring at us. It was a rather tense situation since American "tourists" in that section of India were not a common sight, nor a welcome one. Worse yet, we didn't speak their language, so we were slightly nervous and concerned for our safety.

Suddenly, out of nowhere, we saw another car approaching, a large, luxury car, an especially unusual car for that part of India. We hadn't seen another car the whole time we had been waiting. The driver spotted us along the side of the road and stopped. When he found out what was going on, he came over to us, and we were surprised that he spoke English. In a kind, gentle voice, he said, "Don't be afraid. I'm going to take you where you need to go."

We had never seen that man before, but we got in the car with him. He drove us all the way back to our hotel, a five-hour drive! When we arrived safely back at our hotel, we wanted to pay him for his time and trouble, but he wouldn't hear of it.

I couldn't help but think about that young man my dad had rescued in the airport a few years earlier. Daddy had made an investment; he had stored up God's goodness. Daddy had sowed all those seeds. Now his generosity came back to him when he needed it.

God is keeping a record of every good deed you've ever done.

God is keeping a record of every good deed you've ever done. He is keeping a record of every seed you've ever sown. You may think it went unnoticed, but God saw it. And in your time of need, He will make sure that somebody is there to help you. Your generous gifts will come back to you. God has seen every smile you've ever given to a hurting person. He's observed every time you went out of the way to lend a helping hand. God has witnessed when you have given sacrificially, even giving money that perhaps you needed desperately for yourself or your family. God is keeping those records. Some people will tell you that it doesn't make any difference whether you give or not, or that it doesn't do any good. But don't listen to those lies. God has promised that your generous gifts will come back to you.[4] In your time of need, because of your generosity, God will move heaven and earth to make sure you are taken care of.

One day I was thinking about all the seeds our church has sown down through the years. I don't say it arrogantly, but the church has given an enormous amount of money to help hurting people. There's no telling how many lives we've touched. Beyond that, for nearly half a century, Lakewood has been a lighthouse, not only to our own city, but beaming a message of hope and encouragement to people all over the world.

In June 2001, the Houston area was hammered by a tropical storm that resulted in devastating floodwaters covering much of the lower-lying parts of the city. Lakewood Church was one of the few areas not underwater, and almost immediately, rescue workers began transporting people to the church as an emergency shelter. We had never planned to house hundreds of people on our church property, nor were we set up to do so, but the need was there and the people were coming, so members of the church worked round the clock to accommodate the crowds of people who had been forced out of their homes by the rapidly rising floodwaters.

A television network covering the flood did a "live" report from our parking lot, and during the course of the interview, the reporter asked a Lakewood staff person what we needed. "Food, clothing, blankets, and supplies," the worker replied.

Within hours, all sorts of supplies began pouring into the church from members of our own congregation, and others around the city as well as the nation. As a result, we were able to feed, house, clothe, and take care of thousands of temporarily displaced people in our community. I'll never forget seeing the cars and trucks lined up for miles bringing supplies, food, blankets, and all kinds of things to the church to be distributed to the uprooted families. We finally had to ask people to stop bringing supplies. We didn't have any more room for them! The materials were piled all the way to the ceiling. For several weeks, our church's main job was to serve the flood victims in our community. Later, we were able to help many of them rebuild their homes and get their lives back on track once again.

The spirit of our church has always been to give. Is it any wonder, then, that God was there for us in our time of need? All of our gifts, all of our generosity, all those seeds that we had sown down through the years had been stored up. And when we needed it the most, God just reached over and out of our own harvest. He met our needs.

When God reaches into your harvest, will there be anything there? Are you sowing any seeds of kindness? Are you keeping God first in your finances? Are you living to give, or are you living to get?

A skeptic once said to me, "Joel, it sounds to me like you're saying that if I don't give, and if I don't ever do any good deeds, then God won't ever meet my needs."

"No, you must understand. God's love is unconditional and His grace is unmerited favor," I replied. "God gives us all many things that we don't deserve, and could not possibly earn, no matter how many good deeds we do. But I am saying that our gifts, our acts of kindness, get God's attention in a special way."

God Sees Your Gifts

In the Bible, there's a story about a Roman army captain named Cornelius. The Bible says, "He was a good man. He prayed often and he gave much to the poor."[5] One translation (*The Living Bible*) says, "He was a generous giver." Cornelius and his family became the first recorded Gentile household to receive the good news and to experience salvation after the resurrection of Jesus.

Why was he chosen? Why did God pick him for such an honor? The Scripture tells us Cornelius saw an angel in a vision who said to him: "Your prayers and your alms have come up for a memorial before God."[6] *The Living Bible* says, "Your prayers and charities have not gone unnoticed by God!" Friend, don't let anybody convince you that it doesn't make a difference to give. The reason Cornelius was chosen was because of his giving spirit.

In the same way, when we give, it gets God's attention. I'm not suggesting that we can buy miracles. I'm not saying you have to pay God to meet your needs, but I am saying God sees your gifts. He sees your acts of kindness. Every time you help somebody, God sees. And as with Cornelius, it pleases God when you give, and He will pour out His favor in a new way in your life.

In your time of need, put some action behind your prayers. If you are believing for a promotion at work, don't just say, "God, I'm counting on You. God, I know You'll do it." Sow some seed. Do more than pray. Why don't you do as Cornelius and go out and feed the poor, or do something to get that seed in the ground? Your gifts will go up as a memorial before God.

Maybe today you are believing for your marriage to be restored or some other relationship to be improved. Perhaps you are hoping to buy a new home or to get out of debt. Sow a special seed that relates to your specific need. We can't buy God's goodness, but like Cornelius, we can exercise our faith through our giving.

Every time God puts a bigger dream in Victoria's and my hearts, every time He enlarges our vision, after we pray about it, we sow a seed in faith. We may just sow a seed by giving our time to some project, or maybe we'll sow a special offering, maybe we'll just bless another person in a special way. But we do something to put some faith behind our prayers.

Victoria and I had been married a few years when we decided that we wanted to sell our townhome and buy a house. We put the town-home on the market for six or eight months, but we never had a serious offer. Hardly anybody looked at it, even though we were praying regularly, asking God to help us sell it.

We really wanted the other house, but we couldn't afford it until we sold our townhome. Finally, we decided we needed to do more than pray. We needed to sow a special seed in faith, believing for that town-home to sell.

At the time, we were making double mortgage payments on the townhome, in an attempt to pay the principal down sooner. We decided to make the one required payment, and we'd sow the second part of that money as a seed, believing for God's favor. We did that faith-fully for several months, believing for the townhome to sell. After about the fourth month, we got a call from our Realtor. She said, "I have good news! I've got a contract for your house."

"That's great," I said. "How much is it for?"

She said, "Let me just come by your house and talk to you about it."

My heart sank. Usually when the Realtor wants to talk to the seller about a received offer, that means the offered price is low. But when she arrived at our home, we were pleasantly surprised that the contract was for the full price we were asking for our townhome. We thought we'd have to discount it thousands of dollars. But I believe, because we sowed a seed in faith, God not only brought us a buyer, but He did more than we could ask or think. He gave us even more than we were hoping for!

That's just how our God operates.

The Scripture says, "When we give, God is able to make it all up to us by giving us everything we need and more so that there will not only be enough for our needs, but we will have plenty left over so that we can give joyfully to others."[7] God has promised us that when we give, He will give back to us, then add some more.

Maybe you are in a situation similar to the one Victoria and I were in, where you are praying and believing and hoping for something to change, but thus far, nothing has happened. Perhaps you need to sow a special seed. Sow your time. Sow a special offering. Do something out of the ordinary as an expression of your faith. If you will do that, your gift will go up as Cornelius's gifts did, as a memorial before God. He'll begin to pour out His favor in a new way.

**Do something out of the ordinary
as an expression of your faith.**

Friend, if you want to live your best life now, don't hoard what God has given you. Learn to sow it in faith. Remember, when you give, you are preparing the way for God to meet your needs now and in the future. When you are generous to others, God will always be generous with you.

PART 7

CHOOSE TO BE HAPPY

CHAPTER 30

Happiness Is a Choice

Having worked through the first six steps to living your best life now, you may be tempted to think that your best life is still a long way off. Actually, nothing could be further from the truth. Your best life starts today! God wants you to enjoy your life right now. The seventh step to enjoying your best life now is to *choose to be happy today!* You don't have to wait for everything to be perfectly straightened out in your family or with your business, or for all your problems to be solved. You don't have to forgo happiness until you lose weight, break an unhealthy habit, or accomplish all your goals. No, God wants you to be happy right where you are, right now.

Happiness is a choice. When you get up in the morning, you can choose to be happy and enjoy that day, or you can choose to be unhappy and go around with a sour attitude. It's up to you. If you make the mistake of allowing your circumstances to dictate your happiness, then you risk missing out on God's abundant life.

You may be going through tough times, or you may have major obstacles in your path, all of which give you good reason to be unhappy or upset. But being unhappy won't change anything for the better. Being negative and sour isn't going to improve anything either. You might as well choose to be happy and enjoy your life! When you do that, not only will you feel better, but your faith will cause God to show up and work wonders in your life. God knows that we have difficulties, struggles, and challenges. But it was never His intention for us to live one day "on cloud nine," and the next day down in the dumps, defeated and depressed because we have problems. God wants us to live consistently. He wants us to enjoy every single day of our lives.

To do so, you must stop fretting about the future. Quit worrying about how everything is going to turn out. Live one day at a time; better yet, make the most of this moment. It's good to have a big-picture outlook, to set goals, to establish budgets and make plans, but if you're always living in the future, you're never really enjoying the present in the way God wants you to.

When we focus too much on the future, we are often frustrated because we don't know what's coming. Naturally, the uncertainty increases our stress level and creates a sense of insecurity. We need to understand, though, that God has given us the grace to live today. He has not given us tomorrow's grace. When we get to tomorrow, we'll have the strength to make it through. God will give us what we need. But if we're worried about tomorrow right now, we are bound to be frustrated and discouraged.

You must learn to live one day at a time. By an act of your will, choose to start enjoying your life right now. Life is too short not to enjoy every single day. Learn to enjoy your family, your friends, your health, your work; enjoy everything in your life. Happiness is a decision you make, not an emotion you feel. Certainly there are times in all of our lives when bad things happen, or things don't turn out as we had hoped. But that's when we must make a decision that we're going to be happy in spite of our circumstances.

Happiness is a decision you make, not an emotion you feel.

Many people live in constant turmoil. They're always upset, always frustrated, always having some kind of major challenge that's keeping them from being happy. They can't sleep at night; they're too worried. They don't like the people they work with. They get aggravated over the smallest things. When they have to sit in traffic or something doesn't go their way, they get all bent out of shape and lose their cool.

It's extremely important that we know how to live a life of peace. If we're going to do that, we need to be flexible and willing to make some adjustments. When things happen that would normally bother us, we have to put our foot down and say, "No, I'm not going to let that take my peace. I'm going to rule over my emotions. I'm not going to allow myself to get upset and aggravated. I'm going to choose to be happy."

It's the Little Things

Normally, it's not the big things in life that get us upset; often, the little things bug us the most. But if we don't learn how to deal properly with the little things, they'll end up turning into big things. Say you drive home from work after a long day at the office, and when you pull in to park your car, you see that your kids have left their toys in the driveway. You have to stop, get out, and move the toys. You're tired, it's hot, and you get sweaty moving all that stuff. It's a natural opportunity to get upset and frustrated. But you need to recognize what's going on. That's the enemy trying to steal your peace and ruin the evening with your family by getting you irritated over something relatively small in the grand scheme of life. You've got to make a decision that you're not going to allow the matter to escalate; don't allow yourself to get upset.

"Joel, I can't do that. I'm just a real high-strung person," you may say. "I get upset easily." No—you can do whatever you want to do. God said He would never let us go through something that is too difficult for us to handle. If your desire is great enough, you can stay calm and cool no matter what comes against you in life.

God gives us His peace on the inside, but it's up to us to make use of that peace. Especially in the pressure points of life, we have to learn how to tap into God's supernatural peace. The way you do that is by choosing to keep a good attitude. You've got to choose to stay happy.

One day Victoria took my car down to the car wash to have it cleaned for me. I have a white 1995 Lexus that formerly belonged to my dad. Even though the car is getting old, it hardly has a scratch on it so it looks much newer.

On this day, Victoria drove it through our usual car wash—one of those with supposedly supersoft brushes that are hardly even supposed to touch the car. Unfortunately, something was slightly out of alignment, because not only did it take the dirt off my car, it put a scratch from the front bumper all the way up the hood and over the roof to the back windshield!

When Victoria got home, she stopped in the garage to survey the damage (I think she was secretly praying for a miracle!). Our son,

Jonathan, came out, and when he saw what had happened, he came running into my office to announce the news.

It was a Saturday afternoon, and I had been studying and praying, getting my mind and heart prepared to speak at three services that weekend. I was trying to stay in a peaceful, calm, quiet atmosphere, but then came Jonathan! "Daddy, Daddy!" he called out. "You're not going to believe what has happened. Mama has totally ruined your car!"

"Jonathan, thank you for being so diplomatic," I said. "Next time, you can just hit me with a two-by-four!"

I was joking, of course, but I knew I had to make a decision. Was I going to get angry and allow this accident to steal my peace and my joy? Was I going to allow this circumstance to ruin my whole weekend? Or was I going to rule over my emotions and not allow myself to be upset and agitated? Was I going to keep my peace, knowing that God was still in control?

I went out to the garage and when I saw the car, I had to admit, the scratch was awful. But I simply made the decision not to get upset; I was going to stay happy. As I ran my fingers over the scratch from hood to trunk, I decided to look at the bright side. I said to Victoria, "Well, I'm the only guy in Houston that's got a Lexus with a racing stripe right down the center."

When negative things happen to us, no matter how much we rant and rave, it's not going to change anything. No matter how much we murmur and complain, it's not going to make anything better. I knew no matter how depressed I got about that car, or how much I flew off the handle at the car-wash people, it wasn't going to make that scratch go away. I decided that I might as well keep my peace. I might as well stay happy.

The Bible says we are like a mist, a vapor; we're here for a moment, then we're gone.[1] Life is flying by, so don't waste another moment of your precious time being angry, unhappy, or worried. The psalmist said, "This is the day the Lord has made. I will rejoice and be glad in it."[2] Notice, he didn't say, "Tomorrow, I will be happy." He didn't say, "Next week, when I don't have so many problems, I'm going to rejoice." No, he said, "*This* is the day." This is the day that God wants you to be happy.

"I'm just waiting on God to turn my situation around," I hear someone saying. That may sound good, but the truth is, God is waiting on you. If you'd change your attitude and start enjoying where you are right now, God would show up and begin to work in your life. If you're always waiting for some *event* to make you happy, you're going to spend your whole lifetime waiting. Something will always be "not quite right" in your life. You will always find some reason not to be happy.

I've heard people say, "As soon as I get married, I know I'm going to be happy then." But friend, if you're not happy before you get married, you are definitely not going to be happy *after* you get married. Women have said to me, "Joel, if you'll just pray for me to find a man, I know I'll be happy." They come back a few months later and say, "Joel, if you'll just pray for me to get rid of this man, I know I'll be happy!"

The marriage partner is not really the problem. No other person can ultimately make you happy. You must learn how to be happy within yourself.

Granted, you may have some problems; things in your life may not be perfect. Maybe you wish you were more handsome or more beautiful, more gifted and talented. You may wish you'd been born with a lot more in your favor. But you can't let those superficial things steal your happiness. You have to say, "God, I know You made me who I am on purpose. This is Your plan, and You have given me what I have to work with. I'm not going to complain or be negative. I'm not going to go through life wishing things were different, wishing I was somebody else. Father, I'm going to take what You've given me, and I'm going to make the most of it. I'm going to be happy with who You made me to be. I'm going to enjoy my life in spite of my shortcomings."

Don't take for granted what God has already given you. Have a grateful attitude. See the best in every person and in every situation and learn to be happy right where you are. Here's the key: Bloom where you are planted. You may not be where you want to be in life today. You may not have the perfect marriage. You may not have the perfect job. Life may not have turned out exactly like you'd hoped, but you must make a decision that you're going to make the most of that situation. Learn to be happy in spite of your circumstances.

Bloom Where You're Planted

I was walking in the woods one day when I came to a big, open field that was full of tall weeds. Everywhere I looked, all I could see were ugly, brown, dried-up weeds. But when I went a little farther down the path, I noticed one beautiful flower standing in the midst of all the weeds. It was so colorful, so vivid and, amazingly, it had blossomed right there in the midst of those drab, dreary weeds. I thought, *That is exactly what God wants us to do, to bloom wherever we're planted.*

You may live or work around a bunch of weeds, but don't let that stop you from blooming. Realize that your environment does not prevent you from being happy. Some people spend all their time trying to pull up all the weeds. Meanwhile, they miss much of their lives. Don't worry about things you can't change. You can't change the traffic in the morning. You can't fix everybody at work. You can't make all your family members serve God. But you shouldn't let that keep you from being happy. Bloom anyway, and focus on the things that you can change. You can change your own attitude. You can choose to be happy right where you are.

Don't worry about things you can't change.

Keep a good attitude and keep blossoming right where you are. If you'll make the decision to stay faithful and be content, at the right time God will change those circumstances. He'll get you out of those old weeds and put you in a better place. But if you refuse to bloom where you are, your progress will be stifled. God has planted us somewhere specifically so we might bear much fruit. And it's not so important where we are. What matters is: Are we bearing good fruit? Are we letting our lights shine? Are we being good examples? Can people see the joy of the Lord radiating from our lives? If you will keep blooming right where you are, then you can rest assured in God's perfect timing. He will transplant you. He'll put you in some new soil so you can bear even more fruit. But if you're not happy where you are, you will never get to where you want to be.

Appreciate Today

Some people are convinced that life is simply a series of problems to be solved. The sooner they get through with this problem, the sooner they will be happy. But the truth is, after you successfully make it through this problem, there will be another problem to face. And after you overcome that obstacle, there will be something else to overcome. There's always another mountain to climb. That's why it is important to enjoy the journey, not just the destination. In this world, we will never arrive at a place where everything is perfect and we have no more challenges. As admirable as setting goals and reaching them may be, you can't get so focused on accomplishing your goals that you make the mistake of not enjoying where you are right now.

I've heard parents say, "Well, as soon as my children get out of diapers, I'm going to be happy." A few years go by, and they say, "As soon as they go off to school, I'll have some free time. Then I'm going to be happy." A few more years go by. "When the children graduate, things will slow down. That's when I'm going to start enjoying my life." Meanwhile, life passes by. "As soon as I get that promotion, as soon as I close this big business deal, as soon as I retire . . ." No, you need to learn to enjoy your life now, every day, every part of life's journey.

Big events will not keep you happy. They may make you happy for a while, but after that wears off, like an addict looking for a fix, you're going to need something else. Maybe you have allowed yourself to slip into the habit of waiting for everything to be calm, serene, and settled before you lighten up and grant yourself permission to enjoy life. You're waiting for your problems to be solved. You're waiting for your spouse to become more spiritual. You're waiting for that child to change, for the business to grow, or for the mortgage to be paid off.

Why not be happy right now? Don't go many years down the road and then realize, when it's tragically too late, that one event or achievement, or even a series of them, did not bring you lasting happiness. Appreciate today. Enjoy life's journey.

These are the good old days. Twenty years from now, hopefully, you will look back and say, "That was a great time in my life!"

You may be saying, "But I have so many problems. How can I enjoy my life?" You need to realize that every person has problems; you are not unique in that respect. We all go through things at times that we don't understand. Although you may think your problems are enormous, tragic, or devastating, somebody—possibly many people in the world—have it much worse than you do. Your life compared to somebody else's is a bed of roses. Don't ever take for granted what God has done for you. You may have some obstacles today, but some people would give anything in the world to have your life. Some people would give anything to have your health or your prosperity. Living in America, we have so much for which we should be grateful. We should stop emphasizing what's wrong and start thanking God for what's right.

The apostle Paul wrote more than half of the New Testament while incarcerated, often in tiny prison cells not much bigger than a small bathroom. Some historians and Bible commentators believe that the sewage system of that day ran right through one of the dungeons in which he was imprisoned. Some commentaries state that it's possible that he could have written some of the great passages of what we now know as the New Testament standing in raw sewage that at times came all the way up to his waist. Yet Paul wrote such amazing faith-filled words as, "I can do all things through Christ who strengthens me."[3] And, "Thanks be to God, who always causes us to triumph," and "Rejoice in the Lord always. Again I will say, rejoice!"[4] Notice, we are to rejoice and be happy at all times. In your difficulties, when things aren't going your way, instead of having a pity party and thinking about how unfair life is treating you, instead of feeling sorry for yourself, make a decision to rejoice in the Lord. Choose to be happy! Choose to stay full of joy.

When you rejoice in the midst of your difficulties, you're giving the enemy a black eye. He doesn't know what to do with people who keep giving God praise despite their circumstances. Our attitude should be: *I don't care what comes against me in life. I'm going to stay full of the joy of the Lord. I've made up my mind that I'm going to live my life and be happy. I'm going to enjoy my life to the fullest.*

We need to understand that the enemy is not really after your dreams, your health, or your finances. He's not primarily after your family. He's after your joy. The Bible says that "the joy of the LORD is your strength,"[5] and your enemy knows if he can deceive you into living down in the dumps and depressed, then you are not going to have the necessary strength—physically, emotionally, or spiritually—to withstand his attacks. You will be vulnerable and beatable.

Smile for Your Health

It is a scientific fact that if you go through life in a negative frame of mind, always stressed out, worried, and full of fear, your immune system will weaken, making you more susceptible to sickness and disease. Scientists have discovered that every person develops cancerous cells in his or her body every week. But in the tremendous immune system God has given us, we have cells called the "natural killer cells." These cells are designed specifically to attack and destroy abnormal cells. Studies have shown that fear, worry, anxiety, stress, and other negative emotions actually weaken those natural killer cells. In other words, if you go through life uptight and stressed out, you will weaken your own immune system, making yourself more susceptible to sickness and disease.

On the other hand, people who are happy and have a positive outlook, people who laugh on a regular basis, develop more of these natural killer cells than the average person. Think of it! When you stay full of joy, your immune system functions at its peak performance level, just as God intended. The Bible says, "A merry heart does good like a medicine." One translation says, "A cheerful mind works healing," and that Scripture continues to be confirmed by modern science.

**One of the healthiest things you can do is learn
to smile more often.**

One of the healthiest things you can do is learn to smile more often. When we smile, it sends a message to our whole body, setting the tone for our lives. Studies tell us when we smile, certain chemicals are released that travel throughout our system, relaxing us and helping us stay healthy. Whether you have a reason to smile or not, make up your mind that you are going to smile anyway.

I was in the front lobby at Lakewood Church one day when a little boy came up to me with a serious, troubled expression on his face. He looked me up and down, and then said, "I want to know something about you."

"Okay," I responded. "What would you like to know?"

Without missing a beat, the boy replied, "I want to know why you smile so much." He said it so sternly, I almost got the impression that there was something wrong with smiling so much!

Nevertheless, I answered, "Well, I smile because I'm a happy person. Do you smile very often?"

The little boy thought about it, and said, "Only when I'm eating ice cream." A lot of adults are similar to that little fellow. They only smile when everything in their lives is sweet and creamy. But if they would lighten up, God might do a miracle in their lives.

Learn how to laugh. Quit being so uptight and stressed out. A relaxed attitude will not only lengthen your life, it will make it much more enjoyable.

That in itself is reason enough to quit complaining and start rejoicing. The more you thank God for what you have, the more He will give you what you don't yet have. Paul said, "I have learned how to be content no matter what my circumstances are."[6] The Amplified Bible says, "I have learned how to be content (satisfied to the point where I am not disturbed or disquieted) in whatever state I am."[7] Notice, Paul had to learn how to be content, just as he learned how to stay full of joy. These responses did not happen automatically. Paul had to make some decisions that resulted in contentment.

Be Content Where You Are

Now, being content doesn't mean you should sit back, fatalistically accepting life's problems or troubles; it doesn't mean you should live life like a wandering generality, unmotivated and undisciplined. Nor does being content mean you lack passion or you are devoid of a drive and desire to want things to change for the better. No, being content simply means you trust God enough that you don't get frustrated when things don't go your way. You don't allow circumstances to steal your joy and keep you from being happy. You can choose to stay happy and content no matter what comes against you in life. You can decide not to let little things get the best of you.

If you are always discontented, something is wrong. If you get up each morning and you dread going to work, dread driving in the traffic, dread dealing with the boss, dread doing what you do all day, and dread coming home, either your attitude needs to change or you need to change your occupation!

On the other hand, in most cases, God is not going to change your circumstances until you change. If you don't learn to be content where you are, you're never going to get to where you want to be. You may not have all the money you want today. Things may be tight, and you may be struggling. But as long as you complain all the time, talking about how poorly life's treating you and how you're never going to get ahead, your sour attitude will keep you right where you are.

You may not be everything you want to be. You may not have everything you want to have, but you must learn to be content, regardless of your circumstances. You must trust that God is at work in your life. You need to believe that you are making progress. You are growing. The Bible says God changes us little by little. Don't be upset or discontented; know God is in control.

The Bible says, "The steps of a good man are ordered by the Lord."[8] If God is ordering your steps, that means where you are right now is exactly where God wants you to be.

"Oh, Joel, that couldn't be true," you say. "I've got too many problems. I'm too uncomfortable in this place. This can't be God's plan for me."

God has you there for a reason. You may not understand it. He may be trying to do a work in you. He may be trying to teach you, to push you, to stretch you, to see how you're going to respond in that difficulty. Or, God may have put you in that situation to be a part of the work He is doing in someone else's life. God may be using you to influence other people. But whatever it is, you might as well choose to be happy, knowing that God is directing your steps and He has you there for a reason.

Isn't it interesting, we believe that God is guiding us as long as we are getting what we want and we're "living on the mountaintop," relatively unscathed by the warp and woof of life in the valley below. But we need to understand that the Lord is directing our steps even when it seems things are not going our way. You may be in a stressful situation today. You may be living with a spouse or a child who is difficult to get along with. Or perhaps because of politics at the office, you are not being treated fairly, or possibly you are having to work two jobs in order to make ends meet. You may be thinking, *This doesn't seem right. God, I don't understand it.*

The Scripture says, "Since the Lord is directing our steps, why try to figure out everything that happens along the way?"[9] Friend, you are never going to understand everything you go through in life or why certain things come against you. You simply must learn to trust God anyway. You must learn to keep a good attitude, knowing that God is in control.

Back in the late 1990s, two former college basketball players—both twenty-seven years of age; one stood 6'7" and the other 6'5"—were headed to Kenya to work on a missions project. This was their first trip overseas, and they were extremely excited about it. They had prayed for many months, asking God to use their lives and asking that everything go smoothly on this trip.

When the plane was about to land in London, the weather was too foggy, forcing the plane into a holding pattern above Heathrow. After circling for a couple of hours, the two young men missed their connecting flight to Kenya. They were extremely disappointed as the next flight wasn't for eight or nine hours. They were a bit irritated and said so. "God, we don't understand this. We spent all that time praying for things to go smoothly. The whole church was praying for us, but now we start off with a setback."

When it finally came time for the next flight to leave, there were no seats available except in first class. The airline seated the two big fellows right up at the front of the plane, with plenty of leg room, so they were happy about that. But about midway through that flight, the plane took a nosedive and started streaking toward the ground at full throttle. People aboard the plane were screaming as the flight attendants scrambled to keep the passengers from panicking. They thought for sure they were going to die.

The young guys up front maintained their wits enough to pray: "God, it's bad enough we missed our flight, but now we're on this plane, and it's about to crash. God, we really don't understand this, but use our lives somehow."

About that time, they heard some noise that sounded like a struggle in the cockpit. They looked at each other and said, "We have nothing to lose. Let's find out what's going on!" A flight attendant opened the cockpit door, and there was a deranged man—a big man who stood over 7' tall—attacking the pilots and trying to gain control of the plane. The two pilots, who were 5'4" and 5'7", were desperately trying to stop the madman, but they didn't have a chance.

When the two basketball players saw what was happening, they wrestled the attacker to the ground and pulled him out of the cockpit. By the time they were able to subdue him, the plane had fallen all the way from 30,000 feet to less than 4,000 feet. Had the pilots not been able to regain control, within seconds the plane would have crashed, most likely killing everyone aboard and possibly people on the ground.

Sometimes God will put you in an uncomfortable situation so you can help somebody else. God delayed those two young men on purpose. He put them in first class, right up front, so they could help save that entire plane. God knows what He's doing. He can see the big picture; He can see the future. And He has you exactly where He wants you today. Quit questioning Him and start trusting Him. Just know that God is in control. He has your best interests at heart. He's directing your steps.

Quit questioning [God] and start trusting Him.

Your responsibility is to choose to be happy, regardless of what comes your way. You may work around somebody who gets on your nerves and annoys you. You may be thinking, *God, I shouldn't have to put up with this. I don't understand this. Why don't You get this person out of my life?* But have you considered that God may have put you there on purpose to help do a work in that person's life? Maybe you are exactly what that person needs. Maybe God is counting on you to be a positive influence, to speak a word of encouragement, to let your light shine so He can make a difference in that person and change his or her heart.

Choose to be happy. Choose to keep a good attitude. Remember, happiness is a choice you have to make. And even when you don't understand it, know that God is at work in you and He's working through you. Make up your mind that from today forward, you are going to bloom where you are planted and enjoy every single day of your life.

CHAPTER 31

Being a Person of Excellence and Integrity

For many people, mediocrity is the norm; they want to do as little as they possibly can and still get by. But God did not create us to be mediocre or average. He doesn't want us to just barely get by, or to do what everybody else is doing. God has called us to be a cut above. He's called us to stand out in the crowd, to be people of excellence and integrity. Indeed, the only way to be truly happy is to live with excellence and integrity. Any hint of compromise will taint our greatest victories or our grandest achievements.

What does it mean to be a person of excellence and integrity?

A person of excellence and integrity goes the extra mile to do what's right. He keeps his word even when it's difficult. People of excellence arrive at work on time. They give their employers a full day's work; they don't leave early or call in sick when they are not. When you have an excellent spirit, it shows up in the quality of your work, and the attitude with which you do it.

God doesn't bless mediocrity. He blesses excellence.

God doesn't bless mediocrity. He blesses excellence. The Scripture says, "Whatever you do, work at it with your whole heart, not unto men, but do it unto God knowing that God will reward you."[1] Notice, whatever we do, we should give it our best effort and do it as if we were doing it for God. If we'll work with that standard in mind, God promises to reward us.

If you want to live your best life now, start aiming for excellence and integrity in your life, doing a little bit more than you are required to do. If you are supposed to be at work at eight o'clock, get there ten minutes early and stay ten minutes late. Go the extra mile. A lot of people show up at work fifteen minutes late, then they wander around the office, go get some coffee, and finally get to their desk or worksite thirty minutes later. They spend half the day talking on the phone, playing games, or sending jokes on the Internet, and then they wonder, *God, why don't You ever bless me? Why don't I ever get a promotion?*

God doesn't bless mediocrity. God blesses excellence and integrity.

"But Joel, everybody's doing it. Everybody gets to work late at my office. Everybody plays on the Internet when the boss is gone. Everybody takes extra-long lunch breaks."

Maybe so, but you are not like everybody else! You are called to live a life of excellence. You represent Almighty God. How you live, how you conduct your business or do your work, whether you're on time or not, is all a reflection on our God.

Start making the more excellent choices in every area of life, even the mundane. For instance, you may be driving a car that hasn't been washed in six weeks. Your trunk or backseat may be filled with so much junk—everything from your sports equipment to your office equipment—you can barely close the door! I'm not condemning anybody—Victoria and I have children, too—and sometimes our car looks like a storm hit it. But I don't like driving a car like that. Not only does it represent God poorly, but it makes me feel unkempt, undisciplined, sloppy, and less than my best. Many times before I leave the house, I'll take a couple of minutes and clean out the car, not because I want to impress my friends, but because I feel better driving a clean car. You need to take pride in what God has given you.

You may say, "Well, Joel, I'm just driving an old clunker. No use in my washing this."

No, if you will start taking care of what God has given you, He'll be more likely to give you something better. Similarly, you may not live in a big, new, beautiful home. You may have an older, smaller home, but at least you can keep it looking nice. Make sure it looks like a person of excellence lives there.

A while back, I was driving through a certain section of Houston and I noticed that many of the people didn't take care of their homes.

The yards weren't mowed; the weeds were overgrown, and things were stacked and stored everywhere, on the side of the house, in the front yard, wherever space was available. The entire neighborhood looked messy. As I continued driving, I came to one particular house that stood out among the rest. The yard was mowed, everything was neatly in order, and the home looked beautiful. When I got to the church, I commented about that house in that neighborhood. Somebody said, "The people who live in that house are some of our most faithful members."

That didn't surprise me a bit. God's people are people of excellence. The people who live in that home could have said, "Nobody else is taking care of their property in this neighborhood, why should we?" But they chose to be people of excellence, and they stood out from the crowd.

You may be in a situation today where everybody around you is compromising their integrity or taking the easy way out. Don't let that rub off on you. Be the one to have an excellent spirit. Be the one to stand out in the crowd.

Take care of what God has given you. My grandparents lived in a little wood-frame house that Granddaddy built way back in the 1930s. It couldn't have been more than a thousand square feet, but every time I went over there, the place was spotless inside and out. The yard was always immaculate. The bushes were perfectly trimmed. Granddaddy kept the outside of that house painted, and Grandmother kept the inside neat and clean. My grandparents didn't have a lot of money, but that didn't matter. They were people of excellence. They knew they represented God, and they were intent on being a positive reflection.

The same should be true of us. You are made in the image of Almighty God, and how you present yourself in your personal appearance is not only a reflection of how you feel about yourself, it is a direct reflection on God. When you put on a fresh, clean outfit, you'll go out feeling confident. On the other hand, if you leave the house looking sloppy and wearing dirty, disheveled clothing, you're not going to feel good about yourself.

One day Victoria asked me to run to the grocery store and pick up something so she could finish making dinner. I had just finished working out, and I was hot and sweaty. I was wearing an old T-shirt, and my hair was all messed up. But I didn't really feel like changing clothes.

I thought, *Okay, I'll run up to the grocery store and try to get in and out of there quickly, so hopefully nobody will see me.* I drove to the store, still in my workout clothes. I pulled in the parking lot and was about to hop out of the car when God spoke to me. I mean, if God has ever spoken to me, He spoke to me right there! Right down inside, I'm sure He said, "Don't you dare go in there representing Me like that!" He said, "Don't you know that I'm the King of kings?"

I turned around, went back home, took a shower, combed my hair, brushed my teeth, and put on some clean clothes. Then I went back to that grocery store and picked up that TV dinner Victoria wanted!

Seriously, we need to remind ourselves that we represent Almighty God, and He does not appreciate laziness or sloppiness. When you go to the mall, and you accidentally knock those clothes off the rack, don't act as though you don't see them and just leave them lying on the floor. A person of excellence will pick them up and put them back on the appropriate rack. When you're at the grocery store and you suddenly decide you don't want that box of cereal, don't just stick it over by the potato chips. A person of excellence takes it back to where she found it.

"But Joel, those stores have employees who are paid to do those things," I hear somebody saying. That doesn't matter. You do what is right, as unto God.

A person of excellence doesn't park in a parking spot designated for handicapped persons, just so he can run in and pick up something real quick. People of excellence go the extra mile to do what's right, not because somebody's watching them, not because they have to, but because they are honoring God.

People of excellence take care of other people's property as if it's their own. If you are in a hotel room, don't set a glass of water on that wooden table when you know it will stain. You wouldn't do that at your own house. Be a person of excellence and respect other people's property. When I used to travel a lot, many times I'd leave the hotel room with all the lights on, the air conditioner going full blast, and the television blaring. I thought, *No big deal. I'm paying for this room. I can do what I want.* But something inside said, *Joel, that's not right. You don't waste electricity at your home. You should treat other people's property the same way you'd want them to treat yours.*

Understand, neglecting those little things will not keep you out of heaven; in most cases, it won't even cause you serious problems or make you miserable in this life. But those subtle compromises of integrity will keep you from God's best. They will prevent you from ascending to your highest level. They will keep you from living your best life now. God desires people who will go the extra mile to do what is right even when nobody is watching.

**Subtle compromises of integrity
will keep you from God's best.**

People Are Watching You

I was in a store parking lot one windy day, and when I opened my car door, the wind blew out several pieces of paper onto the ground. I didn't really need the papers, but I didn't want to litter, either. Each time I went to pick them up, a gust of wind blew them about fifteen or twenty feet in all different directions. I thought, *Now, I don't want to go chasing around the parking lot all day, trying to pick up that paper!* I glanced at the lot and noticed there was already plenty of other trash out there. I was in kind of a hurry, too. I came up with several good excuses why I shouldn't waste any more time chasing kites. I had almost talked myself out of retrieving the trash when I decided, *No, I will do the right thing and go pick that stuff up.*

I wandered around that parking lot pursuing my papers. Every time the wind kicked up, the paper flew even farther. I was saying to myself, "What in the world are you doing out here? Just leave it. The store probably has a street sweeper that comes by every night!"

But I kept collecting papers until I felt certain I had all that had flown from my car—and several that had flown from other people's cars! When I finally got it all gathered up, I came back to my car. I hadn't realized it, but there was a couple sitting in the car parked next to mine. They rolled down their windows when they recognized me. We talked there for a couple of seconds. Then the young woman smiled and said, "We were watching to see what you were going to do about all those papers that flew out of your car."

I thought, *Thank You, God, that I obeyed and did the right thing!*
Whether you realize it or not, people are watching you. They're

watching how you dress, how you take care of your home, how you treat other people. They're watching you at work. What do they see? Are you a good representation of our God? Are you striving for excellence? Or are you compromising in so-called insignificant areas?

God wants us to be people of integrity, people of honor, people who are trustworthy. A person of integrity is open and honest. He doesn't have any hidden agendas or ulterior motives. A person of integrity is true to his word. He keeps his commitments. He doesn't need a legal contract; his word is his bond. People of integrity are the same in private as they are in public. They don't go out and treat their friends and coworkers kindly and then go home and treat their family rudely or disrespectfully. No, when you have integrity, you'll do what's right whether anybody is watching or not.

Every day our integrity is tested. If the bank teller gives you too much money in return, are you going to have integrity and go back and make things right? Or are you going to go out of there saying, "Thank You, Jesus! You did it again!"

Do you call in sick at work so you can stay home and take care of your personal business? When the phone rings and it's somebody you don't want to talk to, do you tell your child to lie? "Tell them I'm not home!"

"Oh, Joel, that's just a little white lie," some people say. "It's not hurting anything." No, lies are not color coded in the Bible. In God's sight, there is no such thing as a white, gray, or black lie. A lie is a lie. If you're not telling the truth, that's being dishonest. Sooner or later, it will catch up to you. What you sow you will eventually reap.

Understand this: If you will lie about the little things, before long you'll lie about bigger things. We read about the large companies that have come tumbling down because of fraud and financial misdeeds. Those people didn't start off by stealing millions of dollars. Most likely, they started off compromising a hundred dollars here, a thousand dollars there. Then, when the opportunity came, they compromised in millions. Don't kid yourself, if you will compromise in something small, eventually you will compromise in more serious matters. Compromise is a downhill slide. And theft is theft, whether it's a dollar, a thousand dollars, or a million dollars. If you're taking home your company's office supplies, that's being dishonest. If you're not giving your company a full day's work, that's not integrity. If you're having to stretch the truth in order to get that new account, that is deceit, and God won't bless that. We need to live honestly before our God and before other people. I heard somebody put it this way: "Don't do anything that you wouldn't feel comfortable reading about in the newspaper the next day."

When I go to the video store, if I have to hide from someone the movie I am renting, then something is wrong. If my credit report were to be made public today, would I be embarrassed because I never pay my bills on time? If my coworkers were interviewed on television, would they say I'm a person of honor, somebody they can count on, somebody they can trust? Or would they say, "That guy will stab you in the back every time. He's only out for himself"?

God wants us to be people of excellence and integrity. If you don't have integrity, you will never reach your highest potential. Integrity is the foundation on which a truly successful life is built. Every time you compromise, every time you are less than honest, you are causing a slight crack in your foundation. If you continue compromising, that foundation will never be able to hold what God wants to build. You'll never have lasting prosperity if you don't first have integrity. Oh, you may enjoy some temporary success, but you'll never see the fullness of God's favor if you don't take the high road and make the more excellent choices. On the other hand, God's blessings will overtake us if we settle for nothing less than living with integrity.

Are we willing to pay the price to do the right thing?

Of course, we all want to prosper in life. But the real question is: Are we willing to pay the price to do the right thing? It's not always easy. Are we paying our honest debts? Are we being aboveboard in our business decisions? Are we treating other people with respect and honor? Are we being true to our word? Integrity and prosperity are flip sides of the same coin. You can't have one without the other.

God may be reminding you about paying a bill that you've swept under the rug. Maybe it's about getting to work on time consistently; maybe you know you should be more truthful in that business deal. Start making things right. Step up to a higher level of integrity in those areas. God is calling us out of mediocrity and into excellence.

The Bible says if we will be faithful in little things, then God will trust us with more. How can God trust me to do the right thing with millions of dollars, if I won't do the right thing with a hundred bucks? Yet too many people are letting the little things keep them from moving higher.

You may not think it makes any difference when you don't pay your bills on time, or when you tell those "little white lies." You may think it doesn't make a difference if you treat your friends one way and your family another. But if you don't learn to pass those little tests, then God won't promote you. If you don't learn to do what's right in the little areas, God can't trust you with more. Remember, our lives are an open book before God. He looks at our hearts. He looks at our motives. God sees every time you go the extra mile to do what's right. He also sees the times that you compromise and take the easy way out.

I heard about a guy who left early from work one day to go to his grandmother's funeral. The next morning at work, his boss came up and said, "Do you believe in life after death?"

The employee looked puzzled and finally said, "Well, yes; I do."

The boss said, "Boy, that makes me feel a whole lot better."

"Why? What are you talking about?"

The boss said, "Well, yesterday after you left to attend your grandmother's funeral, she stopped by to visit you."

That is the opposite of integrity! Be open and honest and tell the whole truth. If you want to take your child out of school one day to go to a ball game, don't write the teacher a note the next day and say, "Please excuse little Johnny from school. He just wasn't feeling well." God can't bless that.

"But Joel, he might get in trouble."

I would rather get in trouble with men than get in trouble with God. Besides, you never really lose if you take the high road. Learn to listen to your conscience. God put that inside you so you would have an inner rule by which to know right from wrong. When you start to compromise, you will hear that alarm go off in your conscience. Don't ignore it. Do what you know in your heart is the right thing.

Moreover, a person of integrity says what he means and means what he says. People should not have to try to figure out what you *really* meant. Be straightforward in your statements and conversations.

Integrity is more than not telling a lie. A person of integrity will not deceive or mislead in any way. Often it's easy to tell part of the truth while conveniently leaving out something we know might have a negative impact. That is not speaking with integrity. We need to be open and honest even when it's difficult.

Say you are trying to sell your automobile. A man approaches with his checkbook in hand. He's excited; he likes your car; he's ready to sign on the dotted line. But then he looks at you and says, "Let me ask you one last question: Have you ever wrecked this car?"

Like a computer hard drive, your mind whirrs through the possible answers. Although *you* have never wrecked it, your wife, child, and mother-in-law have all had major accidents in the car. You start to reason it all out, thinking, *Well . . . technically, the man asked if I have ever wrecked it. . . .* So you look at him and smile. "No, I've never wrecked this car."

If you listen carefully, you will hear a resounding alarm going off in your conscience. And if you are a person of integrity, you will say, "But yes, the car has been wrecked."

A person of integrity will tell the whole truth. "But Joel," I hear you protesting. "That's just not the way business is done nowadays. If I tell the man the truth, he may not buy the car. I may lose this sale."

Yes, you may lose a few sales in the short term, but in the long term, you will fare much better. Even if that person doesn't buy what you are selling, because you responded in integrity, God will make it up to you. He will send somebody along to buy the car for more money. He'll give you a promotion at work. He'll help you get a better deal on that new car you're trying to buy. Friend, God is in charge of the whole universe. If you will honor Him by walking in integrity, He will make sure that you are blessed in abundance. Scripture says, "God holds victory for the upright and He guards those who walk in integrity."[2] If you want God to guard you, if you want God to bring victory into your life, you must make a decision that you are going to be a person of integrity.

A businessman worried, "If I told the whole truth, I'd lose some of my best customers. I may lose some of my biggest clients."

"No," I said. "If you will consistently do what is right, even if you do lose some customers, God will bring you bigger and better clients.

There's no limit to what God will do in your life when He knows that He can trust you."

"I know people at my workplace, and they lie, they cheat, they stab people in the back," said a young woman working for a stock brokerage. "It's not hurting them one bit. In fact, they're getting way ahead of me."

"Don't be deceived," I replied. "One day that is going to catch up with them. I promise you this: If you'll make a commitment to integrity, in the long run you'll go further, you'll be happier, you'll be more fulfilled. God will promote you. He holds victory in store for you when you walk uprightly. When you refuse to compromise, He is guarding your path. If you just sink down to their level and do what everybody else is doing, stabbing people in the back, cutting corners here and there, you may think you're gaining, but in the end you'll be the one to suffer. In the end you'll be the one to lose out."

Commit to Excellence

I heard a story about a wealthy man whose friend was a builder. This builder was down on his luck and hadn't had much work lately, so the wealthy man felt sorry for him and decided to help him out. He gave him a set of plans and a check for $300,000. He said, "I want you to build me a new home. I don't have time to bother with it. I'm turning it all over to you. You make all the decisions. I trust you. If you do a good job, I promise to pay you well."

This builder was so excited. He could finally start making some money. But he got to thinking, *If I cut a few corners here and there, maybe I could pocket some of that $300,000.* So he went out and bought the cheapest concrete he could find. He had the cement mixer water it down so it would stretch further. He saved four or five thousand dollars right there. Excited, he went out and found the cheapest lumber he could find. Some of it was bent and warped and crooked. He didn't care. It was going to be hidden behind the walls. Nobody would ever see it. He did the same thing with the plumbing, the electrical work, and so on, cutting corners and saving money. When the house was completed, he had saved nearly $40,000, which he discreetly deposited in his own bank account.

He called his wealthy friend to come take a look at the house. The purchaser was quite impressed. On the surface, the home looked beautiful. He never guessed that the builder had cut corners, compromising the integrity of the whole house.

The builder was ecstatic as he noted the pleased expression on the owner's face. He couldn't wait to see how much he was going to get paid. After all, he knew the owner was a very generous man.

As the wealthy man walked to the front door, he turned with a twinkle in his eye and said to the builder, "You know, I don't really need this home. I already have a beautiful home. I was just trying to help you out and do you a favor." He handed the builder the keys, and said, "Here, my friend. This is for you. You've just built yourself a brand-new home."

That builder nearly passed out. He thought, *If I had known it was going to be my own home, I would have built it a whole lot better!*

The truth is, whether we realize it or not, we all are building our own homes. We may cut corners here and there, but it's not hurting anybody except ourselves. Those poor decisions will weaken our foundations, causing us all kinds of problems in the future. Everything may look fine on the surface, but what really counts is what's going on within the walls, behind closed doors. What do we do when nobody is watching? Are we watering down our foundations because of a lack of integrity? Are we cheating people here and not paying taxes over there, compromising right and left? What kind of materials are we putting into our own homes?

**Whether we realize it or not,
we all are building our own homes.**

This builder got into his new house and three months later, he was having foundation problems. Six months after that, cracks appeared in the walls. The plumbing wouldn't work right. It cost him far more than the $40,000 he'd "saved" to fix all those problems. If he had it to do over again, he would do it right the first time.

In the same way, when we compromise to get ahead or sully someone else's reputation so we can be promoted, we may think we're gaining, but in the end it will bring nothing but problems. We'll suffer dire consequences. We have to live in our own homes. I can't build your home; you can't build mine. No, we each have to take responsibility for our own decisions. I don't know what you do behind closed doors. You don't know what I do. But as people of integrity, we should have the same character in private as we do in public. We don't put on our Sunday face in church and then go out and compromise all during the week. It's not enough to talk the talk. We've got to walk the walk.

You may be tempted at work to make a personal long-distance call on your company's phone lines. "Aw, go ahead," a coworker says. "Everybody does it. Nobody's going to see you. Nobody will know whether it was a business call or not."

No, a person of excellence and integrity does what is right, even when nobody is watching. People of excellence do what's right because it is right, not because somebody is forcing them to do it. Friend, there are a lot of things you can get away with in life and still be acceptable in society's eyes. You can compromise your personal integrity or that of your company; you can cheat people or be dishonest. You can lie, steal, compromise your morals, and you can cut corners here and there. But the question is: How high do you want to go? How much of God's favor do you want to see? How much do you want God to use you? God cannot promote you or bless you if you are not living in integrity.

A few years ago a friend of mine was in the process of changing jobs. He was an executive, and he landed a great position at a new company. He was excited about the new job, but it wasn't scheduled to start for three or four months. When he gave his company notice, they agreed that he should work right up until that new job started.

My friend was a hard worker, diligent and very intelligent. He always gave the job his best. Nevertheless, during that three-month period, while things were winding down at his former place of employment, I expected that he'd sort of kick back and take it easy, maybe go in late, maybe take some time off. After all, he wasn't trying to impress anybody there.

But he did just the opposite. He went in earlier than ever and stayed later. He started new projects; he gave it his best effort. I was really impressed. One day I was talking to him about it, and I said, "You're working harder than ever. How come?"

He said, "Joel, I was planning on taking it easy till my new job began, but one day I went to work feeling kind of lazy, giving a half-hearted effort, and God spoke to me right down inside. He said, 'Son, if you don't continue to honor this company by giving them your best effort, you're not going to excel at that new position.' When I heard that, I knew I had to give it everything I've got."

My friend realized who his real Boss is. He was not working for the company or for his supervisor, he was working unto God, not unto men. God is the One keeping the records. He's the One who will reward us. He's the One who can promote you. We shouldn't act nobly simply because somebody is watching us. We should do what's right because God is watching us. Do what's right because you are a person of excellence and integrity.

If you've made some mistakes in ethical matters, do the honorable thing and make it right as best you can. If you will be committed to excellence, God will help you to get out of that mess. But He's not going to help you if you won't walk in integrity.

My dad was a person of excellence and a man of integrity. When he was in his early twenties, he once bought two suits on credit. But he moved away and never paid them off. Year after year went by, and he'd forgotten all about it. One day he was praying, and God brought that unpaid bill up in his spirit and reminded him about those two suits. Daddy felt so badly; he decided to do his best to make it right. This was some thirty or forty years after the fact, but he called Fort Worth and tried to contact the place where he had bought those suits. It was no longer in business, but that didn't stop Daddy. He asked the company next door if they knew the name of the man who had owned the business. They gave him the man's name, but, they said, "he died a number of years ago." Daddy didn't give up. He dug in the phone book, made call after call trying to track down some of that man's relatives. He finally got in touch with one of the man's sons, and Daddy sent him a check for several thousand dollars, not just for the two suits, but he included interest as well. Why did he do it? Because Daddy was a person of excellence and integrity. He honored God by keeping his word.

When you make a commitment to excellence and integrity, God will reward you. When you are committed to doing what's right, you are sowing seeds for God's blessings. You will never go wrong by taking the high road and doing more than is required.

A few years before my dad went to be with the Lord, we decided that we were going to remodel the platform area at Lakewood Church. At the time, I was working behind the scenes in the television production department. I'm a perfectionist, so I wanted the new set to look the best that it possibly could. We worked several months with the architects and the designers, and after they got it all drawn up, I had a mock-up made of everything. I wanted to see it through the camera before we built anything permanently. We brought up a big sphere and positioned it at the right height where eventually we constructed a large revolving globe. Then we had the designers position the mock-up of the podium, and we brought my dad in and sized it just for him, fine-tuning every detail. When we got it all built, we spent several weeks working on the lighting. Victoria used to ask me, "Joel, why are you spending hours and hours adjusting one little light, maybe just one little slash of color across the curtain?"

"Because I want it to be right," I'd reply. I was committed to doing the best I could do. I was committed to excellence. Little did I realize that one day I would be the one standing on that same platform, behind that same podium. I didn't realize it then, but I was building my own house. Looking back, I'm glad I put forth the extra effort. I'm glad I gave it everything I had.

Have that same commitment to excellence. Start doing what you know in your heart is the better thing. Don't settle for mediocrity. Don't just do what you have to do to get by. Be a person who goes the extra mile. Be a person who does a little bit more than he has to do. Remember, you and I are representing Almighty God. Let's be done with lazy, mediocre, sloppy living, and let's move up to higher levels. If you will live with a commitment to excellence and integrity, happiness will be a natural by-product, because God will reward you far beyond your grandest dreams!

CHAPTER 32

Living with Enthusiasm

A woman shopping in Houston happily hummed a tune as she collected the items she wished to purchase and approached the cashier to pay. The clerk, noticing the shopper's effervescent personality, just stared at the shopper for a long moment as though she was wondering what was wrong with her. Still eying her somewhat curiously, the clerk finally offered an obligatory "How are you doing today?"

That's all it took. The enthusiastic woman nearly bubbled over. "How nice of you to ask! I'm doing great. I am so blessed. I'm excited about this day!"

The clerk looked at the woman quizzically for a moment, and then said, "Let me ask you a question. Do you go to Lakewood?"

"Why, yes I do," the shopper said. "How did you guess?"

The clerk shook her head and smiled. "I should have known. Everybody that comes in here like you is from Lakewood."

God's people should be the happiest people on earth!

When I first heard that story, I chuckled, but then I thought, *What a great compliment!* That's the way it should be. God's people should be the happiest people on earth! So happy, in fact, that other people notice. Why? Because we not only have a fabulous future, we can enjoy life today! That's what living your best life now is all about.

Live with Enthusiasm

Living your best life now is living with enthusiasm and being excited about the life God has given you. It is believing for more good things in the days ahead, but it is also living in the moment and enjoying it to the hilt!

Let's not be naive. The pressures of modern life constantly threaten to take a toll on our enthusiasm, causing it to quickly evaporate if it is not continually replenished. You probably know some people who have lost their passion. They've lost their zest for life. Once they were excited about the future. They were excited about their dreams, but they've lost their fire.

Perhaps even in your own life you've seen evidence of dwindling enthusiasm. Maybe at one time you were excited about your marriage. You were deeply in love, so full of passion, but now your marriage has become stale and stagnant. Or maybe you were excited about your job. You loved going to work, but recently, it's become dull, routine, and boring. Maybe at one time you were excited about serving God. You couldn't wait to get to church. You loved reading your Bible, praying, and spending time with fellow believers. But lately you've been thinking, *I don't know what's wrong with me. I don't have any drive. I don't have any passion. I'm just going through the motions.*

The truth is, much of life is routine, and we can become stagnant if we're not careful. We need to stir ourselves up, to replenish our supply of God's good gifts on a daily basis. Like the Hebrew people in the wilderness who had to gather God's miraculous provisions of manna afresh each morning, we, too, cannot get by on yesterday's supply. We need fresh enthusiasm each day. The word *enthusiasm* derives from two Greek words, *en theos*, meaning "inspired by God." Our lives need to be inspired, infused, filled afresh with God's goodness every day.

Make a decision that you are not going to live another day without the joy of the Lord in your life; without love, peace, and passion; without being excited about your life. And understand that you don't have to have something extraordinary happening in your life to be excited. You may not live in the perfect environment or have the perfect job or the perfect marriage, but you can still choose to live each day with enthusiasm. The Scripture says, "Never lag in zeal, but be aglow and on fire, serving the Lord enthusiastically."[1] Do those terms describe your life? Are you *aglow* with God's presence in your life? Are you *on fire* with enthusiasm? You can be! When you awaken in the morning, do you get up with passion to meet the day? Are you excited about your dreams? Do you go to work each day with enthusiasm?

"Well, I don't really like my job," Darlene complains. "I can't stand driving in the traffic. I don't like the people I work around."

If that sounds familiar, you need to change your attitude. You should be grateful that you even have a job. You need to appreciate and stay excited about the opportunities God has given you. Wherever you are in life, make the most of it and be the best that you can be. If your assignment right now is to raise your children, do it with passion. Do it with enthusiasm. Don't get up and say, "Humph! My friends are out doing something significant, something important, something exciting. All I'm doing is taking care of these kids."

A mother's work is one of the most important jobs in the whole world. But you have to keep up your enthusiasm. You may not have somebody patting you on the back or cheering you on. Your day may not be filled with extraordinary events. There are diapers to change, children to feed, clothes to be washed and pressed, housework that needs to be done; routine, mundane chores that seem to start over the moment you complete them. But in the midst of the ordinary, you can choose to have an extraordinary attitude toward your work. The Scripture tells us to do everything we do with our whole hearts, "to never lag in zeal."

If you work outside the home, don't give your employer a half-hearted effort. Don't dawdle on the telephone, wasting your employer's time and money. If you are digging a ditch, don't spend half the day leaning on your shovel; do your work with excellence and enthusiasm!

"Well, they don't pay me enough, anyway. I shouldn't have to work very hard."

You won't be blessed, with that kind of attitude. God wants you to give it everything you've got. Be enthusiastic. Set an example.

We should be so excited, and so full of joy that other people will want what we have. Ask yourself, "Is the way I'm living attractive and contagious? Will my attitudes, the words I speak, my expressions, the way I handle challenges and setbacks, cause anybody to want what I have?" In other words, are you drawing people to God, because of your joy, your friendliness, your enthusiasm, your attitude of faith? Or do you alienate people, turning them away because you're perpetually negative, discouraged, caustic, or cynical? Nobody enjoys being around a person like that. If you want to point people to God, or simply to a better way of living, have some enthusiasm and be excited about life.

I love the fictitious story of Tom Sawyer. As a young boy, Tom was told he had to go outside and paint the fence. Well, Tom didn't feel like working; he wanted to go play with his friends. But instead of getting all negative and sour, he decided he was going to make the best of that situation. He went out and started painting that fence with enthusiasm and excitement, as though he were enjoying it. His friends came around, and when they saw how much fun Tom was having, they became envious of him. They said, "Hey, Tom! Would you let us try painting that fence?"

"Oh, no," Tom said. "This is my fence. This is my project. You could never do what I'm doing." He played it up real big. And you know the story. When it was all said and done, Tom Sawyer was sitting back watching his friends do all the work, simply because he approached his chore with excitement and enthusiasm.

Who knows what would happen if each of us lived with more excitement in our eyes, with our hearts full of passion, our faces filled with enthusiasm? Instead of dragging around, complaining that you don't want to mow the lawn, put a smile on your face, a spring in your step, start acting as if you're enjoying it. Maybe somebody will come along to help! If not, at least you will feel better about your work. You'll have more energy, and you will get the job done quicker. You will be amazed at how God will pour out His favor, and how the "breaks" will start coming your way, when you start living with enthusiasm. Employers prefer employees who are excited about working at their companies. Your boss is much more likely to give you a raise in pay or a promotion if you have a good attitude and are excited about working, than if you just show up and do your work in a perfunctory manner. In fact, studies show that enthusiastic people often get promoted over other employees who are actually more qualified. The upbeat person is promoted simply because he or she has a good attitude.

Other People Will Notice

Hundreds of people work with us at Lakewood, but regardless of how talented or skilled a person may be, we don't hire anybody who's not excited about our organization. We don't hire a person who doesn't believe in what we are doing. Moreover, we don't encourage employees to remain on our staff if they don't think Lakewood is the greatest place in the world to work. We want only enthusiastic coworkers.

For several years, I noticed Jackie sitting down front at Lakewood Church, week after week. She was always excited about the service, attentive to what was going on, participating with tremendous enthusiasm, and radiating joy from her very demeanor and countenance. I didn't know who she was, but she always looked like she was having the time of her life. When we sang, she would sing with her whole heart. When I'd be bringing a message, I'd look out at the audience, and Jackie would always have a smile on her face. She'd be nodding her head, as though she was encouraging me, "Come on, Joel. Tell me more. You're doing a good job."

When a staff position became available in our Women's Ministry, the first thing I said was, "Somebody go find that lady who sits down front. There's nobody I would rather have represent us than somebody like her!"

We hired Jackie, and she continues to inspire and encourage people. That door of opportunity opened for her simply because she was enthusiastic. She was excited. When you live with passion and are excited about your dreams, other people will notice. It may not even be your own employer who promotes you, but somebody else will notice your positive attitude and will offer you a position that you weren't expecting. All kinds of advantages and opportunities will come your way if you'll simply do everything you do with enthusiasm, with your whole heart.

Growing up, I was fascinated by a traffic policeman who worked over by the Galleria, one of the busy shopping areas in Houston. He directed traffic at one of the busiest intersections in that part of town. During rush hour, the traffic would be so badly backed up, it was not uncommon to have to wait ten or fifteen minutes just to get through that one light. Observing people in their cars, it was plain to see that they were irritated about having to wait so long. But when they approached the policeman, their whole attitude changed.

This officer didn't simply direct traffic. He put on a show! He was so enthusiastic, just watching him was entertaining. It was obvious that he loved what he was doing. He was practically dancing as he directed that traffic, with both arms waving wildly, his hands gesturing, his feet shuffling all through the intersection. He could direct the traffic and moonwalk at the same time!

Amazingly, after inching along in the traffic jam for ten or fifteen minutes, many drivers would pull over into nearby parking lots just to watch the traffic officer perform. He was *enthusiastic*. He wasn't just showing up for work. He wasn't just going through the motions. No, he was passionately fulfilling his destiny.

Don't just go through the motions in life.
Have some enthusiasm.

That's the way you and I should be. Don't just go through the motions in life. Have some enthusiasm. Choose to be happy; live with excellence and integrity, and put a spring in your step. Put a smile on your face. Moonwalk if you want, and let the world know that you are enjoying the life God has given you!

Friend, if you want to see God's favor, do everything with your whole heart. Do it with passion and some fire. Not only will you feel better, but that fire will spread, and soon other people will want what you have. Do you want your life to make an impact? You can change the atmosphere of your home or your entire office with a little bit of enthusiasm. Don't live another day defeated and depressed. Stir yourself up; rekindle that fire.

In the New Testament, the apostle Paul encouraged his young coworker Timothy: "Fan the flame. Rekindle the embers. Stir up the gift that is within you."[2] Paul was reminding his understudy to live with enthusiasm. Give it your all. Don't settle for mediocrity.

You may have to live or work around people who are prone to being negative, who tend to drag you down. But don't let them throw water on your fire. Don't let their lack of enthusiasm squelch your passion. If you live with a deadbeat spouse, make a decision that you're going to be happy and enthusiastic anyway. If you work around people who are always negative, try to overcome that negativity by being positive, encouraging, and uplifting. Fan your flame more than usual to make sure the fire doesn't go out.

When everybody else is down and defeated, when you are all alone with nobody nearby to encourage you, simply encourage yourself. Your attitude should be: *It doesn't matter what anybody else does or doesn't do, I'm going to live my life with enthusiasm! I'm going to stay on fire. I'm going to be aglow. I'm going to be passionate about seeing my dreams come to pass.*

People who see me on television sometimes write to me, saying, "Joel, why do you always smile so much? Why are you so happy? Why are you so enthusiastic?"

"I'm glad you asked!" I respond, and that opens the door for me to tell them about my relationship with God, and how they can have a relationship with Him as well.

Some guy stopped me on the streets in New York City and said, "Hey, aren't you that smiling preacher?"

I laughed and said, "I guess so. That's me. I'm the smiling preacher." I take that as a compliment. Yes, I'm guilty of being happy! I'm guilty of being excited about the future. I'm guilty of living each day with enthusiasm.

God Has Great Things in Store for You

Prior to reading this book, you may have been down in the doldrums or stuck in a rut. Perhaps you were ready to give up on your dreams. You weren't excited about the people in your life or your career. But now you know better! Now, you know that God has great things in store for you. It's time to relight your fire; recapture your enthusiasm and adopt a fresh, positive, happy attitude.

"Yes, but Joel, I've had a rough year. I've gone through so many disappointments. I've lost a lot of good things."

Maybe so, but have you considered this? If it were not for the goodness of God, you might have lost it all. You might not even be here today. Why not be grateful for what you have? Quit looking at what's wrong and start thanking God for what's right. Get up each day expecting good things. Start expecting God's favor. Start expecting His blessings. Be excited about today.

This could be the day things turn around. This could be the day you get your miracle. This could be the day you meet the person of your dreams. This could be the day your child comes back home. That's how you stay enthusiastic, even in tough times. You expect good things. You stay filled with hope.

"What if I do all that and nothing happens?" I hear you saying. "I'll go to bed all discouraged after another disappointment."

No, you can go to bed saying, "God, even though it didn't happen today, I'm still trusting. I'm still believing for good things in my life. I'm still excited, knowing that I'm one day closer to my miracle. I'm one day closer to things turning around. I'm one day closer to a breakthrough."

That's what it means to stay full of zeal. Stay passionate about seeing your dreams come to pass. Stay on fire and aglow. Whatever you do, do it with enthusiasm!

The Bible says, "If you are willing and obedient, you shall eat the good of the land."[3] Notice, we have to be more than obedient; we must be willing—willing to do the right thing, willing to live with a good attitude and with enthusiasm.

It's interesting to watch when the offerings are taken in church. A lot of people will give, but they're not really willing. Their attitude is: *Here, God. Here's the money I owe You. Another hundred bucks. I could have bought a new truck by now.*

Technically, they may be obedient when it comes to giving, but God desires more than mere obedience; He's looking for a willing heart. The Bible says, "God loves a cheerful giver."[4] (One translation says, "An enthusiastic giver.") This truth does not simply apply to money. We should cheerfully give of our time, cheerfully serve other people, cheerfully do good to those around us.

I don't enjoy people giving me things out of obligation or duty, simply because they feel they have to. What if on my birthday my children came up to me and said, "All right, Daddy, here is your gift. We had to spend all our money on this, so if you really want it, you can have it"?

As much as I love my children, I'd say, "No, that's all right. You just keep that gift."

What if Victoria came up to me in the morning and said, "All right, Joel, let's get it over with. Let me give you a hug. Okay, I did my duty for the day."

No, we all want somebody who wants to love us, somebody with a willing heart, somebody who's enthusiastic about being around us. God is the same way. He doesn't simply want us to obey Him out of fear or even respect; He wants us to love Him as our heavenly Father. He wants us to do the right thing because we want to!

He looks at your heart. When you pray, talk to God with a willing attitude. When it's time to attend church services or take part in other opportunities to serve in the community, be excited about it. Don't do it out of obligation, merely because you have to. No, do it because you want to please God. Do it with enthusiasm. Learn to be more than obedient; learn to be willing. Develop a habit of doing the right thing with the proper motives, with a right attitude, and out of a grateful heart.

Learn to be more than obedient; learn to be willing.

One of the main reasons that we lose our enthusiasm in life is because we become ungrateful; we take for granted what God has done for us. We let what once was a miracle become common to us. We get so accustomed to His goodness, it becomes routine; it doesn't really excite us anymore. I heard somebody say, "Don't let your miracles become monuments." A monument is a piece of wood or stone that reminds us of something that once was alive, vibrant, and exciting.

Maybe you used to be excited about the home that God helped you to buy, but now that you've grown accustomed to it, you forget to be grateful for it; you're not excited about it anymore. That's old news.

Maybe you once were excited about that person God supernaturally brought into your life as a marriage partner, but now all the excitement has worn off. Don't allow that sense of a miracle to slip away. Don't get so familiar with each other that you take one another for granted.

During the first year that Victoria and I dated, we were on cloud nine. We laughed. We had fun. We didn't need to do extravagant or expensive things for entertainment. We were happy doing ordinary things. We were in love; we were excited, so everything we did was exciting as far as we were concerned.

On one of our first dates I picked her up a bit early, so we had a few minutes to spare. As we were driving down the highway, Victoria said,

"Joel, let's pull into that new office building over there and take a look at the lobby. I've heard that it is incredibly beautiful."

Now, normally I would think, *Why do I want to go into a building and look at a lobby? I can think of much more exciting things to do.*

But no, I was with Victoria. As long as she was there, it didn't matter. I would have gone and looked around a power plant as long as we were together!

If you are married, you probably felt the same way about your spouse. You were head over heels for that person. You knew God brought you together.

But too often, as time goes by, we take for granted what God has done for us. We get up in the morning and say, "Well, that's just my wife (or husband). No big deal. Sorry, honey, I don't have time to give you a hug. I'm in a hurry. I don't have time to do anything fun tonight. I might miss my favorite TV show, or the ball game." What we once regarded as a miracle has now become commonplace. We've grown cool to it; we take what we have for granted.

But the good news is, that fire can be rekindled. In your marriage, in your career, in your personal relationships, in your life! If you will initiate the changes you've learned about in this book, the excitement will come back. Rekindle that fire. Don't take life for granted.

Don't take for granted the greatest gift of all that God has given you—Himself! Don't allow your relationship with Him to become stale, or your appreciation for His goodness to become common. Get your fire back. Fan the flame more than ever. Live with enthusiasm. Whatever you do, do it for Him, with your whole heart.

Friend, God doesn't want you to drag through life defeated and depressed. No matter what you've been through, no matter whose fault it was, no matter how impossible your situation may look, the good news is that God wants to turn it around and restore everything that has been stolen from you. He wants to restore your marriage, your family, your career. He wants to restore those broken dreams. He wants to restore your joy and give you a peace and happiness you've never known before. Most of all, He wants to restore your relationship with Him. God wants you to live a satisfied life.

God doesn't want you simply to feel a little better for a few days after you read this book. No, God is in the long-term restoration business. He wants you to have a life filled with an abundance of joy, an abundance of happiness. God doesn't want you simply to survive that marriage. God wants to turn it around and restore you with a strong, healthy, rewarding relationship. God doesn't want your business to merely make it through the murky economic waters. He wants your business to sail and to excel! When God restores, He always brings you out better, improved, increased, and multiplied. He has a vision of total victory for your life!

Hold on to that new, enlarged vision of victory that God has given you. Start expecting things to change in your favor. Dare to boldly declare that you are standing strong against the forces of darkness. You will not settle for a life of mediocrity!

It's our faith that activates the power of God.

Raise your level of expectancy. It's our faith that activates the power of God. Let's quit limiting Him with our small-minded thinking and start believing Him for bigger and better things. Remember, if you obey God and are willing to trust Him, you will have the best this life has to offer—and more! Make a decision that from this day forward, you are going to be excited about the life God has for you. If you will:

- *Enlarge your vision;*
- *Develop a healthy self-image;*
- *Discover the power of your thoughts and words;*
- *Let go of the past;*
- *Stand strong against opposition and adversity;*
- *Live to give;*
- *And choose to be happy . . .*

God will take you places you've never dreamed of, and you will be living your best life now!

You Have Hidden Treasure

I read that Africa has more natural resources than any other continent. They have more gold, more diamonds than North America, than Europe, than Asia. But isn't it interesting that Africa is one of the poorest continents? America and Europe have big cities, prosperity, and wealth.

What's the problem?

It's not what you have in you; it's what you're getting out.

Buried on the inside of you right now is hidden treasure. You are full of resources; books, movies, songs, ideas, inventions, and businesses. When God laid out the plan for your life, He deposited in you everything you need to fulfill your destiny. But it's not what you have that matters; it's what you're getting out.

My challenge for you is to make sure you don't die with the treasure still in you.

You have something to offer that nobody else has. You are unique, one of a kind. When God made you He threw away the mold. Don't go around wishing you had somebody else's gift. If you had their gift it wouldn't help you, it would hinder you. You're not anointed to be them; you're anointed to be you. If God wanted you to look like them, have their personality, do what they do He would have made you that way.

You have exactly what you need. You're tall enough. You're talented enough. You're attractive enough. You're smart enough. Quit comparing yourself to somebody else. You have been fearfully and wonderfully made. When you walk in your anointing, confident in who God made you to be, knowing that you've got what it takes, then the treasure on the inside—your gifts, your talents, your potential—will be released. You'll step into the fullness of your destiny.

Ephesians 3:20 says God is "able to do exceedingly abundantly above all we ask or think, according to the power that works in us." Notice it's not according to the power that works in your neighbor, your parents, your pastor, the bank, or the stock market. It's according to the power that works in you. In other words, it depends on what you're believing.

If you go around thinking, "I'm not that talented. I've reached my limits. I'm just average. I come from the wrong family," then the exceeding greatness of God's power is not going to work in you. That treasure will stay buried.

Do yourself a favor: Stop belittling yourself. Stop discounting yourself. When you criticize yourself, you are criticizing God's creation. God didn't make a mistake when He created you. He wasn't having a bad day. You are not lacking. You were not shortchanged. You are not at a disadvantage.

You've been made in the image of almighty God. He's put treasure on the inside. If that treasure is going to come out, then you've got to have the attitude: "I have what it takes. I'm not waiting on it. I'm not hoping to get it one day. I'm not begging somebody to give me a good break. I'm not wishing I looked like my friend. No, I know it's already on the inside. I'm equipped, empowered, talented, creative, and well able."

When you live like that you'll see the exceeding greatness of God's power. This is where Sarah almost missed it. God gave her the promise that she would have a baby, but she was well beyond the childbearing years.

Sarah thought the promise would come through somebody else, which made more sense, because she was so old. She had her husband, Abraham, get together with her maid and they had a child. She said, "Thank you, Lord, the promise came to pass."

But God said, "No, Sarah, I didn't put the promise in them, I put the promise in you. There is treasure buried in your womb." Sarah kept talking herself out of it, thinking, "I'm too old. I don't have what it takes. I don't look like these younger women. They have an advantage."

How many times do we do the same thing? We think, "I'm not talented. I'll never get out of debt. I could never be in management. I could never write that book. I could never build that house."

God is saying to you what He said to Sarah: "I didn't put the promise in somebody else, I put the promise in you."

The treasure is on the inside. It may be buried beneath doubt and fear, beneath disappointments and what didn't work out, or buried under intimidation and low self-esteem. The good news is it's still in you.

You may have talked yourself out of it, but you didn't talk God out of it. God doesn't abort dreams. If you'll get in agreement with God, knowing that you have what it takes, then what God promised you He will bring to pass. Sarah was almost a hundred years old when she gave birth to a baby boy. The treasure came out, not through somebody else, but through her. The power wasn't according to her maid, and it wasn't according to her husband, Abraham.

The greatness of God's power was activated when she chose to believe. She had to rise up and say, "Hey, wait a minute, this is my time. This is my destiny. I'm not going to sit back like I'm second class. I've got something kicking on the inside. I've got potential, gifts, talents, a baby, a promise that's waiting to be released."

I want to light that fire under you. You may have been on the sidelines, celebrating everybody else, content to see the promise come to pass in their lives, and that's good. But God wants to do something amazing in your life. God wants you to be celebrated.

You don't have to sit on the sidelines. You have buried treasure. There are promises that God has spoken over your life, dreams that He wants you to give birth to. It's not too late. You're not too old. It may look impossible, but our God can do the impossible.

When you believe favor is released, when you believe hidden treasure will come forth, like Sarah, you'll give birth to the baby. It's not going to happen through somebody else; you will see the exceeding greatness of God's favor.

When Abraham first told Sarah they were going to have a baby, it was so far out, she laughed. I can hear her saying, "Abraham, a baby? Are you kidding? I've gone through the change of life. That's impossible, it defies the laws of nature."

She was saying, "I'm at a disadvantage, I don't have what it takes." Notice that she was discounting herself and belittling herself. That will keep the treasure buried. I've learned it's just as easy to talk yourself into it as it is to talk yourself out of it. Instead of thinking of all the reasons why you can't accomplish your dreams, zip it up.

Don't ask why you can't get well, why you can't get out of debt, why your marriage is never going to last. Don't think, "I'm too old, it's been too long, I've made too many mistakes." Instead of talking yourself out of it, talk yourself into it.

"I can do all things through Christ. God is making a way where I don't see a way. I am strong, talented, blessed, and prosperous. More than a conqueror."

You may be thinking, "This sounds good but I don't see how I could ever get well. My grandmother died of the same thing. It's been in our family line for five generations."

If you keep thinking and talking like that it's going to be six generations. Why don't you start talking yourself into it? Try thinking like this: "God is restoring health unto me. I will live and not die. The number of my days He will fulfill."

Avoid negative thinking like this: "Well I could never accomplish my dreams. I don't have the connections." Instead, be positive: "The favor of God is on my life. He's bringing the right people, the right opportunities. Something good is going to happen to me."

In the Scripture, God put a promise in Jeremiah that he would be a great prophet and speak to the nations. Jeremiah was young and afraid and he didn't know if he could do it. He started telling God how bad the situation was. He made one complaint after another: "God, people are making fun of me. Whenever I speak, they mock me. I'm afraid. I'm tired. I'm intimidated."

On and on he went. Just when you thought he was going to talk himself out of it, he said in Jeremiah 20:9, "But his word was in mine heart as a burning fire, shut up in my bones."

He was saying, "God, I don't see how it's going to happen. All the odds are against me, but this promise you put in me will not go away. It's like fire. It's alive. I can't get away from it."

You may be at a place where you could easily get discouraged and give up on what God put in your heart. But I believe, like Jeremiah, there is fire shut up in your bones. There is a promise God put in you that will not die. You can ignore it. You can try to talk yourself out of it. Your mind may tell you it's never going to happen, but down deep you'll feel a stirring, a restlessness, a burning.

That's the promise God put in you. God loves you too much to let you be average. He's going to push you into greatness. That treasure on the inside is coming out.

You need to get ready. The gifts, talents, creativity, inventions, businesses, books, songs, movies, and untapped potential are coming out. You're going to step into a new season. You will have the confidence to do things you couldn't do before. You will feel a supernatural strength. Doors will open that no man can shut.

Opportunity is coming your way. Don't shrink back, or feel intimidated. The creator of the universe has not only equipped and empowered you, he also is breathing in your direction. He's breathing favor, healing, restoration, and confidence.

A lot of times, you hear about what you can't do. I'm here to tell you what you can do. You can accomplish your dreams. You can set a new standard for your family. You can overcome every obstacle. You can break that addiction. You can recover from a fall. You're not average. You're not ordinary. You have treasure on the inside.

When I was growing up, our next-door neighbors had a big German shepherd in their backyard. As I related in *It's Your Time,* even though the yard was fenced off, they usually kept him on a leash. I was about nine years old when I was out playing baseball with friends one day and the ball went over the fence into their backyard. I didn't think much about it. I had gone over there many times and never had a problem. I got a little ladder and climbed over the six-foot fence. I picked up the ball and all of a sudden that dog came charging toward me at ninety miles per hour.

For some reason, he wasn't on a leash. My heart sank. I thought, "I'm as good as dead." I turned and ran back toward my fence as fast as I could, praying the sinner's prayer the whole time.

When I got to their fence, all in one motion I grabbed it with one hand and jumped as high as I could and somehow made it over just before the dog got to me. I was just a little boy and I had jumped over a six-foot fence. You know the saying, "White men can't jump"? That day I jumped.

What's my point? That dog helped me discover potential that I didn't know I had. There was hidden treasure in me. I had never jumped that high before and, the truth is, I've never jumped that high since. That's what happens when you put a demand on your potential. You'll be amazed at what you have on the inside.

You may be offered a higher position at work some day. In the natural, it may seem like it's over your head. You'll be tempted to back down and think, "I can't do that. I'm not qualified. I don't have the experience."

It may be over your head, but it's not over God's head. He's already deposited in you exactly what you need. God wouldn't have brought the opportunity and given you the desire if you didn't already have what it takes.

If you'll rise up in faith, with confidence knowing that you are well able, then you'll see new gifts, new talents, new strengths, and new abilities. All these things will begin to come forth. It's in you—you've just got to work with God to get it out.

You may have an opportunity to go back to school, start your own business or maybe even change careers one day. The easy thing is just to play it safe and stay where you are comfortable. But if you're going to unlock that treasure on the inside, you've to be willing to go where you've never gone.

If you want to walk on water, you have to get out of the boat. You can't stay in the safe zone all of your life and expect to fulfill your highest potential. You've got to be willing to take some risk.

I want you to have a new boldness, a new fire. You are full of possibility. There is potential in you, hidden treasure that you have not tapped into. Don't sit around thinking about what you can't do. "Well I could never be in management. I could never get up and speak in public. I could never jump over that fence."

I bet you could if that dog was chasing you. Like me, you could discover things in you that you never knew you had. The apostle Paul told Timothy to stir up the gift. God is saying today, "I'm taking you somewhere you haven't gone before. I'm going to open new doors of opportunity. I'm going to give you new ways to increase."

You may say, "I'm not that talented. I'll never lead my company in sales." Who told you that? The Creator of the universe says you have everything you need to succeed. You are anointed. You are equipped. You are empowered. This is your season to come up higher. God is about to release hidden treasure that's been buried on the inside. Get ready to take a step of faith. Get ready to do something that you've never done before.

I love the singer Susan Boyle's story. You've probably seen the clip of her debut performance as a competitor on the television show *Britain's Got Talent*. She surprised the judges and the world with her incredible voice. What you may not know is that Susan had a difficult life. She was the youngest of nine children. Her father was a miner struggling to keep the family going. When she was born her mother had difficulty delivering her.

Susan went without oxygen during childbirth and was born with challenges. While the doctors were pleased that she survived, they told her parents, "Don't expect anything out of Susan. She's at a disadvantage. She'll never amount to much."

What the doctors couldn't see was what almighty God had placed on the inside. The doctors gave information from a medical point of view. They did their part, but there was a treasure buried in little Susan that nobody could see. Medical professionals said she was disadvantaged, a slow learner, and that she might not amount to much.

But God said, "She is equipped, empowered, unique, one-of-a-kind, and a masterpiece."

Susan, who was later diagnosed with Asperger syndrome, could have listened to the experts and settled for an average life by talking herself out of anything more. "It's not my fault. I'm at a disadvantage. I've got an excuse to settle where I am."

Instead, she had the attitude that says, "There's a treasure in me. I'm not going to sit around in self-pity, focusing on what I don't have. I know there's something that I do have. I've been fearfully and wonderfully made."

Growing up, she took care of her mother who had become ill. She volunteered in the community, helping the elderly. She sang every time she had a chance, at home, at church in the choir, and with friends. At forty-eight years of age, her parents had passed and she was living alone, not sure how to pay the rent.

The odds appeared to be against her. Susan could have gotten discouraged, but early one morning she got on a bus and headed toward a singing competition. She had never traveled that far by herself. She accidentally got on the wrong bus, and ended up taking six different buses to get to the television show.

Susan Boyle walked out on stage to compete against other contestants who were mostly young, hip, and dressed real cool. She was older, reserved, and conservatively dressed. Simon Cowell asked what she wanted to do and she said, "Sing."

Some of the audience members snickered. They thought it was going to be another mediocre performance to endure. But when Susan opened her mouth and sang they were stunned at the beauty of her voice.

Eventually, the whole world listened and marveled at Susan's gifts as a singer. Three hundred million viewers watched the clips of her performance on YouTube, the most in the history of that Internet site. Media from around the world carried the story of the voice that stunned the world.

Today Susan has released several albums that have sold millions of copies. She's been nominated for Grammy Awards, done movie sound tracks, and performed concerts around the globe, many of them for charities.

Here's my point: There is treasure on the inside of every one of you. It doesn't matter what people have spoken about you. It doesn't matter how great the odds are against you, or how many disadvantages you've had. If you'll just be like Susan and not get discouraged, you will overcome. Do not let people talk you out of your dreams. Do not let your thoughts convince you that you are average, ordinary, or nothing special.

Just keep taking steps of faith, being your best, honoring God, talking yourself into it instead of out of it. Then like Susan, you'll see the treasure God put in you released. Your gift will make room for you. You'll go places that you've never dreamed of.

I told the story in *It's Your Time* about this five-year-old boy who loved the piano. Any time he got a chance, he sat down and played. He'd never taken lessons so he had no formal training. He was often told he was too small, too young, but in spite of those comments he continued to practice and practice.

The only song he knew how to play was *Chopsticks*, just a very simple tune. One night his father surprised him with tickets to a concert by a world-renowned pianist, one of the greatest piano players in history. That night as they were walking to their seats the little boy looked behind the curtain and saw this beautiful grand piano. Without anyone noticing, he slipped over, sat on the bench, and began playing his very elementary version of *Chopsticks*.

About that time the curtain began to rise. Everyone was expecting to see this world-renowned master pianist but instead they saw this little boy, hunched over the piano playing *Chopsticks*. He was so caught up in his world he didn't know anyone was watching. When he finally looked up the boy was petrified.

Just as he was about to get up and run for his life, the boy felt two big hands reaching around him. It was the master pianist. He whispered in the little boy's ear, "Keep playing."

As the little boy played his simple rendition of *Chopsticks*, the celebrated pianist began to play a Beethoven symphony piece that was scored in the same cadence and the same key.

Under the direction of the master, the orchestra began to join in. He first brought in the woodwinds, then the brass, then the percussion. The boy's father sat in tears, amazed at what was happening. He never dreamed that the simple, unpolished song he heard in the living room every day would no longer sound like *Chopsticks* but instead become a full, beautifully perfected and inspired Beethoven symphony.

What happened? The master stepped in.

Sometimes in life you may feel like you don't have the talent, the know-how, the ability, or the strength, but the good news is God does. When you use what you have, the Master shows up. He'll put His hands over your hands. He'll bring in the woodwinds.

God will bring in the right people, and the right opportunities. He'll take what you think is very average—average gifts, average talents, average education—but when the Master steps in He will mix His super with your natural and you'll see amazing things begin to happen.

When I first started ministering, my sermons were very basic, very elementary. It was just like the little boy playing *Chopsticks*. I had never ministered before. But I just kept being my best, using what God gave me. The negative thoughts said, "You don't have what it takes. You're not a minister." I replaced those thoughts with, "I can do all things through Christ. I'm equipped, empowered, and anointed."

What happened? The Master stepped in. God put His hands over my hands. He gave me ability that I didn't know I had. He brought out the hidden treasure. You may think you could never accomplish what's in your heart. You don't have the talent, the connections, or the resources.

You may not have any of those things, but God does. When you make a move He'll make a move. I would still be sitting on the sidelines if I had not taken that step of faith. Every voice told me not to do it. I was nervous. I felt inadequate, unqualified, but deep down I knew I had what it takes.

When I got out of the safe zone and over into the faith zone the Master stepped in. If you play it safe all the time you'll never really know what's on the inside.

In the coming days as you stretch your faith you will have a confidence that you didn't have before. You will discover ability that you didn't know was in you. God's will takes your natural and mixes it with His super and instead of playing *Chopsticks* you will hear the woodwinds join in.

You will receive supernatural breaks. Just when you thought it could not get any better, the brass will join in, along with the right people and the right opportunities. Before long it will sound like a beautiful symphony.

The treasure will come out of you. You will know, like me, "This isn't just my ability, my skill; this is the Master joining in. This is God taking my ordinary and making it extraordinary."

Let me ask you this: If your time on earth was up this week, if you went to heaven, is there something we would have missed out on? Is your treasure buried under fear, doubt, disappointments, or what somebody said?

You owe it to yourself, and you owe it to the world to tap into your hidden treasure. It's not too late. You're not too old. You haven't missed too many opportunities.

Like Jeremiah, there is fire shut up in your bones. There are promises God has spoken to you—dreams, gifts, books, businesses—that the Creator of the universe has put in your heart. Don't act like Sarah and talk yourself out of it. Talk yourself into it.

Get up every morning knowing that you have exactly what you need. You're not waiting for it. You're not hoping to get it. You've got what it takes. If you'll do this, you need to get ready because your hidden treasure is coming out.

You're going to discover ability that you didn't know you had. The master will step in and put His super with your natural. Before you leave this earth, I believe and declare you will spend all of your potential. You will release all of your gifts, and you will become everything God created you to be.

Notes

Chapter 1: Enlarging Your Vision
1. See Ephesians 2:7.
2. See Matthew 9:17.
3. See Isaiah 43:19.
4. See Mark 9:23.

Chapter 2: Raising Your Level of Expectancy
1. See Colossians 3:2.
2. Hebrews 11:1 NKJV.
3. Matthew 9:29 AMP.
4. See Proverbs 13:20.

Chapter 4: Breaking the Barriers of the Past
1. See 2 Corinthians 10:4.
2. Deuteronomy 1:6 AMP.
3. See Isaiah 61:7.
4. See Isaiah 54:2.

Chapter 5: Increasing in Favor
1. See Psalm 8:5.
2. See Romans 8:28.

Chapter 6: Living Favor-Minded
1. See 1 Samuel 13:14; Acts 13:22.
2. Psalm 23:6 NKJV.
3. See Genesis 6:8.
4. See Ruth 2:10.
5. See Genesis 39:5, 21, 23.
6. See Job 10:12.
7. See 1 Peter 1:13.

Chapter 7: Who Do You Think You Are?
1. See Genesis 1:26–27; Psalm 8:4–5.
2. See 2 Corinthians 12:9–10.

Chapter 8: Understanding Your Value
1. See Ephesians 2:10.
2. See 2 Corinthians 3:18.
3. See Proverbs 4:18.
4. See Psalm 40:2–3.

Chapter 9: Become What You Believe
1. Story adapted from Denis Waitley, *Empires of the Mind* (New York: William Morrow, 1995), 126.
2. Matthew 9:28 AMP.
3. See Matthew 9:29–30.
4. See Romans 8:28.
5. See Genesis 12:2.
6. See Isaiah 61:7.
7. See Philippians 1:6.
8. Psalm 34:19 NKJV.
9. See Ephesians 6:13.
10. Hebrews 11:1 NKJV.
11. See John 10:10.
12. Luke 18:27 NKJV.
13. See Isaiah 55:8.

Chapter 10: Developing a Prosperous Mind-Set
1. Romans 8:37 NKJV.

Chapter 11: Be Happy with Who You Are
1. Galatians 6:4 NKJV.

Chapter 12: Choosing the Right Thoughts
1. The Hebrew word for "adversary" is *satan*, which means "a person who opposes or fights against another." In the Bible, the word is often used as a proper name for a powerful angel-like being who is the avowed enemy of God and humans. Although Satan has great powers, he is no match for God.
2. I am not minimizing the causes or effects of clinical depression, caused by a genuine physical or psychological malady. But far too many people consider themselves depressed simply because they have encountered problems or obstacles in life. That is not depression, in the truest sense.
3. Isaiah 40:31 NKJV.
4. See John 16:33.
5. See Ephesians 4:22–24.
6. See Proverbs 23:7.
7. See Colossians 3:2.
8. Philippians 4:8 NKJV.
9. See Romans 12:1–2.
10. See 2 Corinthians 10:5.

Chapter 13: Reprogramming Your Mental Computer
1. See Deuteronomy 30:19.
2. See Isaiah 26:3.
3. See 2 Chronicles 20:17.
4. Proverbs 16:7 NASB.
5. See Hebrews 12:3.

Chapter 14: The Power in Your Words
1. See James 3:4.
2. See Proverbs 18:21.
3. See Mark 11:23.
4. See Joel 3:10.
5. See 1 Samuel 17:43–47.
6. See 1 John 4:4.
7. See Isaiah 54:17.

Chapter 15: Speaking Life-Changing Words
1. See Proverbs 6:2.
2. Romans 10:10 NKJV.
3. Proverbs 2:6–9 TLB.

Chapter 16: Speaking a Blessing
1. See Genesis 27.
2. See Genesis 27:28–29.

Chapter 17: Letting Go of Emotional Wounds
1. John 5:6 NKJV.
2. See 2 Samuel 12.

Chapter 18: Don't Let Bitterness Take Root
1. See Hebrews 12:15.
2. See Matthew 15:19–20.
3. Psalm 139:23 TLB.
4. See Matthew 16:14–15.

Chapter 19: Let God Bring Justice into Your Life
1. See Isaiah 61:7–9.
2. See Hebrews 10:30.
3. Romans 12:19 AMP.
4. See Galatians 6:9.

Chapter 20: Defeating Disappointments
1. See Deuteronomy 29:29.
2. 2 Peter 3:9 NASB.
3. See Genesis 50:20.
4. See Matthew 6:33.
5. See 1 Samuel 16:1.
6. See Isaiah 55:9.
7. Mercy Ministries is a Christian organization we strongly recommend and support. Mercy Ministries provides a home free of charge for troubled young women and unwed mothers between the ages of thirteen and twenty-eight who are willing to commit at least six months to deal with life-controlling issues such as premarital pregnancy, drug and alcohol abuse, eating disorders, etc. For more information, contact Mercy Ministries of America, P.O. Box 111060, Nashville, TN 37222-1060; or online at mercymin istries.org.
8. Philippians 3:13–14 AMP.

Chapter 21: Getting Up on the Inside
1. See Ephesians 6:13.
2. See Hebrews 10:35.
3. 1 Samuel 30:6 AMP.

4. Acts 16:25 NASB.
5. See Acts 16:26.
6. Psalm 51:10 AMP.

Chapter 22: Trusting God's Timing
1. See Habakkuk 2:3.
2. See Psalm 31:14–15.

Chapter 23: The Purpose of Trials
1. See 1 Peter 4:12.
2. Ephesians 2:10 NKJV.
3. Isaiah 64:8.
4. Philippians 2:12 NKJV.
5. 1 Peter 1:6–7 TLB.
6. See Romans 8:28.

Chapter 25: The Joy of Giving
1. See Hebrews 3:13.
2. See Isaiah 58:6–8.
3. Genesis 12:2 AMP.
4. Proverbs 19:17 TLB.
5. Matthew 25:40 NKJV.

Chapter 26: Showing God's Kindness and Mercy
1. 1 Thessalonians 5:15 AMP.
2. See I Peter 4:8.
3. See 1 Corinthians 13.

Chapter 27: Keep Your Heart of Compassion Open
1. See 1 John 3:17.
2. See 2 John 1:6.

Chapter 28: The Seed Must Lead
1. Galatians 6:7 NKJV.
2. See Genesis 26:12.

3. See Psalm 37:1–3.
4. Proverbs 11:24–25 TLB.
5. Luke 6:38 NKJV.
6. 2 Corinthians 9:6 NKJV.
7. See Malachi 3:10–12.
8. Proverbs 3:6 TLB.

Chapter 29: Sowing and Growing
1. See 2 Corinthians 8:2.
2. See 2 Corinthians 8:2.
3. Ecclesiastes 11:1–2 TLB.
4. See Luke 6:38.
5. See Acts 10:2.
6. Acts 10:4 NKJV.
7. See 2 Corinthians 9:8.

Chapter 30: Happiness Is a Choice
1. See James 4:14.
2. Psalm 118:24.
3. Philippians 4:13 NKJV.
4. Philippians 4:4 NKJV.
5. Nehemiah 8:10 NKJV.
6. See Philippians 4:11.
7. Philippians 4:11 AMP.
8. Psalm 37:23 NKJV.
9. See Proverbs 20:24.

Chapter 31: Being a Person of Excellence and Integrity
1. See Colossians 3:23.
2. See Proverbs 2:7.

Chapter 32: Living with Enthusiasm
1. See Romans 12:11.
2. See 2 Timothy 1:6.
3. Isaiah 1:19 NKJV.
4. See 2 Corinthians 9:7.

We Want to Hear from You!

Each week, I close our international television broadcast by giving the audience an opportunity to make Jesus the Lord of their lives. I'd like to extend that same opportunity to you.

Are you at peace with God? A void exists in every person's heart that only God can fill. I'm not talking about joining a church or finding religion. I'm talking about finding life and peace and happiness. Would you pray with me today? Just say, "Lord Jesus, I repent of my sins. I ask You to come into my heart. I make You my Lord and Savior."

Friend, if you prayed that simple prayer, I believe you have been "born again." I encourage you to attend a good, Bible-based church and keep God in first place in your life. For free information on how you can grow stronger in your spiritual life, please feel free to contact us.

Victoria and I love you, and we'll be praying for you. We're believing for God's best for you, that you will see your dreams come to pass. We'd love to hear from you!

To contact us, write to:

Joel and Victoria Osteen
P.O. Box 4600
Houston, TX 77210

Or you can reach us online at www.joelosteen.com.

STAY**CONNECTED,**
BE**BLESSED.**

From thoughtful articles to powerful blogs, podcasts and more, JoelOsteen.com is full of inspirations that will give you encouragement and confidence in your daily life.

AVAILABLE ON JOELOSTEEN.COM

today's W❍RD

This daily devotional from Joel and Victoria will help you grow in your relationship with the Lord and equip you to be everything God intends you to be.

Joel Osteen
STREAMING

Miss a broadcast? Watch Joel Osteen on demand, and see Joel LIVE on Sundays.

Joel Osteen
PODCAST

The podcast is a great way to listen to Joel where you want, when you want.

CONNECT WITH US

Join our community of believers on your favorite social network.

PUT JOEL IN YOUR POCKET

Get the inspiration and encouragement of Joel Osteen on your iPhone, iPad or Android device! Our app puts Joel's messages, devotions and more at your fingertips.

Thanks for helping us make a difference in the lives of millions around the world.